3-00

W9-BSX-947

# The Pelican Guide to the
# FLORIDA PANHANDLE

PUBLIC LIBRARY OF
SELMA & DALLAS CTY
1103 SELMA AVENUE
SELMA, AL 36701

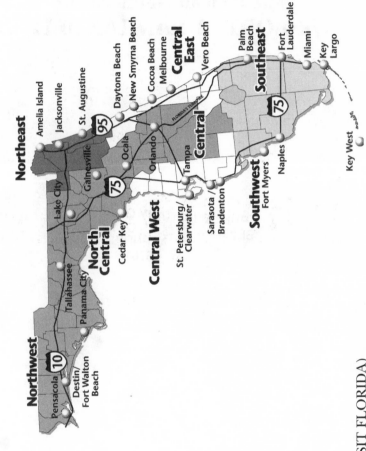

Northwest

Pensacola
Destin/
Fort Walton
Beach
Panama City
Tallahassee

North
Central

Lake City
Gainesville
Cedar Key

Central West

St. Petersburg/
Clearwater
Sarasota /
Bradenton

Southwest
Fort Myers

Naples

Key West

Northeast

Amelia Island
Jacksonville
St. Augustine

Daytona Beach
New Smyrna Beach
Cocoa Beach
Melbourne

Central
East

Vero Beach

Palm
Beach

Fort
Lauderdale

Miami

Key
Largo

Southeast

Central

Ocala
Orlando
Tampa

FLORIDA'S TURNPIKE

(Courtesy of VISIT FLORIDA)

# THE PELICAN GUIDE TO THE
# FLORIDA
# Panhandle

## By Heidi Tyline King

PELICAN PUBLISHING COMPANY
Gretna 1999

Copyright © 1999
By Heidi Tyline King
All rights reserved

*The word "Pelican" and the depiction of a pelican are
trademarks of Pelican Publishing Company, Inc., and are
registered in the U.S. Patent and Trademark Office.*

**Library of Congress Cataloging-in-Publication Data**

King, Heidi Tyline, 1966–
     The Pelican Guide to the Florida Panhandle / by Heidi Tyline
King.
          p.  cm.
     Includes bibliographical references (p.    ) and index.
     ISBN 1-56554-308-4 (pbk. : alk. pbk.)
     1. Florida Panhandle (Fla.)—Guidebooks.   I. Title.
F317.W5K56   1999
917.59'90463–dc21                                           98-45413
                                                                CIP

*All maps courtesy of FLUSA exept where indicated.*

Information in this guidebook is based on authoritative data available
at the time of printing. Hours of operation of attractions listed are
subject to change without notice. Readers are asked to take this into
account when consulting this guide.

Manufactured in Canada

Published by Pelican Publishing Company, Inc.
1000 Burmaster Street, Gretna, Louisiana 70053

# Contents

Acknowledgments . . . . . . . . . . . . . . . . . . . . . . . . . . . .11

1. Introduction . . . . . . . . . . . . . . . . . . . . . . . . . . . . . . .13
   History . . . . . . . . . . . . . . . . . . . . . . . . . . . . . . . .14
   Geology . . . . . . . . . . . . . . . . . . . . . . . . . . . . . . . .16
   Beaches . . . . . . . . . . . . . . . . . . . . . . . . . . . . . . . .18
   Average Temperatures . . . . . . . . . . . . . . . . . . . . .21
   Flora and Fauna . . . . . . . . . . . . . . . . . . . . . . . . . .21
   Natural Habitats . . . . . . . . . . . . . . . . . . . . . . . . . .29
   Florida's Official . . . . . . . . . . . . . . . . . . . . . . . . . .30

2. Tips for Travelers . . . . . . . . . . . . . . . . . . . . . . . . . .33
   Contact Information . . . . . . . . . . . . . . . . . . . . . . .35
   Airlines . . . . . . . . . . . . . . . . . . . . . . . . . . . . . . . .35
   Camping . . . . . . . . . . . . . . . . . . . . . . . . . . . . . . .35
   Canoeing and Kayaking . . . . . . . . . . . . . . . . . . . .37
   Caring for Wildlife . . . . . . . . . . . . . . . . . . . . . . . .37
   Cycling . . . . . . . . . . . . . . . . . . . . . . . . . . . . . . . .38
   Diving . . . . . . . . . . . . . . . . . . . . . . . . . . . . . . . . .39
   Fishing . . . . . . . . . . . . . . . . . . . . . . . . . . . . . . . .40
   Highway Information . . . . . . . . . . . . . . . . . . . . . .41
   Hiking . . . . . . . . . . . . . . . . . . . . . . . . . . . . . . . . .41
   Hurricanes . . . . . . . . . . . . . . . . . . . . . . . . . . . . . .42
   Lottery . . . . . . . . . . . . . . . . . . . . . . . . . . . . . . . . .43
   Packing List . . . . . . . . . . . . . . . . . . . . . . . . . . . . .43

Peak Season . . . . . . . . . . . . . . . . . . . . . . . . . .44
Rental Car Information . . . . . . . . . . . . . . . . . . .44
RV Rental Companies . . . . . . . . . . . . . . . . . . .44
Safety Tips . . . . . . . . . . . . . . . . . . . . . . . . . . . .44
Seasickness . . . . . . . . . . . . . . . . . . . . . . . . . . .45
Smoking . . . . . . . . . . . . . . . . . . . . . . . . . . . . . .45
Sunburn . . . . . . . . . . . . . . . . . . . . . . . . . . . . . .46
Sunscreen . . . . . . . . . . . . . . . . . . . . . . . . . . . .46
Time Zones . . . . . . . . . . . . . . . . . . . . . . . . . . .46
Tipping . . . . . . . . . . . . . . . . . . . . . . . . . . . . . .47
Water Safety . . . . . . . . . . . . . . . . . . . . . . . . . .47

3. Pensacola . . . . . . . . . . . . . . . . . . . . . . . . . . . .49
Introduction . . . . . . . . . . . . . . . . . . . . . . . . . .49
History . . . . . . . . . . . . . . . . . . . . . . . . . . . . . . .49
Pelican Picks . . . . . . . . . . . . . . . . . . . . . . . . . .52
Contact Information . . . . . . . . . . . . . . . . . . . .53
Average Temperatures . . . . . . . . . . . . . . . . . . .53
Transportation . . . . . . . . . . . . . . . . . . . . . . . . .54
Attractions . . . . . . . . . . . . . . . . . . . . . . . . . . . .54
Fishing/Water Recreation . . . . . . . . . . . . . . . .74
Golf . . . . . . . . . . . . . . . . . . . . . . . . . . . . . . . . .76
Tennis . . . . . . . . . . . . . . . . . . . . . . . . . . . . . . .77
Restaurants and Nightlife . . . . . . . . . . . . . . . .78
Accommodations . . . . . . . . . . . . . . . . . . . . . . .80
Shopping . . . . . . . . . . . . . . . . . . . . . . . . . . . . .81
Festivals and Special Events . . . . . . . . . . . . . . .82

4. Okaloosa County . . . . . . . . . . . . . . . . . . . . . . .85
Introduction . . . . . . . . . . . . . . . . . . . . . . . . . .85
History . . . . . . . . . . . . . . . . . . . . . . . . . . . . . . .85
Contact Information . . . . . . . . . . . . . . . . . . . .89
Average Temperatures . . . . . . . . . . . . . . . . . . .89
Transportation . . . . . . . . . . . . . . . . . . . . . . . . .90
Pelican Picks . . . . . . . . . . . . . . . . . . . . . . . . . .90
Attractions . . . . . . . . . . . . . . . . . . . . . . . . . . . .91

Fishing/Water Recreation . . . . . . . . . . . . . . . . . .100
Golf . . . . . . . . . . . . . . . . . . . . . . . . . . . . . . . .105
Tennis . . . . . . . . . . . . . . . . . . . . . . . . . . . . . . .106
Shopping . . . . . . . . . . . . . . . . . . . . . . . . . . . . .106
Bike Rentals . . . . . . . . . . . . . . . . . . . . . . . . . .107
Restaurants and Nightlife . . . . . . . . . . . . . . . . .108
Accommodations . . . . . . . . . . . . . . . . . . . . . . .110
Festivals and Special Events . . . . . . . . . . . . . . .112
Day Trips . . . . . . . . . . . . . . . . . . . . . . . . . . . . .114

**5. Beaches of South Walton/Seaside** . . . . . . . . . . . . .**115**
Introduction . . . . . . . . . . . . . . . . . . . . . . . . . .115
History . . . . . . . . . . . . . . . . . . . . . . . . . . . . . . .116
Contact Information . . . . . . . . . . . . . . . . . . . . .119
Average Temperatures . . . . . . . . . . . . . . . . . . . .120
Transportation . . . . . . . . . . . . . . . . . . . . . . . . .120
Pelican Picks . . . . . . . . . . . . . . . . . . . . . . . . . .120
Beaches . . . . . . . . . . . . . . . . . . . . . . . . . . . . . .122
Attractions . . . . . . . . . . . . . . . . . . . . . . . . . . . .127
Fishing/Water Recreation . . . . . . . . . . . . . . . . . .134
Diving . . . . . . . . . . . . . . . . . . . . . . . . . . . . . . .136
Golf . . . . . . . . . . . . . . . . . . . . . . . . . . . . . . . .136
Tennis . . . . . . . . . . . . . . . . . . . . . . . . . . . . . . .138
Restaurants and Nightlife . . . . . . . . . . . . . . . . .139
Accommodations . . . . . . . . . . . . . . . . . . . . . . .142
Shopping . . . . . . . . . . . . . . . . . . . . . . . . . . . . .145
Festivals and Special Events . . . . . . . . . . . . . . .147
**Seaside** . . . . . . . . . . . . . . . . . . . . . . . . . . . . . . .**149**
Accommodations . . . . . . . . . . . . . . . . . . . . . . .152
Seaside Weddings . . . . . . . . . . . . . . . . . . . . . . .153
Day Trips . . . . . . . . . . . . . . . . . . . . . . . . . . . . .154

**6. Panama City** . . . . . . . . . . . . . . . . . . . . . . . . .**157**
Introduction . . . . . . . . . . . . . . . . . . . . . . . . . .157
History . . . . . . . . . . . . . . . . . . . . . . . . . . . . . . .158
Contact Information . . . . . . . . . . . . . . . . . . . . .160

Average Temperatures . . . . . . . . . . . . . . . . . . . . . .160
Transportation . . . . . . . . . . . . . . . . . . . . . . . . . . .160
The Beach . . . . . . . . . . . . . . . . . . . . . . . . . . . . .161
Spring Break . . . . . . . . . . . . . . . . . . . . . . . . . . .163
Pelican Picks . . . . . . . . . . . . . . . . . . . . . . . . . . .163
Attractions . . . . . . . . . . . . . . . . . . . . . . . . . . . . .165
Fishing/Water Recreation . . . . . . . . . . . . . . . . . .176
Golf . . . . . . . . . . . . . . . . . . . . . . . . . . . . . . . . . .181
Tennis . . . . . . . . . . . . . . . . . . . . . . . . . . . . . . . .183
Restaurants and Nightlife . . . . . . . . . . . . . . . . . .183
Accommodations . . . . . . . . . . . . . . . . . . . . . . . . .186
Shopping . . . . . . . . . . . . . . . . . . . . . . . . . . . . . .190
Festivals and Special Events . . . . . . . . . . . . . . . .191
Day Trips . . . . . . . . . . . . . . . . . . . . . . . . . . . . . .192

**7. Apalachicola** . . . . . . . . . . . . . . . . . . . . . . . . . . .**195**
Introduction . . . . . . . . . . . . . . . . . . . . . . . . . . . .195
History . . . . . . . . . . . . . . . . . . . . . . . . . . . . . . . .197
Apalachicola Oysters . . . . . . . . . . . . . . . . . . . . . .198
Contact information . . . . . . . . . . . . . . . . . . . . . . .201
Average Temperatures . . . . . . . . . . . . . . . . . . . . .201
Transportation . . . . . . . . . . . . . . . . . . . . . . . . . . .201
Beaches . . . . . . . . . . . . . . . . . . . . . . . . . . . . . . .202
Pelican Picks . . . . . . . . . . . . . . . . . . . . . . . . . . .204
Attractions . . . . . . . . . . . . . . . . . . . . . . . . . . . . .208
Fishing/Water Recreation . . . . . . . . . . . . . . . . . .221
Golf . . . . . . . . . . . . . . . . . . . . . . . . . . . . . . . . . .224
Restaurants and Nightlife . . . . . . . . . . . . . . . . . .224
Accommodations . . . . . . . . . . . . . . . . . . . . . . . . .225
Shopping . . . . . . . . . . . . . . . . . . . . . . . . . . . . . .227
Festivals and Special Events . . . . . . . . . . . . . . . .228
Day Trips . . . . . . . . . . . . . . . . . . . . . . . . . . . . . .231

**8. Tallahassee** . . . . . . . . . . . . . . . . . . . . . . . . . . .**235**
Introduction . . . . . . . . . . . . . . . . . . . . . . . . . . . .235
History . . . . . . . . . . . . . . . . . . . . . . . . . . . . . . . .235

Contact Information . . . . . . . . . . . . . . . . . . . . .239
Average Temperatures . . . . . . . . . . . . . . . . . . . .240
Transportation . . . . . . . . . . . . . . . . . . . . . . . . .240
Pelican Picks . . . . . . . . . . . . . . . . . . . . . . . . . .242
Attractions . . . . . . . . . . . . . . . . . . . . . . . . . . . .244
Sports . . . . . . . . . . . . . . . . . . . . . . . . . . . . . . . .270
Fishing/Water Recreation . . . . . . . . . . . . . . . . .273
Golf . . . . . . . . . . . . . . . . . . . . . . . . . . . . . . . . .275
Tennis . . . . . . . . . . . . . . . . . . . . . . . . . . . . . . .275
Restaurants and Nightlife . . . . . . . . . . . . . . . . .275
Accommodations . . . . . . . . . . . . . . . . . . . . . . .278
Shopping . . . . . . . . . . . . . . . . . . . . . . . . . . . . .279
Festivals and Special Events . . . . . . . . . . . . . . .281
Day Trips . . . . . . . . . . . . . . . . . . . . . . . . . . . . .287

Bibliography . . . . . . . . . . . . . . . . . . . . . . . . . . .291
Index . . . . . . . . . . . . . . . . . . . . . . . . . . . . . . . .295

# Acknowledgments

There are so many wonderful people in Florida who are generous with their time, resources, and knowledge. Special thanks to:  '
Anita Gregory, Apalachicola Bay Chamber of Commerce
Kathleen Martin, Beaches of South Walton Tourist
    Development Council
Tracy Louthain, Moore Consulting Group
Sherry Rushing, Okaloosa County Convention and Visitors
    Bureau
Marcia Bush, Panama City Convention and Visitors
    Bureau
Leslie Benz, Skeet Gist, and Sheilah Bowman, Pensacola
    Convention and Visitors Bureau
Robin Knight, VISIT FLORIDA
Melissa Speir, Zimmerman Agency
Jimmy Peacock, who patiently edited the manuscript.

And of course, my husband, Creed, my favorite beach bum.

# 1

# Introduction

It's no secret that Florida is a perennial favorite for both domestic and international tourists. In 1997 alone, 47 million people visited the state. Half of these travelers drove, and as expected Orlando was the number one destination.

Yet surprisingly, the number two hot spot for the drive market was not Miami, Tampa, or even Key West. It was Panama City in the Florida Panhandle, with Okaloosa County ranking close behind.

Curving along the Gulf of Mexico in Florida's northwest corner, the Panhandle boasts the most pristine and least developed beaches in the state. Because of their natural beauty, the beaches are routinely listed among the world's best.

Another reason for Northwest Florida's appeal is its accessibility. Located directly underneath Alabama and Georgia, this part of the state is within a day's driving distance of many points within the Midwest and South. Still, it has only been in the last 10 years that tourists have begun to discover the natural beauty, affordability, and popular pastimes found in the Panhandle. In fact, tourism here has increased progressively since 1991, with most visitors traveling from Georgia, Ohio, Tennessee, North Carolina, Michigan, South Carolina, Alabama, Illinois, Ontario, and Pennsylvania.

Legend has it that in the early 1960s, Walt Disney considered Northwest Florida as a possible site for his new theme park.

No doubt he recognized the area's potential, but he was never given the opportunity to buy land there. It seems that Edward Ball, head of the St. Joe Paper Company that owned the land Disney had his eye on, refused to sell. "We don't deal with carnival people," Ball reportedly said. For the last 30 years, the area has been spared the onslaught of development that has overtaken Orlando, but times are changing.

## History

Indians have inhabited this land for centuries, and by the time Spanish explorer Ponce de Leon arrived in 1513, there were an estimated 10,000 Native Americans scattered throughout the territory. De Leon arrived during Easter, the Feast of the Flowers, and named the area *Florida,* meaning "flowers" in Spanish, and thus began his famous march through what is now the southeastern United States.

Tristan de Luna arrived some years later in 1559 in hopes of establishing a colony at Pensacola. More than 1,500 men came with him, but a devastating hurricane struck the colony two years afterward, and those who didn't die in the storm headed back to Spain. When the colony was reestablished, St. Augustine had been settled, eventually earning the title it now bears of the oldest continuous settlement in America.

During the next two hundred years, Spain, France, and Great Britain jockeyed for possession of Florida, with the United States finally purchasing the territory from Spain in 1821. By this time, many Indians had migrated south to the area in search of refuge from the Europeans who were colonizing the Northern states.

Almost immediately, Andrew Jackson was appointed to establish a new territorial government, and Tallahassee became the capital in 1824.

Also in the 1820s, the Tallahassee Railroad, a predecessor of the Seaboard Air Line Railway, began its 22-mile run between Tallahassee and Port Leon, dependent at first upon mule power. A second railroad was built between Apalachicola and St. Joseph's Bay in an effort to divert river commerce to the boom port of St. Joseph.

Though Florida had been claimed as a U.S. territory, the Seminole Indians continued to resist the influx of settlers on their land, and the Seminole War broke out in 1835. The Seminoles weren't defeated until 1837, when Osceola, their charismatic leader, was betrayed and captured while under a flag of truce. Most of the Indians were forcibly removed to what is now Oklahoma, but a few remained deep in the Everglades, never surrendering. A treaty wasn't signed with them until 1934, and today their descendants remain in South Florida.

Once the Indians had been taken care of, white settlers were free to develop large plantations where their cotton and tobacco crops thrived. When the Civil War broke out, the population of black slaves in Northern Florida was equivalent to the population of white settlers. Florida had become a state in 1845, entering the Union as a slave state concurrently with Iowa, a free state. Because of its ports in Pensacola, Jacksonville, St. Augustine, and Fernandina, the northern half of the state was coveted and eventually captured by Federal troops. Tallahassee was the only Confederate state capital east of the Mississippi not to fall to the Union during the war.

After the Civil War, pioneers continued to move to the area, quietly developing towns near the coast and at railroad junctions. Northwest Florida continued to be Florida's best kept secret until World War II, when activity at area military bases began picking up. Still, growth was slow, and it was mostly visitors from nearby Alabama, Georgia, Mississippi, and Tennessee that fed the tourism industry. For that reason, the area became affectionately known as the "Redneck Riviera," though today's tourist council officials are doing their best to change that image.

Closer to Atlanta than Miami, Northwest Florida is very much a part of the Old South. In the 1930s, *The WPA Guide to Florida* stated that "politically and socially, Florida has its own north and south, but its northern area is strictly southern and its southern area definitely northern."

The same holds true today. Here, boiled peanut vendors set up their portable stands at four-way stops. Antebellum mansions surrounded by hundreds of acres of fertile soil are hidden down dirt roads. Even some of the town names are characteristically Southern. There's Scratch Ankle, so named because smugglers who frequented this bayside town got caught in briar thickets;

Two Egg, named by a grocer whose first customer exchanged two eggs for a pound of flour; and Lick Skillet, origin unknown, later renamed Lamont.

With a distinct Southern flavor, both in atmosphere and geography, the area's inhabitants are friendly, and its setting is spectacular—miles of beaches hug the emerald Gulf, their blinding white sand crunching underfoot like snow. Inland, dense forests are filled with giant oaks standing majestically with wispy strands of Spanish moss tangled in their limbs.

## Geology

Geologists estimate that Florida is one of the youngest parts of the continental United States—only 45,000,000 years old and the last land mass to emerge from the ocean. Known in geological terms as the Floridian Plateau, the area includes the state as well as the surrounding land submerged three hundred feet deep or less in the ocean. During the convulsive age of mountain building, the Floridian Plateau remained comparatively calm, rising and falling in a rolling motion. This formed a downward dip of land mass into the ocean that separates the deep waters of the Atlantic from the deep waters of the Gulf of Mexico.

The hills in the Panhandle are comprised of marine deposits that have been folded and wrinkled in much the same way as rocks in the Piedmont Plateau, yet they are not considered part of the Appalachian Mountains. Small in comparison to hills and mountains north of the state, the hills between Pensacola and Apalachicola include the highest in Florida, one that sits 345 feet above sea level in northern Walton County. The Tallahassee hills region is a narrow, eroded plateau running about a hundred miles from east to west, with topography similar to the red clay hills of Georgia and Alabama. Along the coast, barrier islands protect the Florida mainland from tropical storms and provide habitat for shore birds and other coastal wildlife.

The entire state sits on a limestone formation that resembles a block of Swiss cheese because of the caverns and sinkholes that permeate the limestone. The sinks are caused by water erosion and an interaction of chemicals where the soil meets the limestone. When the limestone underneath the surface erodes, the surface soil slowly sinks into a depression. Sinkholes are

*Florida is one of the youngest parts of the continental United States.*
(Courtesy of VISIT FLORIDA.)

easily spotted because they are round. Three to four hundred new sinkholes are reported each year throughout the state, but most are less than 20 feet wide and therefore go unnoticed.

Springs, lakes, and streams in Florida also result from breaks in the limestone. When the earth caves in, underground waterways are often discovered, exposing streams that seem to disappear into the ground, only to resurface several miles away. Despite such shifts, there is only one cave in Florida, the Florida Caverns in Marianna.

Another familiar occurrence in Florida is the disappearance of lakes. One explanation for this natural phenomena is that the openings in the limestone bottoms become clogged with stumps and logs. When the clog is removed by natural factors, the water is able to drain out of the lake.

## Beaches

Many beaches claim to be the world's best, but those in the Florida Panhandle have scientific analyses to prove their boast. According to research conducted by Dr. Stephen Leatherman, a former University of Maryland geography professor famous for his annual rankings of the country's best beaches, the Sunshine State's northwestern shorelines are some of the world's finest.

Leatherman judges the quality of the nation's 650 public beaches based on the softness of sand, the number of waves and rip currents, the clarity of the surf, the peskiness of the mosquitoes, the number of lifeguards and tall buildings, and the noise level of the beaches. The Panhandle frequently makes the list because of controlled development and a pristine environment.

Officially ranked since 1991, **Grayton Beach State Recreation Area** in the Beaches of South Walton and **St. Andrews State Recreation Area** in Panama City Beach have each topped the list and cannot be ranked again for 10 years. Other Panhandle beaches which have ranked in the top 20 include Franklin County's **St. George Island State Park** near Tallahassee; **St. Joseph Peninsula State Park** on Cape San Blas in Gulf County; and **Perdido Key State Recreation Area** near the Alabama/Florida state line.

Unlike other beaches where the sand is comprised of as many as 20 different minerals, the sand found along the Panhandle consists of pure quartz that has been polished like glass by the undulating waves in the Gulf. Various minerals cause color fluctuations, but since these beaches are created with only hard, crystal-clear quartz, they have the look and texture of sugar.

Some say the sand is so fine because it is hundreds of miles away from its source, the Appalachian Mountains. Over hundreds of thousands of years, quartz from granite formations

*The beaches along Florida's Panhandle are among the least developed and most pristine in America.* (Courtesy of the Beaches of South Walton.)

from the mountains weathered away then washed down to river beds and into the ocean. This journey pummeled the pieces into small bits and buffed raw edges smooth.

Another defining characteristic of Northern Florida's beaches are the massive dunes that sit along the shore. When the sea level rose about 10,000 years ago, large quantities of sand were trapped at the mouth of the Apalachicola River. Afterward, winds transported the sand to the coast and shaped it into its present form.

Sea oats, which have an extensive root system, stabilize the dunes by capturing blowing sand and holding it in place. As the sand accumulates around the grass, it grows upward, creating an extensive root system that can withstand occasional water immersion and sand burial. So important are these plants to the existence of dunes that they are protected by state law. Boardwalks are provided to beach areas to protect dunes from foot traffic.

The dunes are protected because scientists estimate that the state's beaches are eroding at a rate of three feet per year, with erosion most severe along Panhandle beaches. Various types of

*It is illegal to pick sea oats because they stabilize dune systems by capturing blowing sand and holding it in place.* (Courtesy of Judy Doherty.)

barriers have been experimented with to prevent the erosion, which is caused by tropical storms and hurricanes. Many cities affected by Hurricane Opal in 1995 have undergone beach restoration, bringing in sand and planting sea oats along the coast.

Clear, emerald waters are the perfect complement to the blinding whiteness of the beaches. The primary source of Gulf water is filtered first through estuaries like Apalachicola Bay, where most of the silt and other sediments that make the Atlantic less translucent are deposited. The barrier islands also help in keeping the water clear.

Once the water reaches the Gulf, light reflecting off photo-synthetic, micro-algae in the clear water makes it appear green. The variations from green to blue occur at greater depths as a result of all the colors of light except blue being absorbed by the water.

### Average Temperatures

|  | Low | High |
|---|---|---|
| Spring | 63° | 86° |
| Summer | 71° | 89° |
| Fall | 48° | 72° |
| Winter | 44° | 67° |

### Flora and Fauna

The diversity of plants and animals found in the Sunshine State is overwhelming. Over three thousand varieties of indigenous plants have been identified, and native wildlife offers a look at some of the animal kingdom's oddest and most unusual animals.

*Alligators*

One of Florida's most fascinating and frightening creatures is the alligator. In the late 1800s, the skins of alligators were sold for 10¢ a foot; their teeth were made into whistles, key chains, and watch charms. Almost extinct in the 1960s, the few remaining alligators were placed on the endangered species list and bans were placed on hunting them and selling their skins. By 1977, the reptiles' status was upgraded to "threatened," and today they are considered a species of special concern, with regulated hunts and numerous restrictions.

Alligators are typically quite shy and will stay away from humans. But as their territory decreases, "nuisance" alligators find their way to golf courses, carports, and swimming pools.

*Alligators were almost extinct in the 1960s; today they are a species of special concern.* (Courtesy of VISIT FLORIDA.)

Gators are also attracted to dogs and small children who play around the edge of the water. Since 1948, there have been 225 unprovoked alligator attacks on humans, with eight deaths.

Alligators have a keen sense of smell and feed on raccoons, rabbits, snakes (including water moccasins), deer, and birds, and are most active in the spring and summer at night. They kill their prey by grabbing it in their jaws, dragging it under water, and holding it there until it drowns. The Game and Fresh Water Fish Commission receives an average of 8,000 to 10,000 reports of alligator threats each year. Most attacks occur in the water, but alligators have been known to pursue their prey on land—they can run up to 30 miles per hour.

The largest alligator on record weighed 1,043 pounds and was 13 feet, 10½ inches long. To estimate the size of a gator in the water, estimate the inches between its eyes and the tip of its snout; the number of inches is equal to the alligator's length in feet.

## Armadillos

The most likely encounter you'll have with an armadillo is seeing its squashed body along the side of the road. Migrating from Texas, these prehistoric-looking animals have a hard shell on their back and a long, slender nose for digging. While they help control the insect population, they wreak havoc on lawns and gardens. The animals forage at night and like places where the soil is soft and loose. They are harmless, but are the only mammals other than humans to be susceptible to leprosy.

## Herons

With long, spindly legs and sharp, pointed beaks, herons are large, graceful birds that live throughout the state. You'll see them wading along the edge of swamps or sitting in the branches of trees. The most popular types of herons are the great blue and the great white, but there are several different kinds—the flamingo of South Florida is a member of the heron family.

## Jellyfish

It is common to see jellyfish during summer months, but they seem most prevalent in July. These odd sea creatures look like translucent stomachs floating along in the water. The two most prevalent types on the Gulf Coast, the Moon Jellyfish and the Lion's Mane, are not dangerous, but they can inflict serious pain on their victims. If you are stung, pack beach sand on the sting until you can get home, and take care not to rub the area. Clean your skin with alcohol and then apply meat tenderizer or toothpaste to the sting. These products break down the protein in the jellyfish venom. Avoid stepping on jellyfish on the beach since they can sting long after they are dead.

## Lovebugs

If you're wondering what all that creamy, yellowish gunk is on the front of your car, say hello to the lovebug. During May and September, these small, black bugs seem to swarm throughout the state in thick clouds. They are prevalent along the highways because they are attracted to ultraviolet light (UV) combined with automobile exhaust fumes. As expected, many end up on the grills and hoods of cars, and if their squashed bodies are left there to cook in the Florida heat, their residue eats away at the paint.

Lovebugs got their nickname because the male and female fly around in tandem while mating. They have a life span up to six days, most of which is spent mating. Lovebugs don't bite or sting; they are only a nuisance when it comes to keeping your car clean. It appears that cars are also their only predator, since birds find them distasteful.

## Mosquitoes

Where there's water, there's bound to be mosquitoes. *Mosquito* is the Spanish word for "little fly," but anyone who has been bitten by one of these dreaded insects would beg to differ. Like sand gnats, only the females bite; they need blood to develop and lay their eggs. To penetrate the skin, they have long, pointed mouth parts like needles. They inject saliva into their victim's skin so that it mixes with the blood, making it easier to extract. The saliva also enhances blood flow. Mosquito concentration is heaviest during the summer months when humidity is at its highest, and it seems to worsen from dusk throughout the evening. The best way to repel these miniature monsters is to apply mosquito repellent, preferably a brand with DEET. Skin-So-Soft by Avon also works. The old-fashioned way to avoid bites is to wear long pants and shirts with long sleeves.

## Opossums

Like armadillos, opossums don't have much luck crossing the highway; they are blinded by headlights and freeze on the spot, which attributes to their roadside death rate. The state's only marsupials, opossums are so ugly they're cute. Their fur is scraggly and patchy, their straight tail is hairless and skinny, and they will flash their mouthful of teeth when provoked. For the most part, opossums are harmless and rarely seen during the day. If they become scared, they'll roll over and play dead, or "possum."

## Sand Gnats

Also called "no-see-ums" or "flying teeth," sand gnats thrive in salt marshes, freshwater swamps, and anywhere there is wet sand and organic matter—in other words, the entire state of Florida. The gnats range in size from one-sixteenth of an inch to one-eighth inch and are rarely noticed until they have attacked their prey. When they do, they don't bite, but cut into the skin with mouth parts that resemble scissors. This coupled with an itching reaction makes the wound sting and burn. The female gnats are attracted by the carbon dioxide emitted by humans and animals, and they suck blood to develop their eggs. The males don't bite. About the only thing known to ward off the gnats are long-sleeve shirts, pants, and repeated applications of repellents with DEET.

## Sea Turtles

Sea turtles are the gentle giants of Florida's coastline. There are five species: leatherbacks, loggerheads, green turtles, Kemp's Ridley, and hawksbill turtles. In late spring and early summer, they find their way to the beach to lay their eggs above the high-water mark. When a nest is spotted (usually by a volunteer), it is marked off by yellow tape and closely monitored until the fall, when the eggs hatch and the baby turtles dig their way out. These young turtles return to the sea by following reflections of light on the water, and they are easily distracted by bright head-lights, flashlights, and camera flashes. That's why many resorts now turn their beach lights off during this time of year.

Turtles can lay from 300 to 800 eggs in a season in three to 10 different clutches. The majority of these eggs, once hatched, will never make it to maturity since they are easy prey and good eating for raccoons and other predators.

Today, state officials discourage people from bothering a turtle while it is laying eggs, and it is illegal to collect eggs, but back in 1875 when poet Sidney Lanier visited the Panhandle, he recorded in his book, *Florida: Its Scenery, Climate, and History*, that turtle-rolling was a popular sport.

> As she leaves the water to deposit her hundreds of eggs; you see one: you advance, and coolly turn it over on its back—and that is all. You leave it, leisurely pursue your stroll, turn another on its back, leave it, and so on, till you are tired. When you come again on the morrow, there they are. To walk up to a turtle of a morning, after having treated him in this manner overnight, and look steadily in the eye thereof without certain titillating sensations at once in your diaphragm (where you laugh) and in your conscience (where

*Sea turtles are the gentle giants of Florida's coastline.* (Courtesy of VISIT FLORIDA.)

you do not laugh), requires more grim rigidity of the former and more supple elasticity of the latter than some people possess.

## Shells

Over 1,500 varieties of shells have been documented along the beaches of Florida and many of these can be found in the Panhandle. For the best luck, *conchologists,* or people who collect shells, suggest looking along the ends of islands that face passes and channels where currents carry shells to the shore, and going hunting at low tide. Shells also pile up on the oceanside shelf at the bottom of sandbars. Storms and winter weather are also known to stir up shells. Keep in mind that collecting live shells is discouraged.

The state shell is the horse conch (*Pleuroplaca giganta*), also known as the giant band shell because of its pinkish-orange bands. Other noted Florida shells include:

**Atlantic Abra,** a small white clam with a polished shell. Growing to about one-fourth inch, these clams are found in abundance after drastic cold fronts.

**Coquina Shell,** which is small and banded with different colors. These are usually found buried in the sand along the edge of the shore.

**Cross-Barred Venus Clam,** which features a cross-hatched pattern on the outside. Venus clams are the most common shells in Florida.

**Dwarf Surf Clam,** a creamy white shell that is smooth except for fine growth lines.

**Lightning Whelk,** the only Florida shell that spirals regularly to the left.

**Moon Snail,** also called "cat's eye" because of the deep blue color found at the center of a living shell. The color fades after the mollusk inside dies.

**Ponderous Ark,** a type of clam with a black, mossy coating on the outside of its shell. Arks that have rolled around in the waves will be white.

**Slipper Shell,** or boat shell, which resembles a small boat with a seat. You can even float well-shaped slipper shells in water.

*Shells are abundant along the beach, but guests are encouraged to leave them on the shore.* (Courtesy of the Panama City Beach Convention and Visitors Bureau.)

**Van Hyning's Cockle,** one of the largest of Florida's cockle shells. These have a dark red and gold color and are also called heart clams because they look like a heart when they are whole.

### Snakes

Florida is crawling with several different varieties of snakes, only four of which are poisonous. Like alligators, snakes are afraid of humans and usually attack only when provoked. If you are hiking, wear thick boots and step over logs and debris instead of on top of them.

If you stumble across a snake, stand back and slowly walk away. Snakes eat many of Florida's nuisance insects; only poisonous snakes in a threatening situation should be killed. Following are the poisonous snakes found in Florida:

**Coral snakes** are the most deadly snakes in North America. They won't bite unless scared or provoked, and when they do, they bite and chew poison into the victim instead of injecting it. Coral snakes have bands of red, black, and yellow, and are often confused with king snakes that exhibit the same colors. To keep from confusing the two, remember that "red touch yellow, kill a fellow."

**Copperheads** have a pinkish-tan body with brownish-red crossbands. In Florida, they are found only in the Panhandle counties, where they live in heavily timbered areas. Reports of copperhead bites are rare.

**Rattlesnakes** come in three types in the Panhandle. The *Canebrake Rattlesnake* is grayish-brown or pink in color, with dark bands across its body and a rust-colored strip down the middle of its back. Canebrake rattlers live in flatwoods, river bottoms, hammocks, and near cool swamps when the weather is hot. The most dangerous native snake in Florida is the *Eastern Diamondback,* which can fling its body toward a victim as far away as half its body length. A diamondback has a diamond-shaped pattern with a yellow border and buttons at the end of its tail that rattle. Its venom is especially poisonous, and the snake doesn't have to be in a coiled position to strike. Diamondbacks can be found in any habitat with flatlands and brushy, grassy areas. The *Pygmy Rattlesnake* is the smallest of the three. It is gray with red and black spots alternating down the center of its back. Pygmies make a buzzing sound like an insect and are quick to strike their victims. Bites from rattlesnakes can be painful but are rarely fatal.

**Water moccasins** or cottonmouths, are olive-brown to black and are usually found near lakes, swamps, and marshes. When they open their mouths to strike, they reveal a white, cottony interior, hence their nickname.

## Spanish Moss

The wispy, greenish-gray threads of moss hanging from tree branches is Spanish Moss, also called "old man's beard." A member of the bromelaceae family, this moss has no roots; it survives by creating its own food through photosynthesis and trapping and absorbing water.

In the 1930s, the moss was a major industry in Florida because it was used as padding in mattresses, car seats, and couches. When the outside grayish layer rots away, it leaves a very strong filament.

Today, people collect the moss mainly for decorative purposes. If you decide to take some home, microwave it on high for about a minute to kill the thousands of chiggers that live on the moss.

## Natural Habitats

### Flatwoods

The most common type of habitat in Florida, flatwoods are distinguished by longleaf pines, slash pines, and low-growing saw palmettos. The Apalachicola National Forest is a good example of a flatwoods habitat.

### Hardwood Forests and Hammocks

Hammocks, meaning "shady places," are common in hardwood forests. Here you'll find large oak trees draped with Spanish moss and undergrowths of cabbage, sabal palms, and wild azaleas. In North Florida, hardwood forests and hammocks have more species of trees and shrubs than any other plant community in the continental United States. Florida Caverns State Park is a typical hardwood forest habitat.

## High Pine

Once abundant from Texas to the Carolinas, high pine habitats have disappeared in rapid numbers due to logging and urban development. With longleaf pines, low woody shrubs, wringers, and ferns, the remaining areas of this ecosystem require surface fires to maintain their open vistas. The Blackwater River State Forest is a high pine habitat.

## Salt Marshes

Salt marshes appear to be nothing more than flat, grassy meadows. In reality they are active water estuaries teeming with life. The water fluctuates with tidal creeks that flow through the marshes. The sea grasses in the water provide food to a variety of marine life and act as filters for nearby estuaries. Salt marshes are found in inland bays and along the coast east of Apalachicola.

## Scrub

With their gnarled sand pines, evergreen shrubs, and patches of ground lichens, scrub forests are the closest thing Florida has to a desert. Dry, infertile, and sandy soil makes the land extremely valuable in a state where well-drained land is hard to come by. Scrub is also essential for the environment since it acts as a filtering system for rain to replenish the underground drinking water aquifers.

### Florida's Official

| | |
|---|---|
| Animal | Florida Panther |
| Bird | Mockingbird |
| Flower | Orange Blossom |
| Marine Animal | Manatee |
| Reptile | Alligator |
| Saltwater Mammal | Porpoise |
| Shell | Horse Conch |

*One of the most common types of habitat in Northwest Florida is scrub.* (Courtesy of Judy Doherty.)

| | |
|---|---|
| Song | "Old Folks at Home," also called "Suwannee River," by Stephen Foster |
| Tree | Sabal Palm |

# 2

# Tips for Travelers

A hundred years ago, traveling to wild and woolly Florida was equivalent to late 20th-century journeys to Australia's Outback or Africa's remote outposts. Travelers were urged to take special precautions. "Have your teeth thoroughly set in order by a skilful [*sic*] dentist, carry your own towel, and a teaspoonful of carbolic acid or camphor, sprinkled in the room, or an ointment of cold cream scented with turpentine, will be found very disagreeable to these insects, and often equally so to the traveler," wrote Daniel Brinton in his 1869 *Guidebook of Florida and the South for Tourists, Invalids, and Emigrants.*

The WPA's *Florida: A Guide to the Southernmost State* published in 1939 warned travelers "not to enter bushes at sides of highways in rural districts; snakes and redbugs [chiggers] usually infest such places. Do not eat tung nuts; they are poisonous. Do not eat green pecans; in the immature stages the skins have a white film containing arsenic."

Even poet Sidney Lanier lamented that "it is greatly hoped that increased facilities for reaching these favorable regions will soon render them practicable to those who now find the journey too trying."

How times have changed! Thanks to mosquito control, interstate highways, and air-conditioning, Florida's jungle has

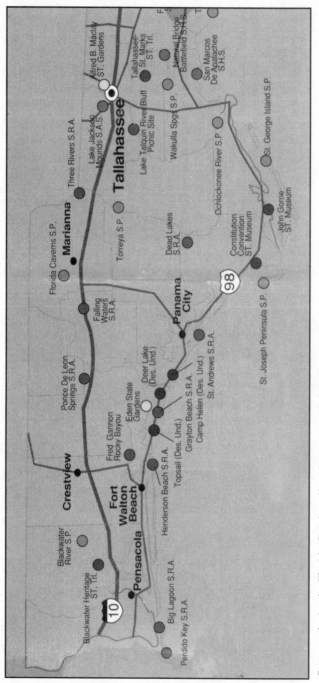

*State parks in the Florida Panhandle.* (Courtesy of the Florida Park Service.)

been tamed so that even the most wary traveler can enjoy the sun and the scenery.

Northwest Florida is one of the last places to be discovered in the Sunshine State, and it offers all the amenities found in its counterparts down south.

## Contact Information

**Florida Tourism Industry Corporation** (661 East Jefferson Street, Suite 300, Tallahassee, FL 32301; 888-7352872, 850-488-5607; www.flausa.com).

**Florida Attractions Association** (P.O. Box 10295, Tallahassee, FL 32302; 850-222-2885).

These folks can provide you with a guide map to all the attractions in the state.

**Florida Chamber of Commerce** (136 South Bronough Street, Tallahassee, FL 32301; 850-425-1200).

A statewide association, the Florida Chamber of Commerce can provide you with a list of contact information for all chambers of commerce in the state. This is especially helpful if you plan to visit rural areas and small cities in the state not represented by a larger tourism organization.

**Florida Hotel/Motel Association** (P.O. Box 1529, Tallahassee, FL 32302; 850-224-2888; www.floridaaccommodations.com).

## Airlines

**Airtran** (800-825-8538)
**Delta** (800-221-1212)
**Gulf Stream International** (800-992-8532)
**US Airways** (800-428-4322)

## Camping

**Florida Association of RV Parks and Campgrounds** (1340 Vickers Drive, Tallahassee, FL 32303-3041; 850-562-7151).

For information on private campsites, request the Official Florida Camping Directory.

*Florida has two sides: the beaches and the wild, untamed backwoods.* (Courtesy of VISIT FLORIDA.)

**Florida Park Information** (Dept. of Environmental Protection, Mail Station 535, 3900 Commonwealth Blvd., Tallahassee, FL 32399-3000; 850-488-9872; www.dep.state.fl.us/parks).

For information on camping and other activities in state parks, request a brochure and price list. You can also ask about a vacation pass that is good for up to 15 days. A family entrance permit covers admission to any of Florida's parks and costs $20.

**Kampgrounds of America (KOA)** (406-248-7444)

This private chain of RV parks also accepts tents.

## Canoeing and Kayaking

**Office of Greenways and Trails** (Florida Dept. of Environmental Protection, 325 John Knox Road, Bldg. 500, Tallahassee, FL 32303-4124; 850-488-3701; www.dep.state.fl.us/gwt/).

The canoe trails in Florida are part of a statewide system managed by the Office of Greenways and Trails. Currently there are 38 canoe trails with over a thousand miles of scenic waterways. A number of these are located in North Florida.

Safety should always be your first concern when canoeing. Be sure to:

- carry drinking water.
- have the proper floatation gear (Florida law requires a Coast Guard-approved, accessible, and wearable personal floatation device for each person in the canoe).
- keep a first-aid kit handy.
- notify someone of your canoe route.
- pack an extra paddle.
- store food and gear in water-tight containers and tie them to the boat.
- take along a flashlight and batteries.

## Caring for Wildlife

While litter is unsightly, it can be deadly to Florida's wildlife. Throw all trash into garbage cans, especially the plastic rings from six-packs. Many animals can get hung in the rings and drown or hang themselves.

If a bird (usually a pelican) swallows your fishing line, do not cut the line, as the bird can get tangled in brush or trees and eventually starve. Instead, gently pull the bird in, using a

*The weather along the Panhandle is conducive to year-round outdoor activities such as cycling.* (Courtesy of Sandestin Resort.)

net to lift it from the water. Have one person hold the bird still and firm, tucking the wings and body underneath one arm while holding the beak shut (pelicans do not bite). Locate the hook and push the barb outside of the skin. Cut the barb and pull the hook out. If the bird has swallowed the line, cut it at the bill and make sure all fishing line is removed from the bird.

When spending time on the beach, be aware of the many animals and birds that live along the shore. Stay away from nesting birds so you won't trample their eggs or young. Report unmarked sea turtle nesting activity, hatching nests, and hatchling disorientations (when hatched turtles head for the light created by development instead of light reflected off the water).

## Cycling

**State Bicycle Office** (Florida Dept. of Transportation, 605 South Suwannee Street, Tallahassee, FL 32399-0450; 850-487-1200).

Many parks and trails throughout Florida are suitable for biking. Bicycles can also be ridden on any roads open to motor

*Snorkeling and diving are popular pastimes along the Panhandle.*
(Courtesy of the Panama City Beach Convention and
Visitors Bureau.)

vehicles. Cyclists under the age of 16 are required by law to wear helmets; helmets are not required by law but strongly encouraged for cyclists over 16.

It is also wise to take steps to prevent your bicycle from being stolen. According to FBI records, more bikes are stolen in Florida each year than in any other state. Use a U-shaped lock, engrave your social security number on expensive parts, and lock your bike in public areas where it is seen by all.

### Diving

**Scuba News** (5395 Lenox Avenue, Jacksonville, FL 32205; 904-384-7336; www.scubanews.com).

The Panhandle offers excellent diving around limestone reefs that stagger downward like giant stairways to the depths of the Gulf. Dolphins play close by, schools of baitfish dart around nearby reefs, and 50-pound amberjack cruise through the area's shipwrecks. Additionally, there are a number of interesting cave systems in the rivers and springs, though most sites will not permit you to take flashlights down with you if you are not certified.

*The deep, blue waters of the Gulf of Mexico provide excellent fishing opportunities.* (Courtesy of the Beaches of South Walton.)

Many dive clubs in the area schedule group dives; consult each chapter for listings.

Summer and fall are the best times of year for beach and reef diving because the winds are generally light. Always check local conditions and updated nautical charts before you dive and make sure to double-check all information with local dive operators.

### Fishing

**Fisheries Management** (Dept. of Environmental Protection, Mail Station 240, 3900 Commonwealth Blvd., Tallahassee, FL 32399-3000; 850-922-4340; www.dep.state.fl.us/marine, www.-dep.state.fl.us/gfc).

Chartering a boat is a common practice along the Panhandle, and whether you take to the rivers and inland waterways or head for the Gulf, you won't be disappointed. Marlin, sailfish, mackerel, dolphin, perch, grouper, speckled trout, redfish, catfish, bass, and bluegill are among the catches you can expect.

In Florida, saltwater and freshwater fishing licenses are required of anglers 16 years and older. There are also restrictions on the size and number of certain species that can be caught. Licenses are available from county tax collectors and local bait and tackle shops. You can also request pamphlets on fishing from the Office of Fisheries.

## Highway Information

It takes about four hours to drive the length of the Panhandle. There are several routes you can take, including Interstate 10, U.S. Highway 90, which winds through inland towns and runs parallel to I-10, and Highway 98, which hugs the coastline. The area is also dissected by roads running north to south from Georgia and Alabama.

- **Yellow** signs indicate warning or directions; **green** signs are for freeway directions and street names; **orange** signs signal roadwork or detours; **brown** signs indicate parks, campsites, and historic sites; **blue** signs provide non-driving information; and **red-and-white** signs mean do not enter or wrong way.
- Speed limits and distances are provided in miles, not kilometers.
- Roads stretching from east to west have even numbers, while those stretching north to south have odd numbers.
- Most state rest areas along the interstates have restrooms, public telephones, and security for at least a portion of the day.

## Hiking

**Florida Trail Association** (P.O. Box 13708, Gainesville, FL 32604; 800-343-1882, 352-378-8823; www.florida-trail.org/~fta).

**Office of Greenways and Trails** (Dept. of Environmental Protection, Mail Station 795, 3900 Commonwealth Blvd., Tallahassee, FL 32399-3000; 850-487-4784; www.dep.state.fl.us/gwt/).

In North Florida, hiking is pleasant for both novice and experienced hikers because the terrain is generally flat but varied in habitats. October through March is the best time to hike in the Panhandle since the humidity tends to be lower, the weather is cooler, and there are fewer insects. The state's Office of Greenways and Trails oversees the network of biking, hiking, horseback riding, skating, and canoeing trails traversing the state, and chooses trails for their scenic, recreational, and historic value. The state is also managing the Rails to Trails program, where abandoned railroad beds are being turned into recreational trails. The Tallahassee–St. Marks Historic Railroad State Trail was the first designated trail in the state.

A private organization, the Florida Trail Association, is undertaking a project to connect 1,300 miles of continuous hiking trails across the state, from Big Cypress National preserve to Gulf Islands National Seashore. Though trails in the Panhandle are among the least developed in Florida, progress is being made in clearing new trails across the area.

### Hurricanes

Even though Florida boasts sunny weather and warm temperatures, it can also claim more rainfall annually than any other mainland state and a frequency of thunderstorms second only to sub-Saharan Africa.

Hurricanes are the most publicized weather occurrences in the state. The hurricane season stretches from June 1 to November 30, with most of the storms occurring in August, September, and October. The last to make its mark along the Panhandle was Opal, which hit in 1995 with winds of 125 mph and gusts of 145. As the third most destructive storm in Florida's history, Opal destroyed 120 miles of coastline from Fort Walton Beach to Panama City.

These dangerous tropical cyclones begin as tropical disturbances with a moving series of thunderstorms. When the storm clouds reach winds from 39 to 74 mph, they elevate into tropical depressions. Above 75 mph, storms become hurricanes. They can cover several hundred miles, generate winds up to 200 mph, and produce torrential rains and tornadoes. There are three phases of a hurricane. The first is a furious gale blowing in one direction, followed by the eerie calm of the center, or eye. The final stage can be just as violent as the first, with winds blowing in the opposite direction.

The most dangerous aspect of a hurricane is the storm surges that accompany it. This dome of water forms in the center of the hurricane as it grows over the ocean. When it reaches the shore, the surge can be up to 20 feet above normal sea level and powerful enough to raze everything in its path.

Florida's entire coastline is prone to hurricanes, but research indicates that the area between the Choctawhatchee Bay and the Perdido River in the Panhandle is more prone to these deadly storms.

If the weather begins to look threatening, tune into local media programs for storm updates and don't hesitate to leave the area if evacuation is encouraged. Telephone directories also contain instructions for hurricane preparation and evacuation. Evacuation routes are marked by signs with a blue drop of water on a white background with arrows indicating safe evacuation directions.

## Lottery

**Florida Lottery** (850-487-7787; www.flalottery.com).

Since its inception in 1988, Florida's lottery has become one of the most successful in America. The most popular game is Lotto, where players select six numbers from 1 to 49 each week, in any order, in hopes that they match the six numbers randomly drawn by a machine. The drawing occurs each Saturday night on a live telecast. If there is no match, the jackpot rolls over to the next week. Jackpots start at $6 million and have climbed as high as $86.04 million.

The lottery also has three-, four-, and five-number games with daily drawings and scratch-off games which can be won instantly. Call and request a list of the most winning numbers.

## Packing List

- Bug repellent (repellents with deet work best for mosquitoes)
- Camera and film
- Cooler with ice cold beverages
- Copies or duplicates of prescriptions or a letter from your doctor verifying your need for a particular medication
- Extra bag for souvenirs
- Eye glasses and sunglasses (look for those without reflective lens)
- Hat or visor
- Medicines and vitamins
- Moisturizing lotion and aloe vera gel
- Sunscreen

- Water bottle
- Windbreaker for cool nights or if you are sunburned

## Peak Season

Unlike South Florida, the Panhandle's high season begins in mid-March with the spring break crowd and ends around Labor Day.

## Rental Car Information

If you plan to rent a car, you will need a valid driver's license, proof of automobile insurance, and a major credit card; some companies also have minimum age requirements. Confirm all reservations in advance.

**Advantage** (800-777-5500)
**Alamo** (800-327-9633)
**Avis** (800-831-2847)
**Budget** (800-527-0770)
**Dollar** (800-800-4000)
**Enterprise** (800-325-8007)
**Hertz** (800-654-3131)
**National** (800-227-7368)
**Thrifty** (800-367-2277)

## RV Rental Companies

**Cruise America** (800-327-7799)
**Go Vacations, Inc.** (800-487-4652)
**Recreation Vehicle Rental Association** (800-336-0355)
**Rental Management Systems** (818-960-1884)

## Safety Tips

Florida has garnered much media attention over the past few years due to crimes committed against tourists throughout the state. While North Florida has a relatively low crime rate compared to other parts of the state, tourists should make safety a top priority. When driving, keep in mind that:
- additional passengers must wear seat belts and children up to three years of age must be secured in separate car seats.

- Florida law requires the use of headlights at dusk and during fog and rain.
- rental cars are prevented by law from having distinguishing license plates, bumper stickers, decals, or other rental information.
- all documentation for the car must be kept available, usually in the glove compartment.
- interstate emergency call boxes are positioned one mile apart.
- lights on emergency or police vehicles are red or blue; do not stop for flashing white lights or flashing headlights.

### Seasickness

Seasickness can occur any time the body experiences motion other than on foot. As a result, almost 90 percent of people suffer from some level of seasickness. Scientists think the condition is caused by sensory mismatch in the brain, when the vestibular system of the inner ear sends messages about body position and movement that contradict information relayed by the eyes. This confuses the brain and causes dizziness, blurry vision, nausea, and other side effects. To counter these unwanted symptoms:

- try non-prescription drugs designed to keep the symptoms under control; to be effective, most drugs should be taken at least an hour before the vessel leaves the dock.
- keep a broad view of the horizon in sight and walk around to try and adjust to the motion of the craft; avoid reading and lying down.
- ask to join the captain so you can focus on the boat's course; this is the same reasoning behind the fact that most automobile drivers never get car sick because they are focused on the road in front of them.
- avoid alcoholic beverages.
- consider purchasing a Sea Band that controls pressure on the acupuncture points (the neikuan points) in your wrists.

### Smoking

As in most U.S. travel destinations, smoking is not permitted in public buildings or on public transportation in Florida.

If you are a smoker, you can request smoking sections in hotels and restaurants.

## Sunburn

Before Coco Chanel popularized tanning in the 1920s, parasols and full-length clothing were standard beach attire. Suddenly, bathing suits became all the rage, and over the years, the suits have grown smaller as the desire for a deep, bronze tan has grown larger.

Now that people are aware of the damaging effects of the sun, dark tans are no longer en vogue. In the Panhandle, the glare from the white beaches and clear waters is highly reflective, so expect to tan or burn quicker than normal. Apply sunscreen generously to your entire body, including exposed skin parts in your hair, your eyelids, and your ears. Avoid suntan oils, and drink plenty of fluids. If you notice your skin turning pink or red, you should get out of the sun. The sun's rays are strongest from 10:00 A.M. to 3:00 P.M., but you can burn as early as 8:00 A.M. and as late at 6:00 P.M.

If you do burn, aloe vera gel helps to soothe and cool skin. A vinegar bath will also help.

## Sunscreen

Regardless of your skin tone, the sun's ultraviolet, or UV, rays can cause serious damage to your skin. Dermatologists recommend that fair-skinned beach bums use a sunscreen with an SPF of 30, which means it will take 30 times longer for skin to burn.

Always apply sunscreen at least 15 minutes before you're in the sun, and if you'll be in the water, make sure the sunscreen is water-resistant; if it's not, reapply after taking a dip. Be sure to use a generous amount, apply it thoroughly, and rub it in. Wear a hat and cover-up to protect sensitive skin.

## Time Zones

Cities located between the Alabama line and the Apalachicola River are in the Central Standard Time zone (CST). Cities east of the Apalachicola River, including Apalachicola, are in the Eastern Standard Time zone (EST).

Daylight Savings Time is observed from the first Sunday in April until the last Sunday in October to take advantage of daylight.

### Tipping

Service charges are usually added to checks for parties of six or more. Otherwise, the standard range is between 15 and 20 percent. Hotel porters and sky caps generally receive a dollar per bag. The bell boy who takes you to your room also receives a dollar.

### Water Safety

Whether you are swimming in a pool or in the ocean, it is always best to use the buddy system. You should also pay attention to the flags dotting the beach. Several cities and many resorts along the Gulf utilize a flag system to inform swimmers of water conditions.

- A **blue** flag indicates calm seas with favorable swimming conditions. You should always exercise caution as there can still be undercurrents.
- A **yellow** flag means that waters may be rough and that undercurrents and rip currents are likely. Rip currents are strong flows of water moving from the shoreline out to sea. They are usually accompanied by high winds and large waves, but can occur on calm days as well. Exercise extreme caution when swimming or wading.
- A **red** flag means danger. You should stay out of the water until conditions change.

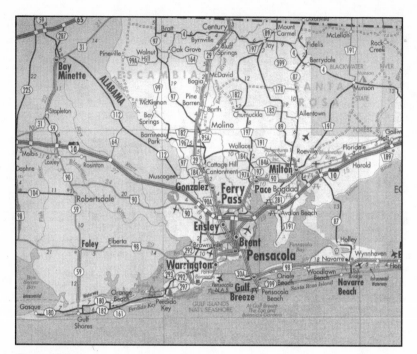

*Pensacola area.*

# 3

# Pensacola

## Introduction

With 40 miles of shoreline, including some of the world's most beautiful beaches, this historic seaport city is shaped geographically and culturally by the waters that surround it. On the map, Santa Rosa Island extends like a bony finger into the warm waters of the Gulf, creating the protected inland harbor of Pensacola Bay. It was the harbor that first attracted the Spaniards to the area in 1559; 250 years later, the U.S. Navy discovered it and promptly set up a naval air station there.

Today, Pensacola is the All-American family destination. The numerous beaches are clean, the entertainment is wholesome, and the accommodations are affordable.

## History

In 1559, six years before America's oldest city, St. Augustine, was founded, Don Tristan de Luna and 1,500 men arrived in Pensacola and established a colony. Within two years, their settlement was destroyed by a hurricane, and those who didn't die in the storm abandoned camp.

In 1698, 139 years after the initial settlement, Don Andres de Ariola and his army of Spanish soldiers tried once again to colonize the area. This time, they succeeded. During the next hundred years, Pensacola changed hands between the Spanish, French, and British—three times in 1718 alone and thirteen times by 1866. The city sided with the British during the Revolutionary War—along with East Florida, they were the only American colonies to do so. Britain laid out and mapped the streets, while Spain built forts to protect the bay and named the streets. Zaragossa, Palafox, Taragona, and Moreno Streets are all legacies of the city's Spanish heritage.

In 1818, Andrew Jackson attacked the town and forced the British to withdraw. Jackson took the city in retribution for Seminole Indian raids into Georgia, but also to assure certain land investments made in the area. Pensacola officially became part of the United States in 1821, and a year later the first Florida territorial legislature under American jurisdiction met here, naming Jackson as the provisional governor. The Navy yard was established in 1825 and remains an economic mainstay to this day.

Like other cities in Florida, Pensacola fought for the Confederacy, but fell to Union forces early in the war. The largest city in Florida before the war, Pensacola sank into a slump from which it did not recover until the late 1800s.

In 1886, Fort Pickens became the holding site for Geronimo, a captured Apache leader. People came from all over to see the Indian, and Geronimo, being a shrewd businessman, would sell the buttons off his coat by day for a dollar each, then stitch more buttons on at night.

It was also around this time that better railroads were built and a well-developed network of river steamboats was established. This revitalized the Navy industry and positioned Pensacola as an important international port of call. The economy was boosted by the Navy once again in 1914, when the Pensacola Naval Air Station was created as the Navy's first flight training center.

Today, Florida's westernmost city has a population of 300,000, with naval operations as the foundation of its economy. Tourism is second.

There are two islands that provide the sugar-sand beaches in the Pensacola area. The first, Perdido Key, lies 15 miles west of Pensacola, the closest beach to the Alabama line. This barrier island is connected to both Alabama and Florida by bridges. Half of the island has plenty of condos, hotels, and restaurants for visitors to choose from. The other half is home to Perdido Key State Recreation Area and Big Lagoon State Park, both part of the Gulf Islands National Seashore.

Santa Rosa, the second island, is basically a giant sandbar always shifting westward. It has two contrasting sides: one is a characteristic Florida shoreline with rolling dunes; the other features the undulating Gulf.

Santa Rosa Sound offers calm bay waters and beaches dotted with scrubby trees and vegetation. The sand dunes on the north side tend to have more vegetation holding them in place and are usually larger in size than their southside counterparts. To the east of the fishing pier on the sound, the clear, smooth water and construction debris left over from the construction of Fort McCree, an early military establishment, now attract a plethora of marine life, making it a perfect spot for snorkeling. Diving is a common activity on the west side of the pier, but divers are cautioned to wear a weight belt since the current from Pensacola Pass can become quite strong.

You can view both sides as you drive along the highway. With its magnificent sand dunes and sea oat preserves, this barrier island is an excellent spot for viewing the more than 280 species of birds that live on the island or stop by while migrating south.

Both ends of Santa Rosa Island are part of the Gulf Islands National Seashore. Pensacola Beach, in the center, was once a federal preserve, but is now where all the commercial beach development is located.

Navarre Beach lies to the east of Pensacola Beach. This small beach is affiliated with Navarre, which sits on the edge of the mainland next to the sound. As one of the few towns in Northwest Florida that began as a tourist community, Navarre is called "Florida's Best-Kept Secret" because it is not as well known as its counterparts along the Gulf. Still, it offers the same immaculate beaches and variety in restaurants and accommodations. Navarre Beach was founded by Col. Guy H. Wyman, a retired army engineer from DeFuniak Springs. He acquired five acres of land along the sound and named it for a province in Northern Spain, a favorite of his wife's.

## Pelican Picks

**Blue Angels** (850-452-4583)

Based at the Pensacola Naval Air Station, these aerobatic aces occasionally perform for the public. It's the outfit that the movie *Top Gun* was based on. Call the public affairs office for a schedule.

**MUFON** (2300 Hallmark Drive, Pensacola, FL 32503; 850-438-3261, 850-429-0216 UFO Hotline number).

In recent years, there have been hundreds of Unidentified Flying Objects reported in the skies of Pensacola and neighboring Gulf Breeze. Consequently, the local Mutual UFO Network, or MUFON, hosts nightly skywatches that begin about an hour after sunset at Shoreline Park South in Gulf Breeze.

MUFON is an international, scientific, non-profit organization composed of people seriously interested in UFO phenomena. There are over 60,000 UFO reports in its files.

The Pensacola/Gulf Breeze MUFON group conducts UFO investigations, sponsors a UFO Abductee Support Group, and hosts meetings on the second Sunday of the month with speakers from around the country.

**Scenic Highway** (Hwy. 90; 850-477-7155).

Snaking above hundred-foot-high red clay bluffs that have been carved out of the coastline by the Escambia River, the Scenic Highway is steeped in Florida history. Historians believe the highway began as an early Indian trail. Later, it became known as the "Spanish Trail," a trade route between El Paso, Texas, and Jacksonville, Florida. English, Spanish, and American settlers made bricks from the bluffs' red clay in the 18th and 19th centuries.

Among the highway's points of interest: *English Point,* where the wreck of a 16th-century Spanish galleon—the one that brought colonists to Pensacola in 1559—was discovered in shallow water just off the bluffs; *Gull Point,* where Florida's first territorial council met in 1822; *Bay Bluffs Park,* a half-mile of cliffs where visitors can descend to the shoreline by wooden stairs and a boardwalk; and *Gaberonne Point*, the site of one of the several brickyards built for easy access to the red clay found in the bluffs. About half of the bluffs have been developed with upscale residential construction, but there are still scattered parcels of land remaining in their natural state.

Because of its unique natural features, recreational opportunities, rich history, and breathtaking beauty, the highway has recently been proposed as the first candidate for the new Florida Scenic Highways Program. If approved, it will be eligible for designation as a National Scenic Byway.

## Contact Information

Free information is available by writing or calling the visitor information center. When you arrive in Pensacola, you can also pick up brochures, pamphlets, and coupons at the satellite information centers located in the T.T. Wentworth, Jr., Museum in Historic Pensacola Village, at Century city hall, and at the Pensacola visitor center at the foot of the Pensacola Bridge.

**Pensacola Visitor Information Center** (1401 E. Gregory Street; 800-874-1234, 850-434-1234, www.visitpensacola.com).

**Santa Rosa County Island Authority** (735 Pensacola Beach Blvd.; 800-635-4803, 850-932-2259; open daily from 9:00 A.M. to 5:00 P.M.; www.pcola.com/penbeach).

**Gulf Breeze and Navarre Beaches Tourist Information Center** (8543 Navarre Pkwy., Navarre, FL 32566; 800-480-SAND, 850-939-2691; open Monday–Friday from 9:00 A.M. to 5:00 P.M., Saturday from 10:00 A.M. to 4:00 P.M., Sunday from 12:00 P.M. to 4:00 P.M.; www.navarrefl.com).

### Average Temperatures

| | |
|---|---|
| Spring | 68° |
| Summer | 81° |
| Fall | 69° |
| Winter | 55° |

## Transportation

As the largest airport in Northwest Florida, the state-of-the-art Pensacola Regional Airport offers 60 flights daily, most of which must connect via Atlanta, Nashville, or Charlotte. A cab ride from the airport to downtown costs about nine dollars; it costs around $17 to reach Pensacola Beach. Renting a car is probably the best way to get around Pensacola once you arrive. Pensacola is intersected by I-10, which means visitors who drive into the city will bypass the two-lane roads that must be traveled to reach other cities along the Panhandle.

**Amtrak** (980 Einberg Street; 800-USA-RAIL, 850-433-4966).

**City of Five Flags Trolley Company** (1515 West Fairfield 32501; 850-595-3228; 25¢ for guided tour).

For a tour of the downtown area of Historic Pensacola, catch the Five Flags Trolley. There are two lines, the Palafox Line and the East Bay Line. The Palafox Line runs Monday through Friday from 7:00 A.M. to 4:00 P.M.; the Bay Line runs until 6:00 P.M. You can get on and off the trolley and switch lines as often as desired. Look for signs in the downtown area.

**Dollar Rent a Car** (2277 Airport Blvd.; 800-800-4000, 850-474-9000).

**Escambia County Transit System** (15151 West Fairfield 32501; 850-436-9383).

There are 280 routes covered by this local bus service, but none to Pensacola Beach.

**Greyhound Bus** (505 W. Burgess Rd.; 800-231-2222, 850-476-4800).

**Pensacola Regional Airport** (Airport Blvd., six miles N of downtown; 850-435-1745).

## Attractions

The Sunshine State's westernmost city offers something for everyone—scenic, relaxing beaches for beach bums, interesting attractions and activities for thrill seekers, and for history buffs, a rich cultural heritage spanning over four hundred years.

Though the beaches continue to be Pensacola's main tourist draw, canoeing opportunities are unparalleled in this region. Eighteen of Florida's largest rivers and hundreds of smaller

*Big Lagoon State Recreation Area is located on Perdido Key.*
(Courtesy of VISIT FLORIDA.)

creeks meander through the Panhandle, creating a diversity of rich coastline that beckons shorebirds and migratory butterflies during spring and fall.

**Big Lagoon State Recreation Area** (10 miles SW of Pensacola on CR 292A; 850-492-1595; open daily from 8:00 A.M. to sunset; $3.25 per vehicle, $1 on foot or bike; www.dep.state.-fl.us/parks/northwest/biglag.html).

The combination of sandy beaches, pine forests, and salt marshes found at the Big Lagoon State Recreation Area provide important habitats for birds and animals. Cardinals, towhees, brown thrashers, and nuthatches are common in the uplands, while great blue herons and other water fowl are frequently seen near Big Lagoon and the park's lake marshes.

Located on Perdido Key, this 69-acre park is ideal for fishing. Redfish, sea trout, flounder, and bluefish are common catches; conditions are also good for crabbing and netting for mullet.

The Big Lagoon is actually the Intracoastal Waterway and is protected by the barrier island of Perdido Key. The 40-foot observation tower at East Beach gives visitors a panoramic view

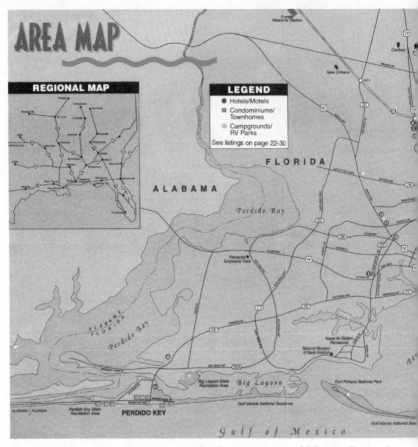

*Pensacola.*(Courtesy of the Pensacola Convention and Visitor Center.)

of Big Lagoon and the Gulf Islands National Seashore across the Intracoastal Waterway.

Besides the Grand Lagoon, Long Pine, and Youpon hiking trails, visitors can also participate in guided nature walks and view interpretative exhibits about the area's natural habitat and native wildlife. A campground, boat ramp, picnic areas, and a swimming beach are among the recreation area's amenities. Outdoor concerts are sometimes held in the pavilion.

**Blackwater River State Park** (15 miles N of Milton; 850-623-2363, 850-623-2364; open daily from 8:00 A.M. to sunset; $3.25 per vehicle, $1 on foot or bike; www.dep.state.fl.us/parks/-northwest/blackwater.html).

Regarded as one of the purest sand bottom rivers in the world, the Blackwater River running through Blackwater River

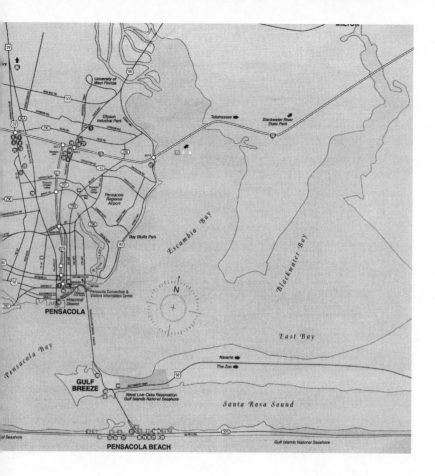

State Park is ideal for tubing and canoeing. A designated Florida canoe trail, the shoals and rapids found here challenge seasoned canoe enthusiasts, while gentler currents in the sheltered marshes and inlets are less intimidating. As one of the few remaining unspoiled rivers in Florida, it remains in a natural state for most of its length.

Contrary to its name, the water in the Blackwater River is not black, but an unpolluted, clear brown, similar to the color of tea, created by decaying leaves and the tannin from cypress trees. Dotted with broad white sandbars and edged with wide sandy banks—both of which are perfect for picnicking—the river runs 58 miles southwest from headwaters in Alabama's Conecuh National Forest before emptying into Blackwater Bay.

The 590-acre park, which runs along the southern border of Blackwater River State Forest, also features a diversity of plant and animal communities. White cedars, bald cypresses, red maples, sweet bays, magnolias, longleaf pines, and turkey oak trees provide a heavily wooded camouflage for the barred owls, opossums, rabbits, raccoons, red foxes, skunks, bobcats, turkeys, and white-tailed deer that roam the park. Water creatures include otters, catfish, brim, and other freshwater fish.

There are two main hiking trails. The *Chain of Lakes Nature Trail* begins at the Deaton Bridge at the park entrance and takes approximately 90 minutes to hike. It runs along the edge of the river and leads through a swamp, past lakes, and through the forest. The trail also winds beside several secluded beaches.

The shorter *Blackwater River Trail* takes about 60 minutes to complete. Starting at a 30-site campground, it too winds through several different types of habitats found in the park.

The park has excellent camping facilities, picnic grounds, fishing, nature trails, and boating. Nearby, the *Blackwater River State Forest*, Florida's largest state forest, is an 183,000-acre woodland with one of the country's finest remaining stands of longleaf pines.

**Blackwater River State Forest** (11650 Munson Hwy., Milton; 850-957-4201; open daily from 7:00 A.M. to sunset; $3 per vehicle; www.dep.state.fl.us/parks).

Abundant wildlife, gently rolling terrain, and shallow, sandy-bottomed creeks are a few of the characteristics of one of Florida's most beautiful forests. With over 183,000 acres, the forest is the ultimate, unspoiled setting for enjoying nature in solitude. Look for armadillos, bears, deer, hogs, opossums, rabbits, raccoons, red and gray foxes, skunks, turkey, quail, and the endangered red-cockaded woodpeckers, which live in the cavities of old, longleaf pines. If you prefer a bit more civilization, visit the areas surrounding Krul and Bear Lakes.

The *Krul Recreation Area* is the busiest day-use area in the forest. It includes the clear, spring-fed Krul Lake, which is restricted to swimming only. There are boardwalks with platforms and ladders, a picnic area, and a campground with fire rings, water, and electricity.

*Bear Lake* is a 107-acre lake full of shellcrackers, sunshine bass, bluegills, channel catfish, largemouth bass, and warmouths. There are two boat ramps, a fishing pier, and a large area designated for bank fishing. The Bear Lake campground offers both non-electric and electric sites, some of which overlook the lake.

For hiking, the *Jackson Trail,* now part of the *Florida National Scenic Trail* and the Recreational Trails System, is a 21-mile trail broken into segments as short as three-fourths of a mile. This is the same path used by Gen. Andrew Jackson during his 1818 journey to the newly established Florida territory.

The *Sweetwater Trail* intersects Jackson Trail and leads over a swinging bridge spanning Sweetwater Creek and across Bear Lake Dam. This 4.5-mile jaunt starts just past the Krul Lake campground.

Horseback riding is another popular pastime. Designated horse trails dissect the area, taking riders through forests of oaks, junipers, and longleaf pines. *Coldwater Horse Trail* has stables for 72 horses and 124 dog kennels, which is convenient since many major bird-dog field trials are held here.

Like the Blackwater River State Recreation Area, the forest also offers excellent canoeing on the Blackwater River, Sweetwater and Juniper Creeks, and East Coldwater Creek. Some of the canoe trails can take a full day to complete. Finally, hunting is allowed in the forest during season.

**Civil War Soldiers Museum** (108 S. Palafox Place; 850-469-1900; open Monday–Saturday, 10 A.M. to 4:30 P.M.; $4 for adults, $2 for children ages 6–12).

This museum chronicles America's bloodiest war through letters, photographs, and artifacts from Confederate soldiers. The Pensacola room highlights the involvement of local soldiers and features a 23-minute film, *Pensacola and the Civil War.*

The founder, Norman Haines, is a local doctor, so it's no wonder that one section of the museum focuses on primitive surgical procedures and equipment.

Civil War buffs will enjoy browsing through the adjacent bookstore, which offers five hundred titles in all genres on the war.

**Fort Barrancas** (Hwy. 98E, Gulf Islands National Seashore; 850-934-2600; open daily April to September 9:30 A.M. to 5 P.M., fall hours are sporadic; free).

Now part of the Gulf Islands National Seashore, the restored Fort Barrancas, its batteries, and redoubts, were erected to protect the harbor during the tumultuous battles of Pensacola's illustrious past.

This strategic coastal site was the focal point for many of Pensacola's battles during its various military occupations. The first fort, Fort San Carlos de Austria, was built by the Spanish in the late 1600s. A little over 20 years later, it was destroyed by the French during a battle. After the Treaty of Paris was signed in 1763, the British occupied Pensacola and erected a second fort on top of a nearby *barranca,* or bluff.

In 1781, the Spanish overtook the Brits and reclaimed the fort. By that time, it had fallen into disrepair, and instead of renovating it, the Spanish decided to build a new third fort on the bluff with a distinct battery, the Battery de San Antonio, at water level. In the War of 1812, the Brits destroyed the Spaniard's fort once again, sparing the Battery de San Antonio. Still in Spanish hands, the fourth fort was constructed, Fort San Carlos de Barrancas.

In 1821, the United States claimed the coastline and destroyed the fort, only to build a fourth one on the same site. It is this fourth fortification that still stands. The base of the fort itself has an octagonal armory and chapel dating to 1845. The Battery de San Antonio dates from 1797 and was the last Spanish fortification built in Florida. The Advanced Redoubt next to Fort Barrancas was built in the mid-1800s to provide protection from land attacks.

While Fort Pickens was occupied by Union troops during the entire Civil War, Fort Barrancas was occupied by the Confederacy until 1862.

**Fort Pickens** (Hwy. 98E, Gulf Islands National Seashore; 850-934-2635, 850-934-2622; open daily from 9:30 A.M. to 5:30 P.M. April–October, and 8:30 A.M. to 4:00 P.M. November–March; free).

Located at the western end of Santa Rosa Island and part of the Gulf Islands National Seashore, Fort Pickens is an imposing pre–Civil War fort built by slave labor in the early 19th century. The moated pentagonal brick fort has intact walls 40 feet high and 12 feet thick; 20 million bricks were used to build the structure.

A small, on-site museum just inside the main fort entrance tells the story of how the fort was built to protect the naval shipyard in Pensacola from attack, and includes displays of native plants and animals as well as weaponry dating from the 1890s to the 1930s.

The fort features eight concrete batteries, now overgrown, which once housed weapons for defense during the Spanish-American War, World War I, and World War II. Some types of rapid-fire weaponry used here were capable of hurling a 54-pound projectile more than five miles out across the sea. As one of the three forts built in the 1820s to guard the entrance to Pensacola Bay, Fort Pickens was held by Union troops throughout the Civil War.

The fort is most famous for one of its prisoners: Geronimo, the Apache leader, and 17 of his followers who were imprisoned here in 1886. As noted, during his stay, Geronimo would shrewdly sell the buttons off his coat for a dollar each to the tourists who would come to gawk at him every day. Each night he would stitch more buttons onto the coat. He and other Apache prisoners stayed in rooms along the south wall, which have since collapsed.

Besides water activities along the seven-mile beach area, there is an on-site aquarium, nature exhibits, hiking and bike trails, a fishing pier, a concession area, and a popular campground. Cottages, motels, and condominiums are located nearby. Complimentary guided tours of the fort are offered Monday through Friday at 11:00 A.M. and 2:00 P.M., and on Saturday and Sunday at 2:00 P.M.

**Gulf Islands National Seashore** (Hwy. 98E, Gulf Breeze; 850-934-2600, 850-924-2600; open daily from 8:00 A.M. to sunset; free except for Perdido Key and Fort Pickens areas).

Encroaching development along the Panhandle's pristine shoreline prompted Congress to create the Gulf Islands National Seashore in 1971. The seashore spans a total of 150 miles, which includes portions of islands and keys from Horn Island in Gulfport, Mississippi, to Okaloosa Island near Destin. West Florida has 52 miles of protected shoreline—the largest tract in the state. Pensacola sits in the heart of the seashore, with the barrier island of Perdido Key to the west and Santa Rosa Island

*Costumed interpreters at Historic Pensacola Village teach visitors about life of yesterday.* (Courtesy of the Pensacola Convention and Visitor Center.)

to the east. With 5.5 million visitors each year, the seashore is one of America's most popular national parks.

In all, the Gulf Islands National Seashore includes six distinct areas: Perdido Key State Recreation Area (including the Big Lagoon State Recreation Area), Fort Pickens at the western end of Santa Rosa Island, the Santa Rosa Day Use Area near Navarre Beach (including Casino Beach and Quietwater Beach), the Historic Forts sections on the Pensacola Naval Air Station, the Okaloosa area east of Fort Walton Beach, and the Naval Live Oaks Reservation on the mainland just east of Gulf Breeze.

Headquarters for the seashore are located at the Naval Live Oaks area, which also houses a small museum. Among the habitats to observe: freshwater marshes and swamps, salt marshes, marine habitats, and coastline areas.

**Historic Pensacola Village** (Zaragossa and Taragona Streets; 850-595-5985; open 10 A.M. to 4:30 P.M. Monday–Saturday, Sundays from 1 P.M. to 4 P.M.; $5.50 for adults, $4.50 for seniors and children 4–16; www.uwf.edu/~archaeo/).

A petrified cat, a portable toilet, and an assortment of glass bottle traps for mice, mosquitoes, and flies aren't the typical exhibits one would expect from a tour of Florida history. Yet perhaps it is the odd, everyday items such as these on display throughout Historic Pensacola Village that best tell the story of life in early Florida.

Located next to Pensacola Bay in the heart of the *Seville Square Historic District,* the village consists of restored and reconstructed examples of the area's coastal vernacular architecture. Quaint wooden houses, a stately brick church, and fully restored, old-fashioned warehouses line the quiet streets. Careful planning has even been considered for landscaping, with the grounds surrounding the museums featuring historical flower and vegetable gardens. The village is an on-going project of the Pensacola Preservation Society and the state of Florida.

The village sits atop the *Colonial Archaeological Walking Trail,* a series of outdoor exhibits and ongoing excavations conducted by archaeologists from the University of West Florida. Dating between 1752 and 1821, the site is revealing a military compound occupied at one time by Spanish, British, and American soldiers. In essence, the village offers a chronological walk through time.

Begin the tour at *Tivoli House* on Zaragossa Street, a short walk from visitor parking on Taragona Street. Reconstructed during the U. S. Bicentennial from photographs and an archaeological dig, the Tivoli House was originally built in 1805 as a boarding and gaming house. Today, it houses the gift shop and information center, and the only money that changes hands is for museum tickets and gift shop purchases.

Across the street—almost on top of the sidewalk—sits *Julee Cottage,* a weathered wooden house with pegged framing and beaded ceilings. It was bought in 1805 by Julee (JEW-lee) Panton, a free woman of color, and was later owned by a succession of free black women. Legend has it that Julee petitioned the king of Spain for a grant of property on the basis that her livelihood was derived from making candles and pastries. Today, it houses Pensacola's black history collection.

Compared to Julee Cottage, the neighboring *LaValle House* looks quite comfortable. With its high-pitched roof and wide porch, the four-room house is one of the most notable examples of French Creole architecture in Pensacola. It was built in the early 1800s as a rental duplex property by Charles Lavalle and Marianna Bonifay, a French woman who migrated from the Caribbean Islands, and moved to its present site to preserve it.

Through extensive testing, curators were able to determine the original colors of the house. The outside is celery green trimmed in a rusty, brick red, while the interior walls are ochre and rust, a vibrant color combination derived from local clays popular in the early 19th century.

"Ordinary" household items on display include a fancy waffle iron heavier than a suitcase, a holder used for storing hard cones of sugar, and a rope bed and mattress filled with hair and Spanish moss.

The LaValle House also displays the ingenious glass bottle traps used to capture an assortment of vermin still common in these parts. Designed to hold sugar water or pieces of corn or cheese in the bottom, most of the bottles feature wide, inverted lips that make it hard for critters to escape.

The most amusing contraption is a *commode voyage,* a round, leather container designed exactly for the purpose suggested by its name, even though it was commonly called a hat box by "ladies of distinction."

The *Lear–Rocheblave House,* a rambling two-story structure that stretches the length of the block, is located down the street next to the Old Christ Church on the corner of Adams and Zaragossa Streets.

Built in 1832, *Old Christ Church* is the oldest church in Florida still standing on its original site. Union soldiers used it as a hospital and barracks during the Civil War. Today, it houses the archives of the Pensacola Historical Society.

Past the church is the *Dorr House,* an 1850's Greek Revival house with Victorian-era trim and Gulf Coast features such as the brick piers and "jib" windows, which raise from the floor to create additional ventilation and a walk through to the second-story porch.

Clara Barkley's marriage to Eben Dorr in 1849 united two leading Pensacola merchant families of British ancestry. When Eben died in 1870, Clara built this home to raise her five children. Though the original paint and wallpaper were never discovered, and while most of Mrs. Dorr's furnishings are no longer in the house, the design scheme is true to period style. With its upholstered furniture and fine, hand-painted china, the comfortable interior offers a stark contrast to the more primitive lifestyle exhibited in the Lavalle House.

Besides displays of residential architecture and tools, Historic Pensacola Village also features primitive examples of industrial architecture and development. In the masonry warehouse at the corner or Church and Taragona Streets, the *Museum of Industry* contains exhibits of prevalent industries of the 19th century, including machinery from the Piney Woods Sawmill that was used during the lumber boom, and photographs and tools from the shipping and railroad industries. It was the combination of these three entities that heavily influenced the development of early Pensacola.

Another 19th-century warehouse, now the *Museum of Commerce,* sits on Zaragossa Street next to Tivoli House. It replicates a Victorian era streetscape with a print shop, a pharmacy, a toy store, and a hardware store; some of these are actually open for business.

Somewhat out of the loop in the Palafox Historic District but still an interesting site to visit is the *T.T. Wentworth, Jr., Museum* in Pensacola's former city hall, a Renaissance Revival-style building on Jefferson Street. Wentworth's eclectic collection of license plates, dinosaur bones, household items, and even a petrified cat is the largest of its kind ever given to the state of Florida by an individual. The third floor contains *Discovery,* a hands-on museum experience for children.

*St. Michael's Cemetery,* the only burial ground in Pensacola until 1876, is also close by. Those resting here include Stephen Mallory, Secretary of the Confederate Navy, and Dorothy Walton, wife of George Walton, who signed the Declaration of Independence.

One of the newest sites in the village is the Pensacola *City of Five Flags Exhibit* in the *J. Earle Bowden Building.* Highlights of this display are recovered treasure and oddities from a 16th-century shipwreck, including stone cannonballs, the oldest piece of Spanish armor ever found in America, fragments of Aztec pottery, glass, and coins.

During the summer, guided tours are offered daily and

*The National Museum of Naval Aviation features a variety of aircraft.* (Courtesy of VISIT FLORIDA.)

costumed interpreters are stationed throughout the village. In the winter months, a self-guided walking tour map is available free of charge.

**National Museum of Naval Aviation** (1750 Radford Drive, Naval Air Station; 800-327-5002, 850-452-2389, 850-453-2024 for information about the IMAX Theatre; open daily from 9 A.M. to 5 P.M. except Thanksgiving, Christmas, New Year's; free, the IMAX Theatre costs $4.50 for adults and $4 for senior citizens, children under 12, and active duty military personnel; www.naval-air.org).

This museum is not only the nation's first aviation museum, but it has grown into one of the world's three largest. Located in the Pensacola Naval Air Station, the 300,000-square-foot museum houses a collection of 150 aircraft once flown by the Navy, Marine Corps, and U.S. Coast Guard. Among the selection: an NC-4, which in 1919 became the first plane to cross the Atlantic by air; an F-14 Tomcat; the F6F Hellcat, the famous WWII fighter; and the Skylab Command Module.

Not to be missed is the museum's IMAX Theatre and "The Magic of Flight," which is shown daily on the hour. Narrated by Tom Selleck, this $4-million film includes vivid sights and startling sounds in such dramatic style that viewers feel they are in the cockpit.

A unique museum feature is the street of memories, which highlights life on the homefront during the 1930s and 1940s. Replicas of a barber shop, pawn shop, restaurant, and house line the street, each with period furnishings and accessories like vintage newspapers and magazines, candy bars in their original packaging, and canned goods with original price tags.

Several dramatic exhibits are displayed throughout the museum. The most stunning is the seven-story Blue Angel Atrium where four Blue Angel Skyhawks are suspended in diamond formation from the ceiling. Should the actual Blue Angels be practicing, you might catch a glimpse of them through the incredible glass ceiling.

There is also a motion-based simulator where visitors can strap themselves into cockpit trainers for pretend test flights. Upstairs, visitors will find recreations of an aircraft carrier deck and a WWII landing strip. Former aviators and other ex-military personnel give tours and often share anecdotes and personal experiences aboard the aircraft.

In addition to the exhibits and displays, there is the Naval Aviation Technical Library & Research Center with extensive holdings on aviation and space travel. Future plans for the museum include a proposed National Flight Academy. Similar to Space Camp, the academy will be a one-week co-ed school of aviation for 7th- and 8th-grade students.

**Naval Live Oaks Reservation** (Hwy. 98E, Gulf Islands National Seashore, Gulf Islands; 850-934-2613; open daily from 8:30 A.M. to 5 P.M.; free).

In 1828, President John Quincy Adams set aside the 1,400-acre Santa Rosa Live Oak Timber Reservation to provide timber for building naval vessels. The live oak—so dense that is was called "ironwood"—was a superb building material for sea vessels. Both the USS *Constitution* (whose nickname was "Old Ironsides" because of the wood) and the USS *Constellation* were built with timber harvested from this reserve.

Today, what remains is a historic remnant of the nation's first timber preserve. This is also the headquarters for the Gulf Islands National Seashore, where you can pick up brochures and maps of the seashore and view exhibits of Indian artifacts and displays about early ship-building techniques. Several trails shaded by live oak canopies and a picnic area make this part of the seashore a pleasant respite from the intensity of the Florida sun.

**North Hill Historic District** (Wright Street to Blount Street and Reus Street to Palafox Street; 850-595-5985; www.virtualp-cola.com/downtown).

Developed by turn-of-the-century affluent families, this residential area occupies the site where the Spanish recaptured Pensacola from the British in a bloody battle in 1781. Today, the area consists of 50 blocks and contains over five hundred homes. It is one of the most intact residential historic districts in Florida. Queen Anne, Neoclassical, Tudor Revival, Craftsman Bungalow, Art Moderne, and Mediterranean Revival are among the architectural styles found in North Hill. Keep in mind that a walking or driving tour is probably the best way to see this area, since most of the homes are private residences.

*Christ Episcopal Church* (10 W. Wright Street) is an elaborate 1902 Mission Revival church built for the Episcopal parish after it had outgrown the old Christ Church on Seville Square. Though unusual for an Episcopal church to erect a building based on Spanish Colonial style, the design was chosen because of Pensacola's Spanish heritage and its practicality for the climate.

Once the site of Fort McClellan, an earthenworks fortification erected by Union troops, *Lee Square* (Palafox and Gadsden Streets) now symbolizes Pensacola's tribute to the Southern Confederacy. The 50-foot obelisk and sculpture located here was sponsored by funds raised by local residents.

*Fort George* (Palafox and LaRua Streets) was the largest of three fortifications built by the British in Pensacola in 1778. Constructed of square pine logs laid horizontally, the fort has bomb-proof wooden casements for barracks and was surrounded by a dry moat 15 feet wide and 20 feet deep. Excavations have uncovered weapons, brick foundations, and debris from military operations. In the late 19th century, much of the site was lost to residential development. The only undeveloped parcel was bought and preserved by the city of Pensacola in 1974.

**Palafox Historic District** (located on Palafox Street; 850-434-5371, 850-444-8905; free; www.virtualpcola.com/downtown).

Separated from Seville Square Historic District by Taragona

Street, this locally ordinanced historic district was once the commercial and government hub of Pensacola. Although many of the earlier buildings have been lost to fire, hurricanes, or demolition, Pensacola's downtown retains a large number of historical commercial structures, some of which feature New Orleans wrought-iron balconies.

*Plaza Ferdinand VII* has been an open area since Pensacola's first Spanish period. A statue of Andrew Jackson sits on Palafox Street between Government and Zaragossa Streets to commemorate the formal transfer of Florida from Spain to the United States, which was held here in 1821.

Pensacola's former city hall now houses the *T.T. Wentworth, Jr., Museum.* Located on Jefferson Street, the museum is part of Historic Pensacola Village.

The 10-story *Empire Building* at 226 Palafox Place was the tallest commercial-style building in Florida when it was constructed in 1909. The simple, clean forms with vertical bands of windows and relief ornamentation make this building one of the finest examples of this style in the South.

The *Saenger Theatre* is located at 118 Palafox Place. A Spanish Baroque-style building with Renaissance ornamentation, this vaudeville theater opened in 1925 and continues to host performances by the Pensacola Symphony Orchestra, First City Dance, the Choral Society, and the Pensacola Opera. A 1925 Robert Morton pipe organ is still used for recitals and concerts by prominent organists. (Call 850-438-2787 for a schedule of events.)

Once home to the Pensacola city jail and city court, the 1906 Mission Revival building at 407 South Jefferson now houses the *Pensacola Museum of Art.*

**Panhandle Butterfly House** (Navarre Park, Hwy. 98, Navarre; 850-939-3267, 850-623-1930; open from June to September daily from 11:00 A.M. to 4:00 P.M.; free).

One of a handful of butterfly houses in the entire country dedicated to native species, the Navarre Butterfly House is the perfect place to get up close and personal with these beautiful creatures. There is also a freshwater pond with ducks, swans, fish, and turtles; a playground with pirate ship equipment; and a beach for swimming in Santa Rosa Sound.

**Pensacola Greyhound Track** (Hwy. 98 at Dog Track Road; 800-345-3997, 850-455-8595; open Tuesday–Wednesday, Friday–Saturday at 6:00 P.M. with racing beginning at 7:00 P.M., Wednesday, Saturday, and Sunday at 11:30 for matinees; $1 general admission).

Live greyhound racing occurs year round; simulcast horse and greyhound races are held during Saturday. There is a Kennel Dinner Club on property.

**Pensacola Ice Pilots** (Games held at the Pensacola Civic Center; 850-433-7944).

Pensacola's ice hockey team, affiliated with the International Hockey League's Quebec Rafales, plays October through April. Call the ticket office for a schedule and price information.

**Pensacola Little Theatre** (Pensacola Cultural Center, 186 N. Palafox Street; 850-432-2042, 850-432-8621).

A vital part of the Pensacola Cultural Center, the Little Theatre presents performances ranging from musicals to dramas and comedies.

**Pensacola Museum of Art** (407 S. Jefferson St.; 850-432-5682, 850-432-6247; open Tuesday–Friday from 10 A.M. to 5 P.M., Saturday from 10 A.M. to 4 P.M., Sunday from 1 P.M. to 4 P.M.; free).

Once home to the Pensacola city jail and city court, the 1906 Mission Revival building at 407 South Jefferson now houses the Pensacola Museum of Art. Both local and touring art exhibits are on display throughout this two-story, non-profit museum, including an impressive collection of Chinese porcelain.

**Pensacola Symphony Orchestra** (performances are held at the Saenger Theatre; 850-435-2533).

Performing a series of five concerts each season, the Pensacola Symphony Orchestra is comprised of some of the Panhandle's most talented musicians. Call for a schedule and ticket information.

**Perdido River Canoe Trail** (three miles W of SR 98-A at the end of Jackson Springs Road; 850-487-4784).

The Perdido River offers excellent canoeing along its 24-mile canoe trail. The river is the natural dividing line between Florida and Alabama, and winds through south Alabama before emptying into the Perdido Bay. The canoe trail along the river offers easy paddling over clear water with a white sand bottom.

You'll pass several habitats, including flatwoods; lakes, rivers, and springs; freshwater marshes and swamps. Avoid the upper section of the river from Dyas Creek to Three Runs because of poor access and difficult navigation.

**Perdido Key State Recreation Area** (15 miles SW of Pensacola off SR 292; 850-492-4660, 850-492-1595; open daily from 8:00 A.M. to sunset; $3.25 per vehicle, $1 on foot or bike, passes good for seven days; www.dep.state.fl.us/parks/northwest/-perdido.html).

Listed among the best beaches in the nation by Dr. Beach (a.k.a. Dr. Stephen Leatherman from the University of Maryland), this 247-acre barrier island is a pristine nature preserve with wide, white sandy beaches and rolling sand dunes covered with sea oats. Approximately seven miles of Perdido Key is part of the Gulf Islands National Seashore. Another nine miles hugs the Big Lagoon.

First discovered by the Spanish in 1693, Perdido Key, which means "lost island" in Spanish, is flanked by the Gulf of Mexico on one side and the Old River on the other. More than half of the island is preserved from growth by federal and state parks.

The Big Lagoon State Recreation Area is part of the Perdido Key State Recreation Area. In turn, Perdido Key is part of the Gulf Islands National Seashore. The area is only 20 minutes west of Pensacola and is linked to both Alabama and Florida by bridges.

Beaches on Perdido Key are easily accessible from paved roads. There are picnic shelters and a parking lot behind the sign for public beach access.

Each November, songwriters from across the country converge at this state recreation area for the annual Frank Brown International Songwriters Festival.

**Science and Space Museum at Pensacola Junior College** (Bronco Center for Science and Advanced Technology at the PJC main campus; 850-484-1117/1150; $3 for adults, $2 for students).

With daily and evening programs year round, the Science and Space Museum highlights the world of space. The programs vary: journey to the farthest reaches of the universe via the spectacular 3-D DIGISTAR computer graphics projection system or learn about the story of thunderstorms, tornadoes, and

*Perdido Key State Recreation Area is listed among the country's top beaches.* (Courtesy of VISIT FLORIDA.)

hurricanes. A couple of evenings each week the museum takes a fun look at the night sky. Call for a daily schedule.

**Seville Square Historic District** (120 E. Church Street; 850-444-8905).

Pensacola's first permanent Spanish colonial settlement is one of the oldest historic districts in the Southeast. Listed on the National Register, Seville Square Historic District contains a rare concentration of Frame Vernacular, Folk Victorian, and Creole homes, which date from the early to the late 19th century and include some of the oldest in Florida. The simplicity of these buildings represents the traditions of Florida's early years more accurately than any other historic district in the state.

*Seville Square,* an old Spanish plaza shaded by the canopies of live oak trees, sits in the center of the district. Today, the plaza is a two-block park facing the Dorr House, and is ideal for events as small as a family outing or as large as the annual Seafood Festival in September. The Seville Square Historic District is also home to Historic Pensacola Village.

**The Wall South and Veterans' Memorial Park** (Bayfront Pkwy.; 850-433-8200; free).

Overlooking Pensacola Bay, this park was created as a living monument to all veterans who fought in any of the American wars. The highlight of the park is the three-quarter-scale replica of the Vietnam Veterans' Memorial in Washington, DC, complete with the names of all the Americans who lost their lives in the war engraved on the wall. Future plans for this 5.5-acre park include memorials commemorating veterans from World War I to the present.

**Wildlife Rescue & Sanctuary** (105 N. S Street; 850-433-9453, 850-932-7768; free; donations are welcomed).

Abandoned, sick, and injured wildlife are given a second chance at this non-profit refuge for birds and wildlife. If possible, the sanctuary releases recovered animals back to the wild, but those with permanent disabilities become full-time residents. Park volunteers care for the animals and will gladly tell you stories about the critters currently under their care.

**The ZOO** (5701 Gulf Breeze Pkwy., Gulf Breeze; 850-932-2229; open daily from 9:00 A.M. to 5:00 P.M.; $9.75 adults, $5.75 for children ages 3–11; www.the-zoo.com).

More than 700 animals are on display at this 50-acre zoo, which is designed to let visitors get up close and personal with creatures from around the world. Favorite residents include Congo the gorilla, Florida alligators, pygmy hippos, and numerous endangered species such as a white Bengal tiger. Don't miss Ellie the Elephant, who plays music as part of her daily show. She also paints watercolors, which command substantial fees at local charity fund-raisers.

Touted as the "World's Friendliest," the ZOO also has lots of interesting displays and exhibits. For starters, visit the Giraffe Feeding Tower, where you can climb to the top to feed—and possibly get licked—by friendly, long-necked giraffes. The Safari Line Train ($1.25) is another popular attraction that winds through a 30-acre preserve of free-roaming animals. Windows in the commissary allow visitors to see how foods are prepared for the ZOO's inhabitants. A nursery and incubator room for zoo babies and a petting farm round out the animal activities. The gift shop features a simulated rain forest, environmental gifts, and genuine African art.

Last but not least, a manicured botanical gardens flourishing with exotic plants and flowers is an ideal place for an afternoon picnic.

### Fishing/Water Recreation

Home to some of the finest billfishing in the United States, Pensacola offers a variety of fishing options. Daily charters are available for Gulf fishing, and you can rent a boat on the many inland waterways. If you'd prefer, fish off the Three Mile Bridge, known as the "World's Longest Fishing Pier."

**Bonifay Water Sports** (460 Pensacola Beach Blvd.; 850-932-0633).

Besides renting sailboats, jet skis, and catamarans, Bonifay Water Sports provides safety and sailing instructions.

**Key Sailing** (400 Quietwater Beach Blvd.; 850-932-5520).

Located on Quietwater Beach Boulevard, Key Sailing rents jet skis, windsurfers, waverunners, sunfish, and Hobie Cats.

*Charters*

**Abundant Charters** (2112 Pullman Circle; 850-453-5885).
**Lafitte Cove Marina** (1010 Fort Pickens Road; 850-932-9241).

**Lo-Baby** (935 Fairway Drive; 850-455-4892).
**Moorings Marina** (655 Pensacola Beach Blvd.; 850-932-0305).
**Party Board Chulamar** (801 S. Palafox Street; 850-434-6977).

*Diving*

From natural reefs to the remains of sunken ships, Pensacola offers an underwater preserve with water that is warm and remarkably clear—visibility ranges from 30 to 50 feet inshore and as much as 100 feet offshore.

There are fascinating shipwrecks and excellent spawning areas to explore. One example is the USS *Massachusetts,* a popular shallow-water dive resting only 30 feet below the surface. Sunk in 1927, the wreck is relatively intact and can be seen from the surface at low tide.

Farther out is the Russian Freighter *San Pablo,* sunk as a result of a German U-boat attack. It lies in 75 feet of water and is a good place to collect spiny oysters.

**Aquatic Orientations** (31 Hoffman Drive, Gulf Breeze; 850-932-1944).

**Scuba Shack** (719 Palafox Street; 850-433-4319).

**Surf and Sail** (11-J Via de Luna; 850-932-7873).

*Canoeing*

Milton, just north of Pensacola, is called the "Canoe Capital of Florida" because of the network of rivers and streams in the area.

**Adventures Unlimited** (12 miles N of Milton off Hwy. 87; 800-239-6864, 850-623-0235; open daily from 8:00 A.M. to 6:00 P.M., summer hours extended to 7:00 P.M. during the week and to 8:00 P.M. on Friday and Saturday; www.propaddlesports.com/-paddle/advunlimted).

Situated outside of Milton, the "Canoe Capital of Florida," Adventures Unlimited offers canoeing, kayaking, and inner-tubing down Coldwater, Sweetwater, Juniper, or Blackwater Creeks. Not only do these creeks have clear water, but you can stop along the way and picnic or lie out on the sandy beaches along the banks. Stream beds are also covered with white sand, making it easy to see marine life and plants under the water. As the largest outfitter in the county, Adventures Unlimited can arrange hourly, daily, and overnight excursions.

Besides equipment and excursions, there is a trading post, snack bar, RV and camp sites, and a restored schoolhouse-turned-bed-&-breakfast on the property.

**Blackwater River Canoe Rental** (off Hwy. 90 E of Milton; 800-967-789, 850-623-0235).

Canoeing on the Blackwater River is like canoeing on a smooth stream in the ocean. The bottom is made of white sand; so are the banks along the river. At its deepest, the canoe trail is two and a half feet deep, and there are no whitewater rapids, so you basically float the entire way.

The average time for a canoe trip is around four hours, but you can also schedule day-long and overnight trips. This outfitter rents everything you need, from canoes to tents and sleeping bags.

**Bob's Canoes** (Hwy. 191 NW of Milton; 850-623-5457).

### Golf

**Carriage Hills Golf Course** (2355 W. Michigan Avenue; 850-944-5497).

**Club at Hidden Creek** (3070 PGA Blvd.; Navarre; 850-939-4606).

**Green Meadow** (W. Michigan Avenue; 850-944-5483).

**Lost Key Golf Club** (625 Lost Key Drive, Perdido Key; 850-492-1300).

An Arnold Palmer-designed, 6,808-yard course, Lost Key has 18-hole, par-72 play. It's the first course in Florida with "Flora-dwarf" grass.

**The Moors Golf Club** (off I-10, east of Pensacola, Exit 7, one mile north of Hwy. 281, 3220 Avalon Blvd., Milton; 800-727-1010, 850-995-4653).

This public 18-hole, par-70 course features Scottish-style links play. There is also an eight-room lodge overlooking the course, a driving range, and a practice putting green. The Moors hosts the Senior PGA Tour's Emerald Coast Classic each year.

**Perdido Bay Golf Resort** (1 Doug Ford Drive; 850-492-1223).

This 18-hole course was recognized by *Golf Digest* as one of the top 50 daily fee courses in the United States. The former home of the Pensacola Open, Perdido Bay also features accommodations, tennis courts, and a swimming pool.

*Golf is a major attraction for tourists visiting Pensacola.*
(Courtesy of VISIT FLORIDA.)

**Scenic Hills Country Club** (8891 Burning Tree Road; 850-476-0380).

This semi-private golf club was originally designed by Scottish architect Charles Adams; it was later updated by US Open Champion Jerry Pate. The 18-hole course is the site of the Women's Western Open and the Women's Florida Amateur and has hosted the USGA Women's Open.

**Tanglewood Golf and Country Club** (Tanglewood Drive, Milton; 850-623-6176).

**Tiger Point Golf and Country Club** (1255 Country Club Road, Gulf Breeze; 850-932-1333).

This 36-hole, par-72 course has two sides. On the east side, there is an island green on hole five. On the west, the last nine holes are on the water, providing a scenic backdrop for play.

### Tennis

**Pensacola Racquet Club** (3450 Wimbledon Drive; 850-434-2434).

## Restaurants and Nightlife

**The Angus** (1101 Scenic Hwy.; 850-432-0475; open Monday–Saturday 5:00 P.M. to 10:00 P.M., until 11:00 P.M. on Friday and Saturday).

Since 1968, the Bithos family has been serving prime rib au jus, fresh gulf seafood, pasta, and Greek salads to hungry visitors.

**Chan's** (21/2 Via de Luna; 850-932-3525; open daily from 5:00 P.M. to 10:00 P.M., downstairs from 11:00 A.M. to 11:00 P.M.).

Spectacular Gulf views and mouthwatering entrées make Chan's the restaurant of choice for discerning diners. Upstairs, Chan's offers mesquite-grilled steaks, pastas, and of course, fresh Gulf seafood prepared any way you like it. It also has an extensive wine list. Reservations are recommended. Downstairs is more casual with food served throughout the day.

**Cowboy's** (8673 Navarre Pkwy.; 850-939-0502; open daily for lunch from 11:00 A.M. to 2:00 P.M., for dinner from 4:00 P.M. to 9:00 P.M., on weekends from 11:00 A.M. to 9:30 P.M., Sunday brunch from 10:30 A.M. to 2:00 P.M.).

Cowboy's serves great steaks and grub, including huge Sunday brunches with homemade biscuits and gravy, scrambled eggs, bacon, sausage, hash browns and grits.

**Flora-Bama Lounge and Package Store** (17401 Perdido Key Drive; 850-492-0611; open daily from 9:00 A.M. to 2:30 A.M.; www.florabama.com).

Situated on the beach at the Florida–Alabama line, this raucous country-western bar is known for outrageous events like the annual mullet-tossing contest and the winter Polar Bear Swimfest. Each November, the bar hosts a nationally renowned festival of songwriters. Mobile, Alabama's native son, Jimmy Buffett, has been rumored to drop in when he's visiting the Panhandle.

**Flounder's Chowder and Ale House** (800 Quiet Water Beach Road; 850-932-2003; open daily from 11:00 A.M. to 2:00 P.M.).

The quintessential beach bar and restaurant, Flounder's offers fresh, charbroiled seafood in a casual setting. Enjoy live entertainment from the reggae bands who perform in the Jamaican-style beach bar.

**Hopkins' Boarding House** (Spring and Strong Streets; 850-438-3979; open Tuesday–Friday from 5:00 P.M. to 7:30 P.M., Saturday–Sunday from 11:00 A.M. to 2:00 P.M.).

Enjoy old-fashioned Southern cooking like pork chops and turnip greens served up family-style at this Victorian boarding house restaurant.

**Jerry's Cajun Café** (corner of Creighton and 9th Streets; 850-484-6962; open Monday–Thursday from 11:00 A.M. to 8:00 P.M., Friday–Saturday from 11:00 A.M. to 9:00 P.M.).

A locals' favorite, Jerry's is known for its nightly specials— jambalaya, crawfish étouffée, po-boys, and chicken New Iberia.

**Jubilee Restaurant & Entertainment Complex** (400 Quietwater Beach Boardwalk; 850-934-3108; open daily from 11:00 A.M. to 10:00 P.M., on Saturday until 11:00 P.M., Sunday from 10:00 A.M. to 10:00 P.M.).

Selected as one of Florida's top 200 restaurants, Jubilee offers five-star gourmet dining with a Cajun flair. The menu changes weekly.

**Marina Oyster Bar** (505 Bayou Blvd.; 850-433-0511; open Tuesday–Thursday from 5:00 P.M. to 9:00 P.M., Friday–Saturday from 5:00 P.M. to 10:00 P.M.).

This old-school oyster bar is nothing fancy, but the view of the Marina is great, and the food is excellent. Broiled and fried seafood are the house favorites along with the raw bar.

**McGuire's Irish Pub** (600 E. Gregory Street; 850-433-6789; open daily from 11:00 A.M.).

Kosher-style sandwiches, seafood, steaks, chili con carne, pecan pie, and specialty beers from the microbrewery are favorites at this local Irish pub. While the food is good, you won't want to miss the atmosphere, where "feasting, imbibery, and debauchery" are encouraged. The entire restaurant is papered with dollar bills signed by patrons—at last count there was $98,000 hanging on the walls.

**Patti's Seafood Deli** (610 S. C Street; 850-434-3193; open Tuesday–Saturday from 10:00 A.M. to 4:00 P.M.).

A local favorite, Patti's serves up all sorts of Cajun specialties, from gumbos, Creoles, and platters with fish right off the boats. Try one of the po-boys, a sandwich made with seafood.

**Seville Quarter** (130 E. Government Street; 850-434-6211; open daily from 11:00 A.M. until . . .).

This restored brick complex in the Seville Square Historic District is perhaps the most happening place in town. With names like Rosie O'Grady's Goodtime Emporium, Phineas

Phoggs Balloon Works Dance Hall, and End O' the Alley Bar, the seven clubs feature a variety of music ranging from Dixieland jazz and country-western to disco and pop. One price gets you into all the clubs.

## Accommodations

**All Star RV Resort** (Perdido Key Drive off Gulf Beach Hwy., 13620 Perdido Key Drive; 850-492-0041).

One of Pensacola's newest campsites offers a beach-front setting swimming pool, cable TV. Phone hook-ups, laundry room, and showers. All RV spaces are pull-thru and paved; different sizes are available.

**The Beach Club** (1591 Via de Luna; 800-874-9245, 850-932-5331).

Located directly on the Gulf, these luxury condos have private balconies, Jacuzzi tubs, fully equipped kitchens, washers, and dryers.

**Clarion Suites Resort and Convention Center** (20 Via de Luna; 800-874-5303, 850-932-4300).

The 86 luxury suites at this Gulfside resort have the look of a quaint fishing village. Each room has a kitchenette and two televisions, and there is a pool on property.

**The Dunes** (333 Fort Pickens Road; 800-83-DUNES, 850-932-3536).

Every room in this hotel overlooks the Gulf and has its own private balcony. The Dunes also has a heated pool with a waterfall, a café, and lounge on site.

**Gulf Aire Motel** (21 Via de Luna; 850-932-2319).

This modest motel features 23 units on the waterfront with a private beach, gazebo, barbecue grills, and cable TVs. Kitchenettes are available.

**Leichty's Homestead Inn** (7830 Pine Forest Road at Route 10; 850-944-4816).

Six-course breakfasts and homemade desserts are only two reasons to reserve one of the six rooms at the Leichty's Homestead Inn. The Leichtys are hospitable and more than happy to give advice on what to see and do in the area. Each of the rooms in their gingerbread-style home is named for an American patriot.

**Navarre Beach Family Campground** (9201 Navarre Pkwy.; 850-939-2188).

This eight-and-a-half-acre campground features white sand beaches, pull-thru sites, a large swimming pool, playground, pavilion, cable TV, and a boat ramp and pier. There are a hundred pitches within the campground.

**New World Landing** (600 S. Palafox Street; 850-432-4111).

The 16 rooms in this quaint inn are named for historic Pensacolians such as Geronimo and Andrew Jackson. Each room reflects the nationality of its namesake. The rooms overlook the courtyard, Palafox Street, or the bay.

**Pensacola Grand Hotel** (200 E. Gregory Street; 800-348-3336, 850-433-3336).

Adjacent to the Pensacola Civic Center, the lobby of this Pensacola hotel is the renovated Louisville and Nashville train depot. Ticket and baggage counters are still intact, and old railroad signs remind guests of the days when steam locomotives chugged up to the doors.

**Realty Marts International, Inc.** (1591 Via de Luna; 800-874-9245, 850-932-5376).

Boasting the widest selection of vacation rentals on Pensacola Beach, this agency handles rental property in all price ranges. It also offers affordable golf packages with 11 area golf courses.

**Sandpiper Inn** (23 Via de Luna; 850-932-2516).

This inn has contemporary motel rooms and cottages directly across from the Gulf. Some kitchenettes are available, and there is a pool on property.

**Two Tom's Bed and Breakfast** (7984 Navarre Pkwy.; 850-939-2382).

Sitting on four acres—complete with a duck pond—this modern brick and frame home is located east of the toll bridge to Navarre Beach. The B&B offers a full breakfast and shared baths.

### Shopping

**Cordova Mall** (5100 N. 9th Avenue at Bayou Blvd.; 850-497-5355; open Monday–Saturday from 10:00 A.M. to 9:00 P.M., Sunday from 12:30 P.M. to 5:30 P.M.).

One of Pensacola's largest, Cordova Mall has 140 specialty shops and four anchor stores: Dillard's, Gayfers, Montgomery Ward, and Parisian.

**9th Avenue Antique Mall** (380 N. 9th Avenue; 850-438-3961; open Monday–Saturday from 10:00 A.M. to 6:00 P.M., Sunday from 12:00 P.M. to 6:00 P.M.).

Listed on the antique trail and just across from the visitor's bureau, this antique and collectibles mall houses 38 shops under one roof.

**Pensacola Historical Museum** (115 E. Zaragossa Street; 850-433-1559; open Monday–Saturday from 10:00 A.M. to 4:30 P.M.).

Looking for books with a Pensacola slant? Head for the gift shop at the Pensacola Historical Museum. It has books and materials on local history and ecology and souvenirs with a Pensacola appeal.

**Quayside Market** (712 S. Palafox Street; 850-433-9930; open Wednesday–Saturday from 10:00 A.M. to 5:00 P.M., Sunday from 12:00 P.M. to 4:00 P.M.).

This restored waterfront warehouse is the South's largest cooperative art gallery. You'll find handicrafts, antiques, collectibles, fancy coffees, and imports.

**University Mall** (off Davis Hwy.; 850-478-3600; open Monday–Saturday from 10:00 A.M. to 9:00 P.M.).

With more than 70 stores under one roof, including JC Penney and McRae's, this mall provides an ideal afternoon respite from the Florida sun.

### Festivals and Special Events

*March*

### Mardi Gras

Going strong for over 50 years, Mardi Gras events in Pensacola begin in the early part of January and continue up until Ash Wednesday. The main parades on Palafox Street and Via de Luna on Pensacola Beach take place the weekend before Fat Tuesday. Call 850-473-8858.

### Emerald Coast Classic

This annual Senior PGA Tournament is held at the Moors Golf Club in Milton. More than 40,000 people turn out to see their favorite senior golfers. Most of the top 35 golfers show up for the tournament. Call 850-438-7700.

## May

### Springfest
More than 60,000 people flock to downtown Pensacola each May for a weekend-long street party full of rock, jazz, country, blues, and alternative music performed by local and international stars. Former guest stars include the Neville Brothers, Widespread Panic, and Blood, Sweat, & Tears. Call 800-874-1234, 850-434-1234.

## June

### Fiesta of Five Flags
This 10-day festival each June celebrates Pensacola's rich heritage under five nations. In all, five flags have flown over Pensacola—Spanish, French, British, Confederate, and U.S. Boat and street parades, music, ethnic festivals, treasure hunts, and sandcastle contests are among the scheduled activities. Call 850-433-6512.

## September

### Boggy Bayou Mullet Festival
This down-home folk-fest has 275,000 attendees each year who eat more than 11 tons of mullet. Call 800-322-3319, 850-651-7131.
### Pensacola Jazz Festival
The annual two-day event features jazz performances from local, regional, and national artists. Call 800-874-1234, 850-434-1234.
### Seafood Festival in Seville Square
An extravaganza of arts and crafts, food, musical entertainment, and, of course, lots of seafood, the Seville Square Festival is an annual September event. Call 850-433-6512.

## October

### Pensacola Interstate Fair
When fall is in the air, it's time for the Pensacola Interstate Fair, which ranks among the top 50 fairs in the world. Call 800-874-1234, 850-434-1234.

*November*

### Frank Brown International Songwriters Festival

Held in early November, this 10-day festival draws up to 150 songwriters of blues, country, gospel, and rock music. The songwriters perform their music throughout the week in various venues around Pensacola. Call 850-492-7664 or 334-980-5116 for more information.

### Great Gulf Coast Arts Festival

This weekend arts festival attracts over two hundred artists from across the country who display and sell their artwork. More than 100,000 people show up for the festival, which is held in Seville Square. Call 800-874-1234, 850-434-1234.

### Pensacola Beach Air Show

Every November, the Blue Angels, the Navy's six-jet Flight Demonstration Team, perform thrilling aerobatics in the Pensacola Beach Air Show. Call 850-452-4583.

# 4

## Okaloosa County

### Introduction

Halfway between Pensacola and Panama City, Okaloosa County has been eager to pin publicity slogans on this luminous stretch of beach and its verdant waters, giving it names like the *Emerald Coast* and *Miracle Strip*. In reality, there is no slogan or marketing ploy that can amply describe the beauty awaiting visitors. The sun shines virtually year round—an average of 343 sunny days are reported each year—and the sand here is so white that according to legend, mercenaries sold it as sugar during World War II. There are 24 miles of beaches, 60 percent of which are preserved and protected. And the fishing? Well, in any one season, there are at least 20 species of game fish available.

### History

Native Americans once inhabited the entire coastline, as the Indian Temple Museum in Fort Walton reflects. They built a temple mound here that served as a ceremonial center from 1200 to 1700 AD, though construction may have started as early as 700 AD. Created from 100,000 cubic feet of soil, clay, and shell, the mound is now a National Historic Landmark. The Indians also gave Okaloosa County its name, meaning "black water" or "pleasant place."

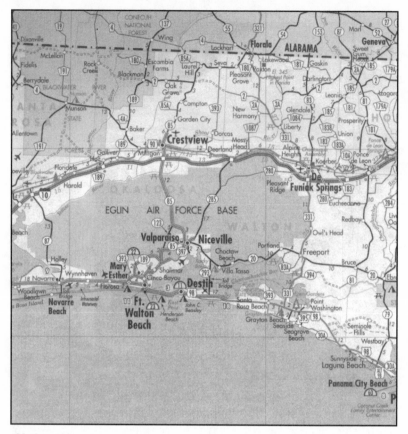

*Okaloosa County.*

When the Europeans arrived between 1500 and 1700 AD, conflicts between cultures arose and continued as the settlers spread throughout the Southeast. Renegade pirates acting in defiance of their mother country's policies added to the turmoil.

In more recent history, Fort Walton Beach had its beginnings in the Civil War when the Confederacy's First Florida Infantry, also known as Walton's Guard, camped along Santa Rosa Sound in front of a large Indian mound in the area that is now downtown Fort Walton Beach. After the war, John Thomas Brooks returned to homestead 111 acres. He was the first white settler here, and in tribute, the town was named Brooks Landing.

*The Emerald Coast gets its name from the smooth, emerald waters of the Gulf.* (Courtesy of VISIT FLORIDA.)

By the turn of the century, a school and post office had been established, and the town's name had changed to Camp Walton. Camp Walton was gaining fame as a small fishing retreat, but it wasn't until the 1930s when Highway 98 was built and tourists could reach the town by means other than water that tourism began to affect Camp Walton's economy.

Fewer than 90 people lived in Fort Walton in 1940; today, the city is the largest urban development in the county, with a population over 150,000. The last name change occurred in 1953, when Beach was added to Fort Walton. Ironically, the town has never had a fort or a beach.

In tangent with Fort Walton Beach, the neighboring twin cities of Niceville and Valparaiso were also growing as a result of a thriving fishing industry based on the mullet caught in the sandy-bottomed Choctawhatchee Bay. Valparaiso was founded by John B. Perrine, an entrepreneur from Chicago who envisioned it as an ideal city by the sea, a "vale of paradise." Niceville evolved from a tiny fishing village called Boggy. The name was changed in 1910, when the people who lived there thought it an inappropriate name for a growing city.

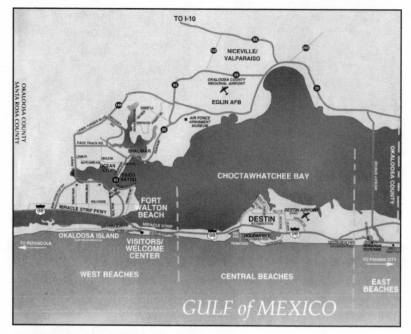

*The Emerald Coast.* (Courtesy of the Emerald Coast
Convention and Visitors Center.)

Destin, ten miles on the other side of the strait from Fort
Walton Beach, was founded by Leonard Destin who moved
there with his family from Connecticut during the 1830s. The
town's East Pass became the site of a skirmish between Union
and Confederate soldiers during the Civil War, and Destin was
forced to move his family to Freeport until the war ended.

In the early 1900s, more families arrived, hoping to earn
a living in the fishing industry. The fish were plentiful, but
the work was tough. Fishing boats were oar- or wind-powered,
and unloading the five thousand or more pounds of fish
from a seine net had to be done by scooping the fish nets out
on the ends of poles. When a hurricane closed East Pass in
1926, residents dug a trench from the overflowing bay to the
Gulf to create a new East Pass, the one still used today.
Though fishermen could now sail out to sea, Choctawhatchee Bay increased in salinity, slowly changing the bay's fish and
plant life.

When East Pass was bridged in 1935, people discovered the excellent fishing in the area, and soon fishermen were converting their seine boats into charter boats. By the 1950s Destin had twenty hotels and "tourist courts."

It wasn't until the last 25 years that the area blossomed as an attractive vacation getaway along the Gulf. Hollywood has even discovered the area, filming *Jaws II* here in 1978 and *The Truman Show* in 1997. Today, tourism in the area is a leading revenue producer, second only to Eglin Air Force Base.

Though much of Okaloosa County's beaches are now protected, the area is tinged with Panama City-style strip malls and high rises, mainly because development began before preservation initiatives were in place.

The best way to gain perspective of this section of Gulf shores is from the sea. On emerald waters with color bands varying from blackish-green to lime to deep blue, you can see the curvaceous line of the shore, the sun-bleached whiteness of the sand, the drifts of dunes and their wispy sea oats that separate the beach from the lively activity beyond.

Okaloosa County can also boast 59 miles of inland waters in and around the Choctawhatchee Bay—an area primed for freshwater fishing and water activities like canoeing and innertubing.

## Contact Information

The welcome center on Miracle Strip Parkway on Okaloosa Island has maps and brochures publicizing attractions and special events. The hours are daily from 8:00 A.M. to 5:00 P.M. during the summer. In the off season, the center is open Monday through Friday from 8:00 A.M. to 5:00 P.M. and on Saturday and Sunday from 10:00 A.M. to 4:00 P.M.

**Emerald Coast Convention & Visitors Bureau** (1540 Hwy. 98E, Fort Walton Beach, FL 32548; 800-322-3319, 850-651-7131; www.destin-fwb.com).

| Average Temperatures | |
|---|---|
| Spring | 82° |
| Summer | 88° |
| Fall | 84° |
| Winter | 70° |

## Transportation

Airports with major carriers in or near Okaloosa County include the Panama City–Bay County International Airport, four miles northwest of Panama City, and the Okaloosa County Air Terminal, one mile east of Destin. There are also airports in Fort Walton Beach, DeFuniak Springs, and Pensacola.

Additionally, both Amtrak and Greyhound provide transportation to the area. Cab rides to the beach from Okaloosa County Airport cost around $12.

**Amtrak** (101 N. Main Street, Crestview; 800-USA-RAIL).

The *Sunset Limited* transcontinental service from Los Angeles stops in Crestview, 26 miles north of Fort Walton Beach.

**Crosstown Taxi** (850-244-7303)

**Greyhound Bus** (101 Perry Ave., Fort Walton Beach; 800-231-2222, 850-243-1940).

**Guardian Rental Cars** (9900 Hwy. 98E, Destin; 850-654-4600 in Destin; 850-863-2992 in Fort Walton Beach).

**Miracle Strip Aviation** (Airport Road; 850-837-6135).

This Destin terminal is for private aircraft only.

**Night Owl Limousine and Towncar Charter Service** (850-650-4848)

**Okaloosa County Air Terminal** (State Road 85, Eglin Air Force Base; 850-651-7160).

**Panama City–Bay County International Airport** (3173 Airport Road; 850-763-6751).

**Pensacola Regional Airport** (Airport Blvd.; 850-435-1746).

**Yellow Cab** (850-244-3600)

### Pelican Picks

**Get in the Wind** (109E Hwy. 98, Destin; 850-654-WIND; open Monday–Saturday from 10:00 A.M. to 6:00 P.M., Sunday from 12:00 P.M. to 6:00 P.M.).

Go fly a kite! With weather as wonderful as what you find in Destin, this old-fashioned pastime provides hours of pleasure. The best places to fly a kite are, of course, on the beach, and summer is ideal because the winds are stronger, but they may be crowded during certain times of the year. Try for late afternoon when most people have left.

To get into the spirit, visit this funky little kite shop. Co-owner Keith Lisk can show you a wide variety of kites to choose from. Stunt kites are the most popular; they come with a thinner, lighter line that is easy to control in the wind.

Open for seven years, Get in the Wind also carries windsocks, flags (including custom-made flags), and feathers.

**Eating Mullet**

You can't visit Northwest Florida without trying this regional specialty. Mullet, oily, bottom-dwelling fish, are bluish-gray or green with small mouths and indistinct horizontal black barrings. The adults migrate offshore in large schools to spawn, but the juveniles migrate inshore. These are the fish you see leaping out of the water. High in iodine content and with virtually no shelf life, they must be prepared soon after they are caught. Fried mullet is the most common way the fish are prepared, but they are also salted and eaten as a breakfast food in place of bacon or canned like tuna. Restaurants that carry local favorites will more than likely have fried mullet and cheese grits on their menu, and local festivals often sell smoked mullet on a stick.

## Attractions

**Air Force Armament Museum at Eglin Air Force Base** (100 Museum Drive on SR 85; 850-882-4062, 850-882-4063; open daily from 9:30 A.M. to 4:30 P.M.; free).

This is the only museum in the world dedicated to the collection, preservation, and exhibition of artifacts and memorabilia associated with Air Force armament and its platforms of delivery. Aircraft exhibits include a P-51 Mustang and P-47 from World War II, an F-80 Shooting Star from the Korean War, and an F-105 Thunderchief from the Vietnam War. There is a wide

*The Air Force Armament Museum at Eglin Air Force Base is the only museum in the world dedicated to the exhibition of Air Force armament.* (Courtesy of Destin • Fort Walton Beach CVB.)

variety of bombs, missiles, and rockets on display, including the AMRAAM and GBU-28 bunker buster developed for use during Desert Storm. In the Gun Vault, you can view weapons ranging from a 1903 Springfield rifle to the GAU-8, which is capable of shooting six thousand rounds per minute. There is also a theater on property showing *Arming the Air Force,* a 32-minute film about the history of Eglin Air Force Base and its role in the development of armament. Volunteers restore all the aircraft as well as man the museum.

**Big Kahuna's Lost Paradise** (1007 Hwy. 98E, Destin; 850-837-4061; water park is open daily from 10:00 A.M. to 5:00 P.M., Grand Prix racetracks until 10:00 P.M.; $27.50 for adults, $25.50 for ages 10 and under).

A 23-acre family entertainment complex, Big Kahuna's boasts the world's largest 54-hole tropical mini-golf course that winds through caves and underneath waterfalls. Water slides, body flumes, whitewater tubing, pools, and rushing rivers are part of this wet-water paradise. There are three go-cart Grand Prix racetracks in the park, Bombs Away with a B-25 bomber, a

Moroccan village with carnival games, and Kiddie Land with rides designed for small children.

**Camp Walton School House** (107 First Street, Fort Walton Beach; open July and August on Tuesday and Thursday from 10:00 A.M. to noon and 2:00 P.M. to 4:00 P.M.; 800-322-3319, 850-651-7131; free).

Though not located on its original site, this is the original one-room Camp Walton school that was used from 1912 to 1936. The first year, 15 children attended school in the building. Church meetings, town halls, and Friday night socials were also held here. Call ahead for tour information.

**Crystal Beach Wayside Park** (2825 Old Scenic 98, Destin; 850-837-6447).

Five miles east of Destin, Crystal Beach Wayside Park sits across a two-lane road from a state-owned, undeveloped, and protected beach.

**Eglin Air Force Base** (850-882-3933, 850-882-3931; tours only for groups with a minimum of 20 people who must have their own bus; www.eglin.af.mil).

As one of the largest bases in the world and the largest in the continental United States, Eglin Air Force Base has 724 square miles of land and 98,000 square miles of water, with a vast testing area in the Gulf of Mexico. More than 16,000 military and civilian personnel are employed on the base. The Son Tay Raiders, a group that attempted to rescue American POWs from a North Vietnamese prison camp in 1970, trained here.

The base no longer provides tours for individuals, but they can be arranged for groups with a minimum of 20 people who can provide their own bus. The tour covers only a minute portion of the base, but it's enough to provide a sense of the kinds of experiments conducted here. The McKinley Climatic Laboratory, an environmental test chamber, can produce temperatures from –65 to 165 degrees as well as 100-mph winds, ice, rain, and snow. There is also a film to watch, *Top Guns of Desert Storm*, which provides an overview of the 33rd Tactical Fighter Wing.

Eglin has over 400,000 acres of diverse habitat traversed by many trails and canoe routes. Contact the *Natural Resources Office* (850-882-4164) for a map of the area and information on permits to hunt, fish, boat, and camp on the Base. Eglin Reservation

Beach, five miles of undeveloped land, is located three miles west of the Brooks Bridge in Fort Walton Beach and is a favorite hangout for local teenagers.

The Eagle and Falcon, two 18-hole golf courses, are available for play with a government ID. Another 18-hole course, Gator Lakes, is located at Hurlburt Field.

**Focus Center** (139 Brooks Street, half a block S of Hwy. 98, Fort Walton Beach; 850-664-1261; open daily in the summer from 1:00 P.M. to 5:00 P.M., on weekends in the off-season from 1:00 P.M. to 5:00 P.M.; $2 per person.)

An acronym for Families of Okaloosa County Understanding Science, the FOCUS Center boasts permanent interactive exhibits that illustrate scientific phenomenon such as magnetism, electricity, fluid dynamics, surface tension, and gyroscopic action. There is a high-tech hurricane exhibit where kids can plot the progression of an actual storm, and a Hall of Life, where visitors can follow a particular system in the body from beginning to end. The Try on a Career room allows children to temporarily live their dream occupation from astronaut to fireman.

**Fort Walton Beach Art Museum** (38 Robinson Drive, S.W., Fort Walton Beach; 850-244-5319; open Sundays from 1:00 P.M. to 5:00 P.M.; free).

This museum houses an eclectic mix of exhibits, from painting, sculpture, and pottery by American artists to artifacts from Cambodia and Thailand.

**Fred Gannon Rocky Bayou State Recreation Area** (4281 Hwy. 20, five miles E of Niceville; 850-833-9144; open daily from 8:00 A.M. to sunset; $2 per vehicle; http://www.dep.state.fl.us/-parks/northwest/rocky.html).

Noted for its extensive mature sand pine forest and abundant plant and animal life, this 357-acre park offers guests a quiet, secluded location for fishing and hiking. Campsites and picnic areas overlook scenic Rocky Bayou, an arm of Choctawhatchee Bay. There is saltwater fishing along the bayou shoreline inside the park, freshwater fishing on Puddin' Head Lake. There are also three trail loops in the park; self-guided booklets that interpret the natural characteristics of each trail are available on site. Boat ramps and swimming are also available.

**Gulfarium** (Hwy. 98 on Okaloosa Island; 850-244-5169; open spring and summer from 9:00 A.M. to 6:00 P.M., fall and winter from 9:00 A.M. to 4:00 P.M.; $14 for adults, $10 for children 4–11, $12 for senior citizens).

One of the first marine parks in America and the second oldest in the state, Gulfarium opened in 1955 as home to Atlantic bottlenose dolphins, California sea lions, Peruvian penguins, and Ridley turtles. Daily performances by trained porpoises take place in a 60,000-gallon tank. There are also shows with sea lions, seals, otters, and penguins, as well as living sea exhibits in which aquarium life can be viewed through underwater windows.

Environmentalists may question using captive marine life as performers, but the Gulfarium prides itself on rescuing, rehabilitating, and releasing many species of dolphin and whales, as well as sea turtles and other injured wildlife, back into the wild.

For an up-close and personal encounter, engage in a "hands-on" experience with Kiwi, a tropical spotted dolphin. For 40 minutes you can sit on a ledge in the water and let Kiwi initiate play. You are not allowed to swim in the water with her.

**Henderson Beach State Recreation Area** (17000 Emerald Coast Pkwy., Destin; 850-837-7550; open daily from 8:00 A.M. to sunset; $3.25 per vehicle; www.dep.state.fl.us/parks/northwest/henderson.html).

As the first acquisition under the *Save Our Coast* program, Henderson Beach State Recreation Area was opened on March 29, 1991. It is named for the previous owners who were concerned with protecting the unique natural features of the area for all to enjoy. This six thousand feet of scenic shoreline, 208 acres in all, is a habitat for sand pines, scrub oaks, Southern magnolias, dune rosemary, and a variety of wildflowers. Wildlife in the park includes protected sea turtles, black skimmers, sanderlings, brown pelicans, and laughing gulls. There are boardwalks throughout to protect the dunes and vegetation.

**Heritage Museum in Valparaiso** (115 Westview Avenue, Valparaiso; 850-678-2615; open Tuesday–Saturday from 11:00 A.M. to 4:00 P.M.; free).

*The Gulfarium was one of the first marine parks in America and is the second oldest in Florida.* (Courtesy of Destin • Fort Walton Beach CVB.)

Housed in an old bank building on the original main street in Valparaiso, the Heritage Museum highlights area history through exhibits featuring eight-thousand-year-old stone tools, early 20th-century iron pots and kettles, and other artifacts of yesteryear. A rare display is a steam-powered, belt-driven cotton gin. There is also a library of genealogical and historical research materials and official Civil War records. The museum offers classes in local history and traditional crafts.

**Historic Fort Walton Beach**

If you are interested in seeing how a coastal Florida town came into being, spend an afternoon walking around historic structures and sites in Fort Walton Beach.

The *Gulfview Hotel* at 12 Miracle Strip Parkway was built in 1906 with architectural characteristics of the buildings constructed here during the early 20th century. It was one of the first hotels in Camp Walton. Later, it was a social gathering spot for guests who arrived by boat. The building has 14 guest rooms with private baths, a lobby, dining room, kitchen, service rooms, and porch.

Built in 1915 on land donated by John Thomas Brooks, *St. Mary's Catholic Church* at 9 First Street Southeast was the first Catholic church in the area. The existing building was used until 1972 when the new church was constructed on Robinwood Drive.

The *Little Chapel in Vandegriff Park* was constructed in the late 1940s for use as the office of the First Methodist Church.

The *Bishop House* at 207 Shell Avenue Southeast is an excellent example of the prefabricated Sears & Roebuck mail-order homes that were common during the early 20th century. The house was built by E. R. McKees, a forest ranger from Niceville. At one time, it was used as a ranger station for Camp Walton. The house is now a private residence.

The *Frances Pryor Camellia Gardens* at 146 Brooks Street was founded in honor of Frances Brooks Pryor, daughter of John T. and Harriet Brooks and the first baby girl born to the new settlers of Camp Walton. As an adult, Frances was a civic leader who founded the Fort Walton Beach Camellia Society. Today, the camellia is the official city flower.

**Indian Temple Mound and Museum** (139 Miracle Strip Pkwy., Fort Walton Beach; 850-243-6521; open Monday–Friday from 11:00 A.M. to 4:00 P.M., Saturday from 9:00 A.M. to 4:00 P.M.; 75¢ for adults, children are free).

With more than six thousand artifacts on display, the Indian Temple Mound Museum outlines 10,000 years of Indian life along the Gulf Coast and Choctawhatchee Bay. Outside, you'll see a six-hundred-year-old, 12-foot high Mississippian-period temple mound, now registered as a National Historic Landmark. Inside the adjacent museum, you'll find artifacts taken from mounds in the area, ranging from effigy vessels, including a burial urn depicting a man sitting in a chair, to a 10,000-piece collection of paleo-Indian projectile points.

**Northwest Florida Ballet** (Fort Walton Beach; 850-664-7787).

Founded in 1969, this professional ballet company performs throughout the Panhandle. In June, the company presents an open-air performance at Liza Jackson Park in Fort Walton Beach. The two other performances of the year, the Nutcracker Ballet in December and a Spring Repertoire, are performed at

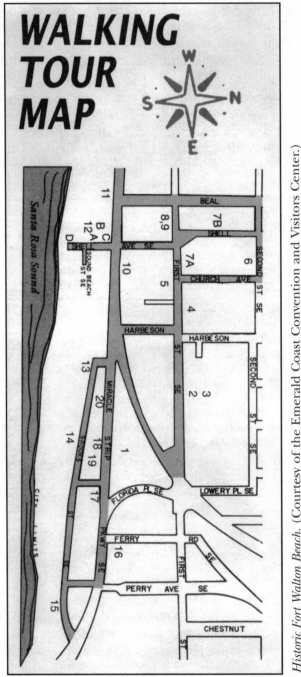

# WALKING TOUR MAP

Santa Rosa Sound

*Historic Fort Walton Beach.* (Courtesy of the Emerald Coast Convention and Visitors Center.)

*The Indian Temple Mound and Museum highlights 10,000 years of Indian life along the Gulf Coast.* (Courtesy of Destin • Fort Walton Beach CVB.)

Fort Walton Beach High School, the Saenger Theatre in Pensacola, and the Marina Civic Center in Panama City. Call for schedule.

**Northwest Florida Symphony Orchestra** (performs at Okaloosa–Walton Community College Arts Center, Niceville; 850-729-6000).

Presenting a series of five or six concerts throughout Okaloosa County each year, the Northwest Florida Symphony is comprised of 80 local musicians. Performances are held at the local community college in the Arts Center's 1,650-seat auditorium. The season generally runs from October through April. Call for ticket prices and schedules.

**Old Destin Post Office Museum** (101 Stahlman Avenue across from the library, Destin; 850-837-8572; open Wednesday from 1:30 P.M. to 4:30 P.M.; free).

Originally located at the intersection of Mooney and Garnier Post Roads, the Old Destin post office serviced the city from 1934 to 1951. Today, the building houses a museum in tribute to Destin's history.

**Pleasure Island Water Park** (1306 Miracle Strip Pkwy., Fort Walton Beach; 850-243-9738; open daily from 10:00 A.M. to 6:00 P.M., until 10:00 P.M. for go-carts; $15 for people over 85 pounds, $13 for people under 85 pounds).

Hours of family entertainment await at Pleasure Island, where you spend your days in the water and your nights playing miniature golf. The par-3 golf course features a pirate shipwreck on a 9-hole course on the bay. There are also batting cages, a pitch 'n putt golf course, and an arcade on site.

**Shoal River Canoe Trail** (originates on SR 285 near Crestview; 850-487-4784, 850-882-4164 for a permit from Eglin Air Force Base).

Beginning near Crestview, this 27-mile trail in the narrow, shallow Shoal River cuts through high banks and passes sand-bars and stands of maple, oak, and cypress trees. The northern border of the trail is on Eglin Air Force Base, so obtain a permit if you plan to canoe the entire trail.

**Stage Crafters Community Theatre** (performances are held at the Fort Walton Beach Civic Auditorium; 850-243-1102).

With four productions each year, including a variety of music, comedy, drama, and mystery, Sage Crafters lives up to its reputation as a quality community theater company. Call for a schedule.

**Yellow River Canoe Trail** (boat ramp off Hwy. 8, originates in Oak Grove; 850-487-4784).

Beginning in the Conecuh National Forest in Alabama, the Yellow River flows swiftly through the Panhandle and empties into Blackwater Bay. The 56-mile canoe trail originates in Oak Grove, passes hardwood forests and cypress-gum swamps, and ends near the northern boundary of Eglin Air Force Base. Obtain a base permit if you plan to enter the reservation at 850-882-4164.

### Fishing/Water Recreation

Known as the "World's Luckiest Fishing Village" because it is home to Florida's largest and best-equipped charter boat fleet, Destin is a fisherman's paradise. For starters, the area offers the quickest deepwater access on the Gulf of Mexico due to a nipple-shaped shelf and curve along the ocean floor. This

*Destin is known as the "World's Luckiest Fishing Village."*
(Courtesy of VISIT FLORIDA.)

offshore shelf dips straight from Destin's East Pass to hundred-foot depths within 10 miles—so close that you can fish and still see the coast in the distance. As the depths increase, the water changes color from deep green to deep blue. Desoto Canyon, a 3,300-foot-deep outcropping of the Mississippi River Delta, is the deepest part of the Gulf and only 42 miles from Destin.

More billfish are caught each year on the Emerald Coast than all other Gulf ports combined. Red snapper, grouper, war-saw, amberjack, scamp, and triggerfish are among the common catches.

Charter boats leave daily from the marinas; quoted prices range from three hundred to eight hundred dollars and most include licenses, coolers, and beverages. Party boats that take out a number of people are an inexpensive alternative for deep sea fishing. Most offer day trips leaving at 7:00 A.M. and returning around 5:00 P.M. They charge from $35 to $60 for people who want to fish and around $10 for those who are along for the ride. Most charters include all supplies and have junk food on board to purchase, but your best bet is to take along your own lunch and beverages. Party boats range in size; some can accommodate up to 80 people. If you don't want to charter a boat, you can fish off the 1,200-foot-long Okaloosa Island Pier or the 3,000-foot-long Destin Catwalk along the East Pass Bridge.

Freshwater fishing is also excellent; second only to Key West in the state for the number of types of fresh fish available.

**Baytowne Marina at Sandestin** (9300 Hwy. 98W, Destin; 850-267-7777).

Powerboat rentals for fishing, skiing, and snorkeling.

**Blackbeard Sailing Charters** (boards one-fourth mile E of Destin Bridge, behind AJ's Restaurant, Destin; 850-837-2793).

Set sail for three hours of casual cruising aboard the *Blackbeard*, a 54-foot, gaff-rigged schooner—the same type of vessel used by pirates and smugglers in the 19th century. Sails leave daily at noon and again at 5:00 P.M.

**Consigned RV's** (101 Miracle Strip Pkwy, Fort Walton Beach; 850-243-4488).

This firm offers pontoon boat rentals.

**Destin Pontoon Rentals** (107 Gregory Ave., Fort Walton Beach; 850-654-2022).

Boats for fishing, cruising the Choctawhatchee Bay, and Gulf excursions are available for rent.

**Emerald Coast Watersports** (Hwy. 98 on Okaloosa Island; 850-302-0021).

Sea Doos, pontoon boats, and jet boats can be rented daily from five locations on the beach. In addition to the Okaloosa Island location, check out the locations in Destin on Highway 98 on the harbor and three beach locations: Holiday Inn, Days Inn, and Rodeway Inn. This outfitter also offers parasailing.

**Emerald Queen Paddle Wheel Boat** (docked at the Lucky Snapper, Destin; 850-837-2930; boards at 5:30 P.M. daily for dinner, 9:00 P.M. for moonlight cruises; $29.95 for adult dinner cruises, $19.95 for children).

Commanded by Capt. Buddy Godwin, the *Emerald Queen* has one feature that most boats lack—air-conditioning on the lower deck. Upstairs, you can take in the sights in the breezy Gulf air. Sightseeing, lunch, dinner, and moonlight cruises are the daily excursions offered by this authentic paddle wheel boat. The sightseeing and lunch cruises last an hour and a half and highlight dolphin, seabird, and marine life sightings. Dinner cruises are two hours long and feature music and dancing.

**Friendship Charter Sailing** (404 Hwy. 98; 850-837-2694).

Sailing instruction and charters are the specialty of Friendship.

**Gulf Islands Sailing Center** (1383 Miracle Strip Pkwy, Fort Walton Beach; 850-664-6710).

Sailboat rentals in a range of classes are available.

**Kokomo Snorkeling Adventure** (Kokomo Motel & Marina, 500 Hwy. 98E, Destin; 850-837-9029; $20 per person for snorkeling, $10 per person for sunset cruise).

Captain Donnie Brown and his crew set sail on the bay for shelling excursions and around the jetties in Destin Pass for a glimpse at marine life. Coolers and cameras are allowed aboard this 50-foot custom cruiser; call for reservations.

**Nathaniel Bowditch** (Harborwalk Marina near the Lucky Snapper, Destin; 850-650-8787; call for daily sailing schedule; $25 for adults, $15 for children ages 4–12, $23 for senior citizens).

Nathaniel Bowditch, an accomplished mathematician in the late 1700s, revolutionized the navigation world with his computations. His namesake, a 54-foot traditional steel schooner, introduces visitors to his love of the sea with three-hour cruises that highlight life along the Gulf of Mexico.

**Sail Away, Inc. of Destin** (boards one-half mile E of Destin Bridge on Hwy. 98; 850-837-4986).

This 65-foot gaff-rigged tops'l steel schooner, the *Flying Eagle,* can accommodate up to 39 passengers for sails on the Gulf. Private charters are available upon request.

**Southern Star** (Harborwalk Marina near the Lucky Snapper, Destin; 850-837-7741; website: dolphin-sstar.com).

The *Southern Star* features sunset and dolphin cruises on the Gulf throughout the year.

*Charters*

**Ben Marler Party Boats** (Emmanuel Boat Dock, Destin; 850-837-6313).

**East Pass Charters** (East Pass Marina, Hwy. 98E, Destin; 850-654-2022).

**Miller's Charter Services/Barbi-Anne** (next to AJ's Restaurant, Destin; 850-837-6059).

**Moody's Cruises** (194 Hwy. 98E, Destin; 850-837-1293).

**Silver Lining** (docked next to A.J.'s Seafood Restaurant, Destin; 850-243-7304).

**Stewart's Outdoor Sports** (4 S.E. Eglin Pkwy., Fort Walton Beach; 850-243-9443).

*Diving and Snorkeling*

The reefs along the Emerald Coast run in short ledges ranging from a few feet to a mile long—attractive conditions for fish and marine life.

The three most popular diving and snorkeling spots along the Emerald Coast are the jetties, the Destin Bridge, and Crystal Beach Pier. Flounder, blue angel fish, grouper, black snapper, amberjack, squirrel fish, blue crabs, sand dollars, and puffers are among the marine life living here.

The jetties are man-made rock structures that hold back sand and keep Destin's East Pass open to boat traffic. Located on the western tip of Holiday Isle, the site is home to abundant marine life. The depth slopes gradually to 40 feet, with visibility ranging from five to 70 feet.

The Destin Bridge pilings are also good for snorkeling. Visit both the jetties and Destin Bridge during high tide for the best visibility and least tidal current.

The Crystal Beach Pier pilings, located about six miles east of Destin, feature snorkeling with a maximum depth of around 12 feet.

At Timber Hole, you'll discover a submerged petrified forest littered with sunken luxury liners, ships, barges, railroad cars, and airplanes—ideal for lobsters, sponges, and sea squirts.

**Aquanaut Scuba Center** (#24 Hwy. 98, Destin; 850-837-0359).

With a 50-foot Barracuda II, the Scuba Center is equipped to carry up to 22 passengers for diving in the Gulf. Several trip options are available; four-hour trips feature two dives along many of the natural reefs in depths up to 65 feet; eight-hour trips have three dives with exploration of Timber Hole or Grayton Beach reefs. Depths range from 75 to 115 feet. Snorkeling excursions and sunset cruises are offered for non-divers as well as all levels of SCUBA instruction.

**Fantasea Scuba and Snorkel** (#1 Hwy. 98 at the foot of Destin Bridge, Destin; 800-326-2732, 850-837-6943).

The *OdysSea,* a 29-foot glass-bottom boat, conducts daily snorkeling tours to Destin's best snorkeling sites. All equipment is included. The company also offers SCUBA classes and sells and rents SCUBA and snorkel equipment. Call for trip schedules and reservations.

**Scuba Tech Diving Charters** (301 Hwy. 98 and 10004 Hwy. 98E, Destin; 850-837-2822).

A favorite of local divers, this outfit conducts two-tank reef or wreck diver and open-water dives in the Gulf.

### Golf

Destin is sometimes referred to as the "Golf Coast" because it sits in the midst of 576 holes. There are also excellent courses in Pensacola and Panama City as well as several dotting the coastline in between. Though golf is a year-round sport in the Panhandle, plan summer outings for early morning or late afternoon, when the sun is not as intense.

**Bluewater Bay Resort** (Hwy. 20, two miles E of Niceville; 850-897-3241).

The 36 holes on this course have been ranked by *GolfWeek* as the "#1 Course in Northwest Florida" for six consecutive years. The lake course utilizes a lake for the seven water hazards that come into play.

**Emerald Bay** (40001 Emerald Coast Pkwy., Destin; 850-837-5197).

Designed by Bob Cupp, this 18-hole championship course was voted one of the top new courses in the country in 1992 by *Golf Digest.* The 6,802-yard, par-72 layout offers breathtaking views of the Choctawhatchee Bay. The course touts a tough slope rating of 135 from the championship tees.

**Indian Bayou** (off Hwy. 98 on Airport Road, Destin; 850-837-6191).

Large elevated greens, wide forgiving fairways, and well-placed bunkers are found on this 27-hole Earl Stone golf course. Water comes into play on many holes, and there is a driving range on site. Located in the heart of Destin, this course is appropriate for all skill levels.

**Santa Rosa Golf and Beach Club** (Hwy. 30A, six miles past Sandestin, Destin; 850-267-2229).

With the area's only Gulf-front holes, this course has 18 challenging holes of golf on a 6,608-yard course. There is a driving range and putting green on site.

**Seascape Resort** (Emerald Coast Pkwy., seven miles E of Destin; 850-654-7888, 850-837-9181).

One of Destin's most popular courses, Seascape offers golfers a wide variety of shot selection. Thirteen water hazards come into play.

**Shalimar Pointe Golf & Country Club** (2 Country Club Road, Shalimar; 850-651-1416).

Ranked as one of the Southeast's Top 50 Development courses by *GolfWeek* magazine, this championship Finger–Dye course borders the Choctawhatchee Bay and features bunkers that resemble dunes, impeccably manicured greens, and fairways with strategically placed bunkers. The 11th and 17th holes have been distinguished by *Links* magazine as two of the hardest holes on the Emerald Coast. Requiring a 149-yard drive from an elevated and forbidding water hazard, the 11th hole is banked by a tough grass bunker and lake to the right and a drastic downslope to the left. An unforgiving dogleg left awaits at the 17th hole. Shalimar has one of the best driving ranges in the area.

### Tennis

**Destin Racquet and Fitness Center** (995 Airport Road, Destin; 850-837-7300).

**Ft. Walton Racquet Club** (23 Hurlburt Field Road, Fort Walton Beach; 850-862-2023).

**Municipal Tennis Center** (45 W. Audrey Drive, Fort Walton Beach; 850-243-8789).

### Shopping

#### Main Street in Downtown Fort Walton

Designated as one of Florida's "Main Street" cities, downtown Fort Walton offers a clean, old-fashioned alternative to today's malls. The old buildings have been renovated and are now home to restaurants and boutiques. The *Islander's Surf & Sport* has everything you need for outwear at the beach (850-244-0451); *Far East Interiors* offers contemporary and traditional furnishings, including rattan and wicker (850-243-0443); and the *British Pedlar* is the place for British foods and gifts with an English flair (850-243-9352). Hours may vary for each individual store.

**Santa Rosa Mall** (300 Mary Esther Blvd., one block N of Hwy. 98W; Mary Esther; 850-244-2172; open Monday–Saturday from 10:00 A.M. to 9:00 P.M., Sunday from noon to 6:00 P.M.).

This contemporary mall houses four department stores—JC Penney, McRae's, Gayfers, and Sears—and 118 specialty shops, including a food court.

**Shoreline Village Mall** (Hwy. 98 and Gulf Shore Drive, Destin; 850-837-0822).

Brick-paved sidewalks and a colorful facade create a pleasant shopping experience at this specialty outdoor mall. Check out the custom designs at Destin T's and the all-white accessories at Callie's Beautiful Whites. Hours vary for each individual store.

**Silversands Factory Stores** (10562 Emerald Coast Pkwy. on 98W, Destin; 800-510-6255, 850-864-9780; open Monday–Saturday from 10:00 A.M. to 9:00 P.M., Sundays from 10:00 A.M. to 6:00 P.M.).

As one of the Southeast's largest and most exclusive designer outlet shopping centers, Silver Sands has 100 stores, from the Coach Factory Outlet and Clifford & Wills to G. H. Bass & Co., Anne Klein, and the Bose Factory Store. And don't forget about Morgan's, a food and entertainment complex for adults and children.

**Sockeyes Beach and Sports** (20011 Emerald Coast Pkwy., Destin; 850-654-8954; open daily from 9:00 A.M. to 10:00 P.M.).

This store carries a little bit of everything from coffee and beach wear to surfing equipment and bicycles.

### Bike Rentals

**Bob's Bicycle Center** (415 Mary Esther Cutoff, Fort Walton Beach; 850-243-5856).

## Restaurants and Nightlife

**AJ's Seafood and Oyster Bar** (one-fourth mile E of Destin Bridge on the harbor, Destin; 850-837-1166; open daily from 11:00 A.M. to midnight).

Well known for live entertainment and seafood "cooked any way you like it," AJ's also features a spectacular view of the Destin Harbor.

**The Back Porch** (1740 Hwy. 98E, Destin; 850-837-2022; open daily at 11:00 A.M.).

This cedar-shingled seafood shack claims to be Destin's original seafood and oyster house. As such, it serves up seafood in a number of ways: fried, grilled, stuffed, broiled, and boiled. The oysters on the half-shell make for a refreshing afternoon snack; the chargrilled amberjack, its signature dish, is flaky and filling.

**Captain Dave's on the Gulf** (3796 Old Hwy. 98, Destin; 850-837-2627; open daily from 5:00 P.M. to 10:00 P.M.).

Huge helpings of tasty seafood, steak, and chicken keep vacationers coming back year after year to Captain Dave's. The restaurant is decorated with a nautical theme, but it's the view of the Gulf that steals the show. The restaurant was built in the 1950s, complete with a tunnel under the highway for customers crossing from the parking lot.

**Fudpucker's Beachside Bar and Grill** (Okaloosa Island in Fort Walton Beach, 850-243-3833; Emerald Coast Pkwy. in Destin, 850-654-4200; open daily from 11:00 A.M. until . . .; www.emeraldcoast.com/~fudpuckers).

Seafood and burgers are the main fare at this casual coastal eatery, but the main attraction is the T-shirts. Fudpuckers is the nickname for the ugly, puckering triggerfish, and Fudpuckers' specialty is—you guessed it—blackened triggerfish.

**Harry T's** (320 Hwy. 98, Destin; 850-654-6555; open daily at 10:00 A.M.).

Overlooking the Destin Harbor, Harry T's is named for a circus trapeze artist who owned the boat house back in the 1920s. As legend goes, Harry T. led the 2,113-passenger rescue of the luxury cruise ship *Thracia,* which sank off the Gulf on April 12, 1927. The restaurant is decorated with the ship's salvaged furnishings—Harry T's reward for his lifesaving heroics—and memorabilia from Harry's circus days. The menu selection is incredible, and the food, ranging from chimichangas to char-grilled grouper, is pretty darn good. There's a popular night-club downstairs that features a nightly live band.

**Hog's Breath Saloon** (541 Hwy. 98, Destin; 850-837-5991; open 11:00 A.M. to 4:00 A.M.; www.hogsbreth.com).

The menu at this raucous watering hole varies from conch fritters and fish toes to oyster sandwiches and hog burgers. The logo, "Hog's breath is better than no breath at all," is a variation from owner Jerry Dorminy's grandmother's saying, "Bad breath is better than no breath at all."

**Magnolia Grill** (255 Miracle Strip Pkwy. SE, Fort Walton Beach; 850-302-0266; open Monday–Saturday from 11:00 A.M. to 9:00 P.M.).

The Magnolia Grill serves up dishes like scallops St. Jacques with fettuccine and crawfish étouffée in an interior similar to a 1950's diner. Take time to absorb the local history on the walls, where you'll find framed vintage photos and old newspaper clippings.

**Pasarda Hall** (17 Industrial Street, Fort Walton Beach; 850-243-7333).

Do-si-do on over to Pasarda Hall, where you can mingle with Fort Walton Beach's square dance clubs. Dancing takes place nightly except for Wednesday and Sunday nights; call ahead for schedules.

**Santa Rosa Bay Brewery** (54 Miracle Strip Pkwy., Fort Walton Beach; 850-664-BREW; open 11:00 A.M. to 3:00 P.M. and 5:00 P.M. to 10:30 P.M.).

In addition to brewing its own beer, the Santa Rosa Bay Brewery offers waterfront dining on seafood and steaks, live entertainment, and pool on handcarved tables.

**Staff's Seafood Restaurant** (24 SW Miracle Strip Pkwy., Fort Walton Beach; 850-243-3526; open daily from 5:00 P.M. to 11:00 P.M. during season, off-season Monday–Thursday from 5:00 P.M. to 9:30 P.M. and Friday–Saturday from 5:00 P.M. to 10:00 P.M.).

An Emerald Coast favorite for decades, Staff's is credited with being the first restaurant in the area, dating back to 1913. The walls have lots of memorabilia from the early days. For dinner, try the house specialty, the seafood skillet, where you'll be served a variety of broiled and buttered seafood. Save room for the homemade bread, made from a secret, 70-year-old family recipe.

## Accommodations

**Abbott Resorts** (800-336-4853)

From economy condos to luxury villas, Abbott boasts the largest selection of vacation rentals on the Emerald Coast. It has a 24-hour central reservations line. Request its beach book, which lists condos, townhomes, motels, B&Bs, and vacation homes, along with coupons from local restaurants and shops.

**Bluewater Bay Resort** (1950 Bluewater Blvd., Niceville; 800-874-2128, 850-897-3613).

Though this resort is not located on the Gulf, you can indulge in 36 holes of golf, swimming pools, 21 tennis courts, playgrounds, nature trails, a 21-slip marina, and a simulated beach on the bay. The resort offers villas, condos, and traditional hotel rooms.

**Destin Beach Club** (1150 Scenic Hwy. 98, Destin; 850-837-3985).

The 47 Gulf-front units at this new Beach Club have private balconies or patios that face the Gulf of Mexico. Many units have fully equipped kitchens. There is a heated pool, a hot tub, and complimentary fitness center passes.

**Henderson Park Inn** (2700 Scenic Beach Hwy. 98; 800-336-4853).

The only beachside bed and breakfast on the Emerald Coast has 35 rooms in its three-story, Gulf-front property. Almost half of the rooms are named after famous French Impressionist painters and include reproductions of their masterpieces.

**Marina Motel** (1345 Hwy. 98E, Fort Walton Beach; 800-237-7021).

Modest but clean, this affordable mom-and-pop motel is located directly across from the public beach at Beasley Park. All units have refrigerators and microwaves, and 16 units have full kitchens. The motel also has a laundromat, a small pool, and a beach on the bay.

**Pelican Beach Resort** (1002 Hwy. 98E, Destin; 888-PELICAN, 850-735-4226).

One of the beachfront high-rise condos, Pelican Beach has 340 one- and two-bedrooms units that can accommodate up to

*The Henderson Park Inn is the only beachside B&B along the Emerald Coast.* (Courtesy of Destin • Fort Walton Beach CVB.)

six people. There is a sauna, steam room, heated lap pool, tennis courts, and beachside pool on property.

**Sandestin Resort** (9300 Hwy. 98W, Destin; 800-277-0800, 800-622-1623; www.sandestin.com).

Located to the east of Destin, this resort actually claims allegiance with the Beaches of South Walton. See that chapter for more details.

**Sundestin Beach Resort** (1040 Hwy. 98E, Destin; 800-336-4853, 850-837-4853).

With one-, two-, or three-bedroom floor plans, beachside SunDestin Beach Resort provides spacious accommodations with magnificent views of the Gulf. These high-rise condos also feature a heated indoor pool, an outdoor pool, a health club, whirlpool, and shuffleboard.

## Festivals and Special Events
*March*

### World Championship Cobia Tournament
During this time of year, thousands of cobia travel from the Caribbean to the upper Gulf waters to spawn, coming closest to the shore along the Emerald Coast. The tournament is held over a two-month span, with as many as 15,000 anglers participating. Call 800-322-3319, 850-651-7131.

*May*

### Billy Bowlegs Festival
This week-long bash has been a Fort Walton Beach favorite since 1954, when the festival began as a tribute to Pirate Billy Bowlegs. No one is quite sure who Bowlegs was, but a popular legend casts him as William Augustus Bowles, a flamboyant plunderer during the American Revolution who settled along the Panhandle to guard treasure he buried in the sand. In 1778, Bowles formed the State of Muskogee which controlled the Gulf shores. The festival's activities include a mock pirate invasion and takeover with militia skirmishes at Fort Walton Landing, fireworks, a boat parade led by Bowlegs on his pirate ship, a treasure hunt, Torchlight Parade, midnight run, and the Bowlegs Golf Tournament. Call 850-244-8191.

**Mayfest**

Following the example of their raucous cousins in Louisiana, folks along the Emerald Coast party Cajun-style at Mayfest, where the spirit of the bayou drifts across to the Gulf. As expected, music and food are the highlights of this festival, and there is plenty to go around. Call 800-322-3319, 850-651-7131.

*August*

**Dog Days Open Billfish Tournament**

Destin is the "Billfishing Capital of the Gulf" and as such, this competition is intense, especially since there is a $30,000 purse involved. Blue marlin, white marlin, and sailfish are reeled in daily. Call 800-322-3319, 850-651-7131.

*October*

**Destin Fishing Rodeo**

More than 30,000 anglers compete each year in this annual fishing rodeo, a Destin tradition for almost 50 years. There are $100,000 in prizes. Whether you are trolling inshore for king mackerel, offshore for marlin and sailfish, or fishing the deep bottoms for red snapper and grouper, you'll be entered in the daily, weekly, and overall prizes. The rodeo is free to anglers who fish aboard registered boats. Call 850-837-6734.

**Destin Seafood Festival**

As the kick-off to the Destin Fishing Rodeo, the Destin Seafood Festival is host to more than 50,000 people annually who attend this weekend celebration. Indulge in every seafood dish imaginable, from barbecued shrimp and fried alligator to shark-kabobs and crawfish cheese bread. The festival is held at the foot of the Destin Bridge. Call 800-322-3319, 850-651-7131.

*November*

**Eglin Air Show**

Kick back and enjoy aerial acrobatics performed by the famed Thunderbirds. There are flightline displays of military might and simulated dogfights from the 33rd Tactical Fighter Wing. The Air Show occurs every other year. Call 800-322-3319, 850-651-7131.

## Day Trips

### Crestview

Located along a section of the Old Spanish Trail, a historical trade route from Jacksonville, Florida, to El Paso, Texas, Crestview was established in the late 1800s by lumbermen, farmers, and ranchers. It is named for its position above the Yellow and Shoal Rivers, which are 235 feet above sea level—among the highest in the state. Call 850-682-3212.

# 5

## Beaches of South Walton/Seaside

### Introduction

The Beaches of South Walton is paradise for discerning travelers who daydream about a perfect beach vacation with nothing to do but relax and no distractions other than the soft lapping of waves along the seashore. What the area lacks in theme parks, family-activity centers, and shopping, it makes up for in solitary stretches of sugar-white beaches, championship golf courses, and gourmet restaurants.

Tucked between the world-renowned fishing village of Destin and the spring break mecca of Panama City, this rare pocket of natural beauty co-exists peacefully with thoughtful development. The beaches have unusually large sea oat-covered dunes and brilliant white quartz sand that squeaks underfoot; they are also among the least developed and most pristine in Florida. One in particular is Topsail Hill State Park, a two-and-a-half mile span of undeveloped beach that has been identified as the most pristine piece of coastal property in Florida. Besides its unspoiled nature, Topsail Hill also features one of the area's eight coastal dune lakes systems—a unique ecosystem found nowhere else in the world.

Besides the beaches and coastal dune lakes, South Walton has six other ecological communities: mesic flatwoods, scrub, scrub

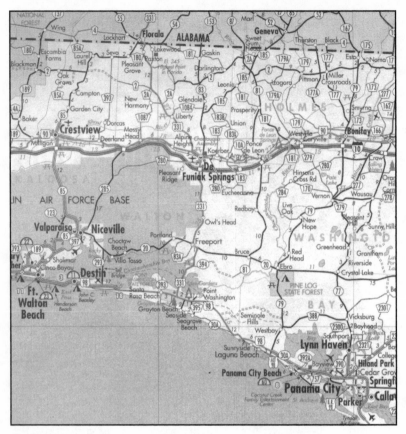

*South Walton area.*

flatwoods, depression marshes, wet flatwoods, and estuarine marsh-
es. Each ecosystem has its own native animals and plants, some of
which are threatened or listed as endangered species. These
include animals like the Atlantic Loggerhead Turtle, Kestrel Tern,
Snowy Plover, Piping Plover, Gopher Tortoise, Southeastern
Kestrel, and Loggerhead Strike Turtle, and plants such as Cruise's
Golden Aster, Large-leaved Jointweed, Conradina, and Godfrey's
Blazing Star. The county also sports 14 fresh- and saltwater lakes.

## History

Like other parts of Florida, the Beaches of South Walton
were once inhabited by Indians, specifically the Euchee and

Choctaw tribes. These tribes were not nomadic, but rather built large villages and were masterful hunters and fishermen. Indian artifacts discovered in the area date back to the 1400s.

In 1824, shortly after Florida was recognized as a U.S. territory, Walton County was created under the territorial governorship of Andrew Jackson. The county was named for Col. George Walton, secretary of West Florida and the son of former Georgia governor George Walton, who signed the Declaration of Independence.

The first permanent white settlers arrived in the late 1800s to harvest timber. They settled at Grayton Beach, the oldest coast community between Pensacola and Apalachicola, and then at Hogtown Bayou, which is now known as Santa Rosa Beach.

Soon, other small towns sprang up. Point Washington, a sawmill community built around the Wesley Lumber Company and now home to Eden State Gardens, was created in 1899. DeFuniak Springs, the county seat, was incorporated in 1901 as a planned railroad town next to Lake DeFuniak for the Louisville & Nashville Railroad (L&N). It also became home to the Winter Assembly of Chautauqua, an extension of the cultural and educational gatherings held each summer in New York.

During World War II, the U.S. military used a deserted stretch of beach at Four Mile Village to test captured German V-2 buzz bombs. Cement bunkers and launch pads from these test sites are still intact along the beach.

It wasn't until 1935 that both electricity and paved roads came to these parts, and it took until 1956 to pave County Road 30A and finally connect all of South Walton's beach communities.

In the following two decades, South Walton began to emerge as a vacation destination for families, many of whom built second homes in the area. When Sandestin was built in the early 1970s, it was the first commercial resort development for the county.

At that time, much of the coastline between Destin and Panama City was nothing more than a desolate stretch of beachfront occasionally interrupted by a house or small string of unassuming condos. Most of the land was owned by the St. Joe Paper Company or by families who had passed it down from one generation to the next. Except for a few clusters of tiny towns that had grown up around early homesteads, there were no convenience stores, no restaurants, and no beach accesses—in fact, the scrub oaks on both sides of County Road 30A grew so dense that few travelers realized the beach lay only a few hundred yards away from the road.

All of that changed in the early 1980s with Seaside, a quintessential small town carefully planned and built around founder Robert Davis's idyllic memories of summer vacations spent at Seagrove Beach, where Seaside now sits. "When I closed my eyes and let my mind wander, I could almost feel the sea breezes evaporating the moisture on my skin. I could recall the special pleasure of relaxing on a porch rocker after a shower at the end of a day on the beach," he recalls in *Seaside,* a pictorial history of his now legendary town.

Determined to recapture the sensory pleasures of life by the sea, Davis, along with world-renowned town planners Andres Duany and Elizabeth Plater-Zyberk, set out to transform the 80 acres of scrub and sand that he inherited from his grandfather into a traditional town where the necessities and indulgences of daily life would be only a short walk away. He also wanted to recreate a sense of community that many of today's modern subdivisions lack.

Seaside was so successful that copycat cottages began popping up all over northwest Florida. This sudden interest in development and the tourism industry it created did wonders for the economy, but locals feared that the natural beauty of the land, once considered "worthless sand and scrub,"would be spoiled permanently.

In 1994, preservation efforts went one step further with the creation of the South Walton Conservation and Development Trust, a 12-member panel of state officials and local citizens that produced a state and county plan for all development in South Walton County until 2025. Under plan recommendations, all development must economically and environmentally enhance the area.

Today, tourists can see the plan in action. Unlike her sister cities, which sprang up during an era when preservation took a back seat to development, the Beaches of South Walton has a look and feel like no other place in the Panhandle. Of the county's 53,000 acres, 23,000 are non-commercial, state-owned property. All residential and commercial construction sites sit well behind the dunes, which are preserved to protect the beaches. There are walk-overs every mile or so to allow beach access without disturbing the sand dunes. And though travelers will find a few chain restaurants and hotels, the majority of businesses along this 26-mile stretch are mom-and-pop operations.

Growth continues today in the Beaches of South Walton with new, innovative developments like Rosemary Beach. Designed by the same team that planned Seaside, this residential community on the east shores of South Walton is heavily influenced by the architectural style of the West Indies. In a July 9, 1997, article, *The Wall Street Journal* recognized the community as one of the hottest spots in the South for a home away from home.

No history of the Beaches of South Walton would be complete without mention of hurricanes. The most recent, Hurricane Opal, wreaked havoc on much of Florida's Panhandle, but for the Beaches of South Walton, damage was minor compared to the destruction just west on Santa Rosa Island. For the most part, many of the majestic dunes that towered above the beach like mountains of sculpted sugar were either destroyed or shifted. Most vacationers, however, can't tell a difference, and now, with massive dune restoration well underway, many of the dunes are slowly growing in stature.

The west end of the Beaches of South Walton is often confused with Destin, and rightly so, since the residential and commercial properties found here have a Destin address. This end is also more developed than the center of South Walton, mainly because development began before preservation initiatives were in place. On the east end, the Beaches of South Walton connects with the outskirts of Panama City Beach. In all, it takes about 40 minutes to traverse the county from east to west.

### Contact Information

**South Walton Tourist Development Council** (Hwy. 331 and Hwy. 98; P.O. Box 1248, Santa Rosa Beach, FL 32459; 800-822-6877, 850-267-1216; www.beachesofsouthwalton.com).

The South Walton Tourist Development Council is housed in a new building on the corner of Highway 331 and Highway 98. Travelers can stop by daily from 8:30 A.M. to 6:00 P.M. to pick up brochures and maps of the area.

## Average Temperatures

Spring    79°
Summer   91°
Fall        81°
Winter    68°

## Transportation

The closest airport to the Beaches of South Walton is the Panama City–Bay County International Airport, located four miles northwest of Panama City, or the Okaloosa County Air Terminal, located one mile east of Destin.

**Amtrak** (101 N. Main Street, Crestview; 800-USA-RAIL).

**Greyhound Bus** (564 James Lee Blvd., Hwy. 90, Crestview; 800-231-2222, 850-682-6922).

**Okaloosa County Air Terminal** (State Road 85, Eglin Air Force Base; 850-651-7160).

**Panama City–Bay County International Airport** (3173 Airport Road; 850-763-6751).

**Pensacola Regional Airport** (Airport Blvd.; 850-435-1746).

### Pelican Picks

**South Walton Turtle Watch** (P.O. Box 4818, Seaside Branch, Santa Rosa Beach, FL 32459; 850-897-5228).

In recent years, human exploitation and habitat destruction have greatly reduced the sea turtle population. To nurture the turtles that return to the Beaches of South Walton each year to lay their eggs, the South Walton Turtle Watch, a volunteer organization, walks the beaches from May through October looking for nests and hatchlings.

Nests are spotted by the flipper swipes made by the female turtle, who digs a flask-shaped shallow pit close to the sand dunes. She lays about a hundred leathery skinned eggs and buries them using her flippers. The process takes around an hour to complete, after which time she returns to the ocean, never to visit the nest again. Once the eggs are laid, they take an average of 62 days to hatch.

When a nest is found, it is staked off and marked with yellow surveyor's tape; it is against the law to disturb a turtle nest.

In October, volunteers begin to watch for hatching turtles. Because of shoreline development, the volunteers try to be on hand to steer the baby turtles toward the water instead of toward land, where bright lights catch their attention and confuse their migration route. Hurricanes also cause major damage to turtle nests. Before Hurricane Opal hit in 1995, 39 nests had been found. After the hurricane, only eight had survived.

If they are lucky, as many as one hundred turtles can hatch from one nest, but unfortunately, only one out of every 10,000 turtles reaches reproduction age. About three days after a nest has hatched, volunteers will excavate it to release any trapped hatchlings and to record data on how many eggs hatched.

Ironically, sand temperature determines the gender of the sea turtle. In South Walton, the sand is cooler than in South Florida, so the hatchlings here are male. As the producer of the largest male population, turtle nesting is Northwest Florida is a vital link in the reproduction process.

**Scenic Highway 30A Bike Path** (800-822-6877)

Completed in 1998, the new Scenic Highway 30A Bike Path connects the diverse communities of the Beaches of South Walton. The off-road paths are eight feet wide and wind along pristine freshwater lakes, undeveloped woodlands, and beach areas. Connecting Dune–Allen Beach to Inlet Beach, nine miles of the path are off-road, while the remaining nine miles are connected to the highway.

Attractions along the trail include Grayton Beach State Recreation Area, Deer Lake State Park, and the historic town of Grayton Beach.

**Walton County Snowbird Club** (Contact Jack Williams; 89 Baird Street, Santa Rosa Beach, FL 32459; 850-267-3848).

Northwest Florida has become a popular migration spot for "snowbirds," the affectionate name for Northerners who winter along the Gulf. The group is basically a social organization designed to help people meet others in the area. They play a lot of golf and sponsor bimonthly scrambles. They host Euchre and bridge nights, hold tennis matches and fashion shows, and occasionally have a dance. The headquarters are at Seascape Resort, but the meetings are held in a variety of places. Dues are five dollars per person for activities from late October through March.

**Bayou Arts and Antiques** (Hwy. 393 by Cessna Park overlooking the bay, Hogtown Bayou; 850-267-1404; open Tuesday–Saturday from 10:00 A.M. to 4:30 P.M.).

This antique shop along Hogtown Bayou has plenty of antiques and knickknacks to browse through, including old and new garden statuary and items chosen especially for beach homes, but the main attraction is the St. Francis Wildlife Chapel next to the store. Hand painted by owners Chick and Cathy Hueffer, the chapel is a quiet place for meditation. Out back is the pet cemetery. Named for St. Francis, the patron saint of animals, the chapel continues an old medieval custom each October of blessing the animals. The blessings were once for farm animals, a family's livelihood; now the blessings are extended to family pets.

If you intend to visit, plan to spend at least a half a day at the compound. There is an art studio on the grounds along with gardens to explore.

### Beaches

When tourism became a viable industry in Walton County, no individual beachfront community was large enough to adequately promote itself as a tourist destination. As a result, the

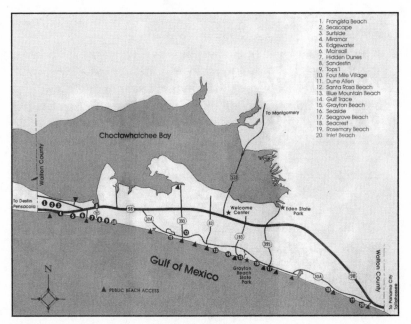

*Beaches of South Walton.* (Courtesy of the Beaches of South Walton.)

fancy name, "the Beaches of South Walton," was created as a marketing ploy by the Tourist Development Council for the numerous coastal communities situated between Destin and Panama City. It was a good choice because there's no doubt that the beaches are South Walton's main attraction.

If you're a bona-fide beach bum, one of the best ways to explore South Walton is to visit a different beach every day—a laid-back tour that will take 19 days to complete. Each beach has a unique story. A few were settled in the late 1800s by some of the area's first homesteaders; others take their name from the developments they border.

**Frangista Beach** is one of the older beaches in the area and was named for the original Frangista Inn, built in 1939. The inn was once used by fishermen to locate their fishing spots in the Gulf. While offshore, they would line up the hotel with another landmark on the beach. If they moved east or west, they could return to the same spot by lining up the landmarks again. This was known as "triangulation."

**Seascape** features Seascape Resort and Conference Center, which was one of the first resorts in the area.

**Surfside** takes its name from a luxurious high-rise in this part of the Beaches of South Walton. The complex has a large walkover that connects the beach to the other side of Highway 98.

**Miramar Beach** is known for its low-rise condos, private homes, and beautiful public beach access. The access was once an old Florida Department of Transportation Wayside Park until Walton County took over its management.

**Edgewater Beach** is distinguished by an unusual cresting-wave shape. The building was developed by a Frenchman who gave it a unique French Riviera look and feel.

**Mainsail Beach** was named for the landmark Gulf-front mid-rise condominium complex. There are also private beach houses, cottages, and low-rise condos.

**Hidden Dunes Beach** is named for the local tennis resort and includes Gulf-front neighborhoods of single-family, private beach homes, many of which are for rent.

**Sandestin Beach** was named for a 2,400-acre beach-to-bay resort. There are homes, condos, luxury hotel accommodations, restaurants, golf courses, tennis courts, fitness and conference facilities, a shopping market, and a marina in this gated complex. The land was originally owned by Winthrop Rockefeller of Little Rock, who planned to build a resort in the 1950s called "Forest By the Sea." He abandoned his plans after he was elected governor of Arkansas.

**Topsail Beach** includes the resort community, Tops'l Beach and Racquet Resort, and the Topsail Hill State Park, located next door.

**Dune Allen** is noted for its multitude of lakes. This quiet community was named for coastal dunes and founders Eric and Jean Allen, who settled Dune Allen in 1946 in hopes of selling vacation cottages. Back then, Thompson Road, little more than a sandy trail, was the only way in and out. It wasn't until the 1950s that County Road 393—Dune Allen's first paved road—connected Santa Rosa Beach to the Gulf of Mexico. Today, Dune Allen features beachfront homes nestled between freshwater lakes and sandy dunes.

**Santa Rosa Beach** is an unincorporated town that encompasses a number of beach communities as well as public beach

*Sandestin Resort is a 2,400-acre beach-to-bay resort.* (Courtesy of Sandestin Resort.)

access along County Road 30A. Santa Rosa was developed at the turn-of-the-century by the Cessnas of Chicago, an industrious family who came South to grow oranges. When citrus canker and poor farming destroyed the groves, and the timber industry failed, the town turned to tourism, which remains the focus of its modern-day economy. Santa Rosa Beach is home to Grayton Beach State Recreation Area.

**Rosemary Beach** is the newest beach to join the string in South Walton County. This beach is a planned development by the world-famous community planners, Andres Duany and Elizabeth Plater-Zybeck, the same planners who designed Seaside.

**Blue Mountain Beach,** the highest point along the Gulf of Mexico in the United States, offers spectacular views of the sunset exploding in fierce reds and oranges over the Gulf. Surprisingly, locals find that this area does have the feel of a mountain, though its small incline will seem more like a tiny hill to visitors unaccustomed to Florida's flat topography. Beach homes and condos are for rent throughout Blue Mountain Beach.

**Gulf Trace** is a quiet beach community of private homes surrounded on three sides by undeveloped state-owned property.

**Grayton Beach** is an eccentric, small town that has changed little in its hundred-year history, partly because it is virtually surrounded by park land and partly because the people who live here have managed to protect it from encroaching development. As a result, this is one of the few places left with an old Florida feel, complete with beaches that are virtually untouched. In fact, Grayton Beach State Recreation Area has been recognized in the past as one of America's top beaches. With oyster shell roads and wooden and cinder block homes, Grayton Beach is the oldest coastal community between Pensacola and Apalachicola and one of North Florida's oldest tourist spots. The Wash-A-Way House, so named because its foundation was swept out by several hurricanes, sits at the end of County Road 283 and is the only structure still standing that supposedly dates back to 1890. It served as a hotel at the turn of the century and was a Coast Guard station during World War II, when soldiers called "beach pounders" would walk or ride mules along the beach to look for German spies or survivors of U-boat attacks. Today, Grayton has a small downtown area lined with eclectic shops, a general store, a coffee house, and the funky Red Bar.

**Seaside,** America's most famous small town, features brick streets lined with pastel-colored cottages. Utopian in look and feel, Seaside is often used for catalog shoots and movie sets. Among its more famous visitors: Jim Carrey, the Bellamy Brothers, and His Royal Highness Prince Charles. Refer to the Seaside section of this chapter for more information.

**Seagrove Beach,** the second oldest beach community in the Beaches of South Walton, is more laid-back and a bit more realistic in feel than its western neighbor, Seaside. Here, visitors will discover 40-foot bluffs overlooking the Gulf, natural sand dunes, and hardwood forests filled with oak, pine, magnolia, hickory, and holly trees. Rental units are also a bit cheaper, but nowhere near the 1940's price of $30 to $40 charged for a week's stay in a Gulf-front home. From the beginning, Seagrove was developed by founder Cube "CB" McGee as a tourist destination, and he even had his own slogan, "Where Nature Did Its Best." The Seagrove Village Market, one of the town's original buildings, still stands along State Road 395, and is the best place along the coast to stop in for staples.

*Seaside is known for its picket fences and tin-topped, pastel-colored cottages.* (Courtesy of Seaside.)

**Seacrest Beach** is considered by locals in the know as a prime spot for making out because of its secluded location and massive sand dunes. If you plan to stay awhile, take a blanket so you can lie on your back and stargaze. Don't get carried away, though; while the beach is usually deserted, there are private beach cottages tucked between the dunes. One of those late bloomers that is catching up fast starts in the area just east of Camp Creek and extends to Rosemary Beach.

**Inlet Beach,** the last in the string of South Walton's beaches, lies at the end of South Walton closest to Panama City and is one of the oldest communities in the South Walton area. This quiet, secluded area with minimal development is named for the large lagoon and inlet lake on its eastern shore, Phillips Inlet.

### Attractions

**Cassine Gardens Nature Trail** (CR 30A, near Grayton Beach; 850-231-5721; free; open daily 24 hours).

As hokey as it sounds, this nature walk, named for the *illex Cassine,* or holly tree, is situated behind Cassine Gardens townhomes. With a boardwalk over marshland, the trail winds past native vegetation and wildlife habitats and joins pristine state forest land.

**Choctawhatchee River Tours** (Black Creek Lodge, two miles off CR 3280; 850-835-4628; $12.50 adults, $6.25 for children ages 5–11; tours begin Tuesday–Friday at 1:00 P.M., Saturday sundown tour begins at 5:30 P.M.; www.allenmedia.com/rivertours).

Get the low-down on life on the Choctawhatchee from the locals. This hour-and-40-minute river tour covers the history of the region, the Indians of the area, and the native plants and wildlife that live along the river. Call ahead for reservations.

**Eastern Lake Bike/Hike Trail** (off CR 395; 850-231-5800; open daily from sunrise to sunset; free).

This three-loop trail through the Point Washington State Forest winds around a variety of natural vegetation and wildlife habitat. There are three-mile, five-mile, and ten-mile trails to choose from for hiking or mountain biking. Call for maps and regulations.

**Eden State Gardens** (CR 395, N of Hwy. 98, Point Washington; 850-231-4214; open daily from 8:00 A.M. to sunset, guided house tours Thursday–Monday from 9:00 A.M. to 4:00 P.M.; grounds are free, house tours are $1.50 adults, 50¢ for children; www.dep.state.fl.us/parks/northwest/eden.html).

The highlight of this state park is the Wesley Mansion, a cultural legacy to North Florida's strong ties to the Old South. Built by William Wesley in 1897 at the height of the lumber boom in this region, the home has been restored with 18th- and 19th-century furnishings. In keeping with early Florida Panhandle architecture, the home is built on piers that allow air circulation under the house while avoiding extreme flooding. Large windows also help to circulate air throughout the building.

Canopies of mature live oak trees laden with frosty, gray-green strands of Spanish moss surround the home, along with gardens brimming with azaleas, dogwood trees, camellias, and hydrangeas. Tucker Bayou, which feeds into the Choctawhatchee Bay, runs only a few hundred yards away from the front of the house.

In its heyday, the mansion and grounds were the hub of the Wesley Lumber Company, with a dry kiln, planer mill, saw mill, commissary, and company-owned houses located on the property. Now, only the house remains. The gardens were the setting for the classic horror film, *The Frogs*.

In 1953, the Wesleys sold the home to Lois Maxon, who donated Eden to the state of Florida in 1968 in memory of her parents.

*In its heyday, Eden State Gardens was the hub of the Wesley Lumber Company, with a dry kiln, planer mill, saw mill, commissary, and company-owned houses located on the property; now, only the house remains.* (Courtesy of the Beaches of South Walton.)

The best time to visit Eden State Gardens is in the spring, when the azaleas and dogwoods are in full bloom.

**Elrod's Fish Camp** (Mach Bayou Road off CR 357; 850-267-2318; open Tuesday–Sunday from 6:00 A.M. to 6:00 P.M.; free).

The Gulf of Mexico isn't the only body of water found in the Beaches of South Walton. There's also the Choctawhatchee Bay, a calm, brackish bay with excellent fishing. Trout, redfish, flounder, black drum, and blue fish are among the common catches. It's also a great place for porpoise watching and crabbing.

The bay is ideal for beginning boaters since most of the fishing takes place in no more than three or four feet of water. The best bet is to rent a boat at Elrod's Fish Camp (it has pontoon boats, deck boats, and John boats), where owner Foster Dugas will provide you with a map and give you free lessons on navigating the bay.

If you're not up to fishing or cruising the bay, buy a cold drink, settle down into one of the rockers on the front porch, and talk Foster into sharing some of his more colorful stories.

Elrod's has an extensive bait and tackle shop with live bait, cold drinks, ice, and snacks. It also provides professional fishing guide excursions on Walton County's lakes and the Choctawhatchee Bay.

**Grayton Beach State Recreation Area** (CR 30A, S of Hwy. 98, Santa Rosa Beach; 850-231-4210; open daily from 8:00 A.M. to sunset, closes at 5:00 P.M. during winter months; $3.25 vehicle; www.dep.state.fl.us/parks/northwest/grayton.html).

This is the pinnacle of all American beaches, at least that's the verdict from Dr. Beach, a.k.a. Dr. Stephen Leatherman, former director of the University of Maryland's Laboratory for Coastal Research. Leatherman rates beaches each year based on scientific and cultural data. Grayton Beach won hands-down in 1994 on qualities such as crystal-clear water, sugar-white sand, unspoiled sand dunes, pristine nature trails, and a safe, uncrowded environment. Once a beach is named at the top of the list, it is retired for 10 years before it is eligible to be judged again.

Besides spectacular beaches, Grayton Beach offers an up-close look at the diverse ecosystems comprising Northwest Florida's coastal areas. Along the self-guided trail, nature buffs can ramble through salt marshes, around 40-foot dunes, and through clusters of Florida scrubs. The trail also provides dramatic examples of dune migration and building, natural pruning, and natural recycling. Upon closer examination of the larger dunes, visitors discover that the bushes growing on them are actually full-size slash pines and Southern magnolia trees with only their tops protruding from the drifting sand.

This 356-acre park offers camping, boating, surf fishing, swimming, nature trails, restroom facilities, and a snack bar. It's also a prime spot for viewing the fall Monarch butterfly migration. In October, it is common to see hundreds of Monarchs stopping over at the park before continuing south to Mexico.

*Grayton Beach was named the top beach in America in 1994.*
(Courtesy of the Beaches of South Walton.)

Situated next to one of the Gulf's oldest townships, Grayton Beach State Recreation Area was obtained through a land lease from the Florida Board of Education in 1964 and was dedicated and opened as a state park in 1968.

**Morrison Springs** (Morrison Springs Road off C1898, just past Bruce; 850-836-4223; open 7–6 weekdays, weekends until 10; $2 per person to swim and snorkel).

With spectacular caverns at depths of 50 to 85 feet and limestone walls that improve visibility to around 100 feet, Morrison Springs is a diver's dream. The spring is set in a cypress-shaded basin of white sand that gradually slopes to 30 feet before dropping off into the caverns. Here, crystal water flows from the lower cavern to the basin and finally out to the Choctawhatchee River. Night dives are allowed, and a complete diving facility is located on site. Equipment rentals are also available, including wet suits, fins, snorkeling equipment, tanks, regulators, and underwater lights. Upon request, PADI-certified diving instruction and checkout dives for students of certified instructions are available, as well as snorkeling and swimming instruction.

Fishing is another pastime at the springs, and is especially good in the channel to the Choctawhatchee River. Pike, bream, catfish, and large freshwater eels are prevalent.

There is also a campground with showers, toilets, and electrical hookups, and one section of the basin is reserved for boat launches.

**Patrone's** (307 DeFuniak Street, Grayton Beach; 850-231-1606; open daily from 10 A.M. to 5 P.M.; free).

It's only fitting that Patrone's, a quirky artist colony and petting zoo, sits in the middle of eccentric Grayton Beach. The cluster of ramshackle wooden booths have been turned into small, rustic studios where painters, potters, and ceramists ply their trade as well as display their eclectic but interesting pieces of art. Out back, get up close and personal with the rabbits, peacocks, goats, pheasants, pigs, and turkeys in the Barnyard Petting Zoo.

Patrone's also includes the Dream Café, which features live music several nights a week; a sno-cone stand, with 53 different flavors; Café Mama, once the town's general store; a bed and brunch; and pontoon and canoe rentals.

**Ponce de Leon Springs State Recreation Area** (one-half mile S of US 90 on CR 181A, Chipley; 850-836-4281; open daily from 7:00 A.M. to sunset; $3.25 per vehicle; http://www.dep.state.fl.us/parks/northwest/ponce.html).

Established in 1970, this 443-acre state recreation area boasts a rich swampland full of cypress trees. The main feature is the distinctive natural spring that produces 14 million gallons of crystal-clear water each day. With a year-round temperature of 68°, the spring has two main boils flowing from a limestone cavity into the center of the pool. The spring runs about 350 feet in length and flows into Sandy Creek, a tributary of the Choctawhatchee River, where the clear spring waters can be seen mingling with Sandy Creek's turbid waters.

Fishing is a favorite pastime at Ponce de Leon State Recreation Area, with plenty of largemouth bass, chain pickerel, and panfish to catch. Swimming is allowed, and there are also nature trails throughout the park.

**Topsail Hill State Park** (7349 Hwy. 98W, Santa Rosa Beach; 850-267-1864; open daily 8:00 A.M. to sunset, closes at 5:00 P.M. during winter months; free).

The sand dunes at this new state park tower as high as 50 feet and are so brilliantly white that it would be easy to mistake them for snowdrifts. Virtually untouched, this parcel of land also

*Patrone's in Grayton Beach is an eclectic artist colony and petting zoo.* (Courtesy of VISIT FLORIDA.)

features fresh-water lakes, pine forests, and a coastal dunes lake system, a unique ecosystem found nowhere else in the world but South Walton County. No wonder Topsail Hill is considered to be Florida's most pristine piece of coastal property. Currently, there are no facilities such as restrooms or snack bars in the park, and no plans to build any. It's also somewhat difficult to reach the beach since the only road in is sandy, narrow, and bumpy. Still, this park is ideal for fishing, swimming, and picnicking, and is a must-see for visitors who appreciate breathtaking beauty and the solitude of a secluded beach—this is Florida at its finest.

**Tops'l Spa** (9011 Hwy. 98W, Destin; 850-267-9222; open daily from 6:00 A.M. to 9:00 P.M.).

*Topsail Hill State Park is considered to be Florida's most pristine piece of coastal property.* (Courtesy of Judy Doherty.)

Tops'l Spa is one of the few full-service spas in the Beaches of South Walton. Guests can undergo massage therapy, skin and body care consultations, dips in heated pools, workouts on a complete line of exercise equipment, and wellness classes at the fitness center.

### Fishing/Water Recreation

The only marina in the Beaches of South Walton is the Baytowne Marina on the bay side of Sandestin Resort. From here, fishing charters for half-day, full-day, and three- to five-day trips can be arranged. You can also find a large fleet of deep sea fishing charters out of Panama City on the east side of South Walton and out of Destin on the west side, which is known as the "Deep Sea Fishing Capital of the World." Grouper, snapper, sea bass, and triggerfish are common catches. Refer to the Okaloosa County or Panama City chapters in this book for more information.

Freshwater fishing is also abundant. Several lakes in the area, along with the Choctawhatchee River and Choctawhatchee Bay, are prime spots for anglers.

*The Baytowne Marina at Sandestin Resort is the only marina located in the Beaches of South Walton.* (Courtesy of Sandestin Resort.)

Campbell Lake, 125 acres, lies only a few hundred yards away from the Gulf of Mexico. Accessible only by sand roads, the lake produces fair bream fishing in the spring and summer months.

Juniper Lake, north of DeFuniak Springs, is a 670-acre fish management area with some of the best bass fishing in the Panhandle. A number of trophy bass are taken each year from the lake. Spring and summer are good times to catch bluegills.

The Choctawhatchee River, flowing 96 miles from the Alabama line to the Choctawhatchee Bay, has access points at Caryville, Ebro, and Black Creek just south of Freeport. Catches include alligator gar, which can produce specimens weighing up to two hundred pounds during season.

Fishing licenses are required for both fresh- and salt-water fishing from land or boat and can be obtained at most local bait and tackle shops or in advance through the county tax collector's office. Call 850-892-8121 for more information.

**Baytowne Marina at Sandestin Resort** (located in Sandestin Resort; 850-267-7777).

**Black Creek Lodge** (Hwy. 331 near Freeport; 850-835-2541).

This rustic fish camp has everything an angler needs, from clean cabins and camper trailer sites to bait, rental boats, and a boat ramp with access to Black Creek and the Choctawhatchee River Basin and Bay.

**Juniper Lake Fish Camp** (Hwy. 83, two miles N of DeFuniak Springs; 850-892-3445).

This modest fish camp has access to Juniper Lake, campsites, trailers, boat rentals, bait, and tackle.

**Kings Lake Campground** (Hwy. 331, four miles N of DeFuniak Springs; 850-892-7229).

Campsites, cabins, bait, tackles, licenses, and boat launching into Kings and Holley Lakes are available at this DeFuniak Springs campground.

## Diving

Like other parts of the Panhandle, the Beaches of South Walton provide excellent diving sites in both the Gulf of Mexico and in the caverns and springs connected to the Choctawhatchee River. In the Gulf, typical diving depths range from 58 to 90 feet and feature natural reefs, artificial reefs, and wrecks. The natural reefs are generally limestone ledges two to six feet in width and covered with sponges and soft corals. There is also an abundance of fish and shells. Visibility ranges from 25 to 40 feet in the summer and 25 to 65 feet in the winter. When Hurricane Opal came through in 1995, many of the reefs were covered with sand; others were completely uncovered. It took about six months for the visibility to rise from zero, and even now, there are still days when visibility is especially poor.

**ScubaTech of Northwest Florida, Inc.** (one-half mile W of Sandestin across from Holiday Travel Park; 850-837-1933; www.prolectron.com/scuba).

ScubaTech is a woman-owned, full-service shop with charters, retail rentals, repair, air and instruction available. Additionally, the store offers reef and wreck diving, shelling, lobstering, spearfishing, and half-day scuba classes.

## Golf

With more golf courses per square mile than any other area in the Panhandle, the Beaches of South Walton is a golfer's paradise. There are 126 holes of golf in all, and the courses offer play for all skill levels and in all price ranges. Many of the courses are consistently ranked as some of America's best. As a result, hotels and resorts in the area usually feature golf packages with discounts on accommodations and green fees—be sure to ask about packages when you make a reservation.

**Emerald Bay Golf & Country Club** (40001 Emerald Coast Pkwy., Destin; 850-837-5197; open 7:00 A.M. to 7:00 P.M.).

This well-maintained, tree-lined golf course features water on nine of its 18 holes. A par-72 course, Emerald Bay has a gorgeous guest house and commands sweeping views of the Choctawhatchee Bay. This semi-private course was selected by *GolfWeek* magazine as one of the Southeast's Top 50 Real Estate Development Courses.

**The Garden** (40091 Emerald Coast Pkwy., Destin; 850-837-7422; open daily 7:00 A.M. to 10:00 P.M.).

With a nine-hole executive golf course and 10-acre driving range, the garden is the only course in the area fully lighted for night play. This facility also offers an 18-hole putting course. Unrestricted walking is available.

**Sandestin Baytowne Course** (9300 Hwy. 98W, Destin; 800-277-0800, 850-267-8155; open daily from 7:30 A.M. to 7:00 P.M.).

This par-72 course has three distinct nine-hole layouts and can be played in any 18-hole combination. The Troon Course is characterized by rolling greens, uniquely shaped bunkers, and a stunning island green. The 466-yard uphill fourth hole of the Dunes Course is considered by many to be the toughest par four in Florida. The 9-hole Harbor Course is a traditional Florida combination of sand and water.

**Sandestin Burnt Pine Golf Club** (9300 Hwy. 98W, Destin; 800-277-0800, 850-267-8000; open daily from 7:30 A.M. to 7:00 P.M.).

This 18-hole, par-72 Rees Jones-designed golf course is playable at various lengths and offers wide landing corridors and optional routes. The course was ranked as one of the top three best new resort courses in 1995 by *Golf Digest*.

**Sandestin's Links Course** (9300 Hwy. 98W, Destin; 800-277-0800, 850-267-8144; open daily from 7:30 A.M. to 6:00 P.M.).

The breezes sweeping off of the Choctawhatchee Bay demand accuracy off the tee and proper club selections for just the right shot. With 18 holes, this course is also surrounded by lagoons and features many greens and tees that utilize the natural terrain of the land.

**Santa Rosa Golf & Beach Club** (CR 30A, three miles east of Sandestin, Santa Rosa Beach; 850-267-2229; open daily from 7:00 A.M. to 7:30 P.M.).

Known as the purest golf course on the Panhandle, hence the nickname, "Nature's Course," this par-72, 18-hole golf club borders the Gulf of Mexico. Unspoiled pines, native vegetation, and sandy beaches are found throughout. Tee times are available for this semi-private course three days in advance.

**Seascape Resort & Conference Center** (100 Seascape Road, Destin; 850-654-7888; open daily from 7:00 A.M. to 6:00 P.M.).

With narrow fairways lined by trees and water and tightly bunkered, undulating greens, Seascape is playable for golfers of all skill levels. Walking is allowed on this 18-hole course after 1:00 P.M. Discount golf packages are available through the resort.

### Tennis

**Sandestin Resorts, Inc.** (9300 Hwy. 98W, Destin; 800-277-0800, 850-267-8000).

Ranked as one of the "50 Greatest US Tennis Resorts" by *Tennis* magazine, Sandestin has 16 courts in all; eight hydrogrid clay, six hard courts, and two Wimbleton-style grass courts. Sandestin is also home to the largest tennis specialty shop in Northwest Florida. The courts and tennis pro shop are situated between the resort's spectacular white beaches and the calm waters of the Choctawhatchee Bay.

**Santa Rosa Golf & Beach Club** (CR 30A, three miles east of Sandestin, Destin; 850-837-9181).

This club features eight clay and hard courts.

**Seaside** (850-267-4224)

Six clay and hard courts are tucked away behind the streets of cottages.

**Tops'l Beach & Racquet Club** (9011 Hwy. 98W, Destin; 850-267-9292, 800-336-4853).

There are twelve courts at Tops'l: two hard courts and 10 lighted rubico courts.

## Restaurants and Nightlife

There are many reasons to visit the Beaches of South Walton, and good food is certainly at the top of the list. Because of the temperate climate, there is an abundance of hearty fruits and vegetables, many with an extended growing season, which means availability for most of the year. The area also boasts fresh seafood that "slept in the Gulf just last night."

Like other Panhandle communities, the Beaches of South Walton offers plenty of beach bars and small restaurants frequented by locals in the know. At these places, you're likely to find Apalachicola oysters on the half-shell and spicy boiled shrimp, a cool but satisfying meal on a sultry summer afternoon.

Yet South Walton also has its share of upscale eateries that are routinely recognized as some of the best restaurants in the state. Here, gourmet chefs infuse Southern, regional influences with spices from Louisiana, the Caribbean, and Asia. Dinners can be a bit pricey; a less expensive but just as tasty alternative is to visit these establishments for lunch. Call for hours before you go; some places do not open for lunch and almost all of them close at some point during the winter months.

**Basmati's Asian Cuisine** (CR 30A, Blue Mountain Beach; 850-267-3028; open Thursday–Monday from 5:30 A.M. to 9:30 P.M.).

As the only Asian restaurant in the Beaches of South Walton, this intimate, upscale restaurant offers Oriental cuisine, fresh Gulf seafood, homemade desserts, and a well-chosen wine list. Entrées can be expensive. Resort wear is standard attire. Basmati's closes in January.

**Bayou Bill's Crab House** (4748 Hwy. 98W, Santa Rosa Beach; 850-267-3849; open daily from 5:00 P.M. to 10:00 P.M.).

Buckets and buckets of fresh steamed seafood, including blue crabs, clams, oysters, and shrimp, are the specialties at this family restaurant. Bayou Bill's is inexpensive and casual. It closes November and December.

**Bud & Alley's** (Hwy. 30A, Seaside; 850-231-5900; open Wednesday–Monday for lunch from 11:30 A.M. to 3:00 P.M., dinner from 5:30 P.M. to 9:00 P.M.).

Bud & Alley's is known for its American, Coastal Southern, and Mediterranean cuisine. Try favorites like the coastal crabcakes meunière or the grilled lamb chops. Everything is fresh, including the herbs, which come from the restaurant's herb garden. Surprisingly, entrées begin at under $10. There is an open-air rooftop deck and live jazz on summer evenings. Dress is casual.

**Café Thirty-A** (CR 30A, Seagrove Beach; 850-231-2166; open Monday–Saturday from 6:00 P.M. to 10:00 P.M.).

Housed in a building that resembles an old Florida Cracker house, Café Thirty-A serves up hearty helpings of pasta, pizza, poultry, and vegetarian dishes. Many of the entrées are prepared over the wood-fired rotisserie and generally cost from $10 to $20. It also features an award-winning wine list. Casual wear is acceptable. The restaurant closes in January.

**Criolla's** (Rt. 283 and CR 30A, Grayton Beach; 850-267-1267; open Tuesday–Saturday from 5:30 P.M. to 10:00 P.M.).

Continually named as one of Florida's top 20 restaurants by *Florida Trend* magazine, Criolla's is a repeat stop for both locals and visitors. Conch fritters, Creole red snapper, key lime cheesecake, paella, barbecue shrimp, and snapper butter pecan are but a few of the mouth-watering entries on the menu. Almost all of the dishes are influenced by the spices and chiles of the Caribbean and South Louisiana. With its contemporary tropical decor, resort wear is suitable for dinner. Criolla's is rather expensive.

**Elephant Walk** (located inside Sandestin Resort; 850-267-4800; open Sunday–Thursday from 5:00 P.M. to 9:00 P.M., Friday–Saturday from 5:00 P.M. to 10:00 P.M.).

Named from an old Elizabeth Taylor movie, the Elephant Walk restaurant at Sandestin is arguably the finest dining adventure in the Panhandle. It's not cheap, but it's one place where you can count on every bite being better than the last.

Feast on Chicken Barbados with its specialty sauce of cherries, cranberries, apples, butter, and rum, or settle for the grouper Elizabeth, sautéed grouper with seasoned jumbo lump crabmeat and toasted almonds in a white wine butter sauce. For dessert, crème brûlée and a cappuccino ice cream sandwich top the list. Elephant Walk closes in January.

**Goatfeathers** (CR 30A in Santa Rosa Beach; 850-267-3342; open daily for lunch from 11:30 A.M. to 2:30 P.M., dinner from 5:00 P.M. to 10:00 P.M.).

Serving up traditional seafood dishes like steamed fish, oysters, and shrimp, this local favorite is convenient and affordable. There is a fresh fish market downstairs and an open deck with a beach view adjacent to the restaurant. Be sure to try the fried pickles—a house specialty. Goatfeathers closes the first three weeks of December.

**Josephine's French Country Inn** (Seaside; 850-231-1940; open daily for breakfast from 9:30 A.M. until . . . , dinner Wednesday–Sunday from 5:30 P.M. to 8:00 P.M.).

Located in Seaside's only bed and breakfast, Josephine's serves delicious breakfasts and gourmet masterpieces for dinner. As the name suggests, French cuisine is a definite mainstay on the menu, but steak and seafood are also well done.

**Morgan's** (Silver Sands Factory Outlet on Hwy. 98E, Destin; 850-654-3320; open daily from 11:00 A.M. to midnight, until 1:00 A.M. on weekends).

Morgan's is a unique, upscale food court in the Silver Sands Factory Outlet—the largest of its kind in the Southeast. Freshly made take-home meals, homemade bakery items, a nostalgic hamburger grill, and wood-fired pizza are among the offerings of the nine food venues. There is also the Harbor Docks Seafood and Brewery, a casual, sit-down restaurant on the second floor. Adjacent to the restaurant are two family entertainment centers with billiards, motion simulation rides, and video games. Entrées are available in all price ranges.

**Pandora's of Grayton Beach** (CR 30A and Route 283, Grayton Beach; 850-231-4102; open Tuesday–Sunday from 5:00 P.M. until . . . ).

If you're hankering for a succulent steak, then Pandora's is the place. Here you'll find specialties such as prime rib and fresh Gulf seafood cooked slowly over an oak fire. Pandora's is moderately priced and features a casual atmosphere. It closes in January.

**The Red Bar in Grayton Beach** (70 Hotz Avenue, Grayton Beach; 850-231-1008; open daily for lunch from 11:00 A.M. to 4:00 P.M., dinner from 5:00 P.M. to 10:00 P.M.).

Eclectic "livingroom-style" furnishings make the Red Bar the funkiest in Grayton Beach. Located in downtown Grayton, the bar is connected to Picolo's, an Italian restaurant.

**Salty Dog's** (CR 30A and Vicky Street, Santa Rosa Beach; 850-267-7108, 850-267-2979; open Monday–Thursday from 11:00 A.M. to 9:00 P.M., Friday–Saturday from 11:00 A.M. to 10:00 P.M.).

The local watering hole in Santa Rosa Beach is Salty Dog's, a casual pub that also serves sandwiches and grilled entrées. Though it sits away from the beach at the corner of Highway 30A and Vicky Street, it is frequented by fishermen, local business people, and tourists in the know. Dress is casual; entrées are inexpensive.

### Accommodations

Unlike other Florida destinations, the majority of accommodations in the Beaches of South Walton are rental homes, cottages, and condos. In all, there are over four thousand lodging units to choose from, many of which are available through local rental agencies. The sooner you book your room, the more apt you'll be to get the type of accommodation you want in your particular price range.

**Abbott Resorts** (800-336-4853)

This real estate company offers the largest selection of vacation rentals on the Emerald Coast. Call the 24-hour central reservations line to request a beach book listing properties and coupons from local restaurants and shops.

**A Highlands House** (4193 Hwy. 30A, Dune Allen Beach; 850-267-0110).

This gracious Gulfside bed and breakfast has private entrances and baths for each of its rooms. Romantic and quiet, Highlands House is a home-away-from-home with all the pamperings expected of a vacation stay.

**Camping on the Gulf Holiday Travel Park** (10005 W. Emerald Coast Hwy., Destin; 850-837-6334; www.campgulf.com).

Directly on the Gulf, Holiday Travel Park has more than a thousand sites available for rental.

**Emerald Coast RV & Golf Resort, Inc.** (7525 Hwy. 30A W, Santa Rosa Beach; 800-232-2478, 850-267-2808).

An inexpensive way to enjoy the Beaches of South Walton is to stay at the Emerald Coast RV & Golf Resort. The property features an enclosed heated pool, tennis courts, a driving range, cable television hook-ups, propane gas, 50 amps of electricity, landscaped sites, concrete pads, and patios.

There is also a nature trail to the beach as well as a beach shuttle.

**Grayton Beach Realty, Inc.** (800-471-8812, 850-231-1223).

In the heart of historic Grayton Beach, this realty offers information on property throughout the Beaches of South Walton.

**Hibiscus Coffee & Guesthouse** (85 DeFuniak Street; Grayton Beach; 850-231-2733).

A combination coffee and guest house, Hibiscus reflects the charming eccentricity of Grayton Beach. Fresh fruit and pastries are frequently served for breakfast; for lunch, guests can enjoy soups, salads, sandwiches, and a variety of coffee drinks from the coffee house. This is the only place in Grayton Beach where you can get an espresso. Each room has a private bath.

**Patrone's Bed and Brunch** (307 Defuniak Street, Grayton Beach; 850-231-1606).

These modest but clean and comfortable studio apartments in the heart of Grayton Beach are available for daily, weekly, and monthly rentals. Each casual apartment has a bedroom, a living room, and a fully-equipped kitchen.

**Sandestin Beach Hilton** (on the beach in Sandestin Resort, Destin; 800-367-1271, 850-267-9500).

Tucked away behind Sandestin Resort, this beachfront luxury resort hotel has commanding Gulf views and all the amenities expected from a Hilton.

**Sandestin Resort** (9300 Hwy. 98W, Destin; 800-277-0800, 800-622-1623; www.sandestin.com).

With its great golf, fabulous tennis courts, and wonderful beaches, you could easily stay a week at Sandestin Resort and find plenty to do without ever leaving. Most guests, however, prefer to use the resort as home base. They'll get out and explore all the great things this area has to offer, then come back to Sandestin to be pampered.

And pampering is what Sandestin does best. Of course, the water sports, bicycle paths, and nature trails are among the area's finest, but nothing beats work-a-day blues like lounging in front of a mesmerizing, blue-green seascape or unwinding at the Sandestin Spa. Here are some other Sandestin "bests" for travelers:

**Sporting Activities:** Sandestin has more golf than you can shake a club at—63 holes in all. There's the *Burnt Pine Golf Club,* a classic 18-hole design by Rees Jones that was ranked as one of the top three best new resort courses for 1995. The *Baytowne Golf Club,* designed by Tom Jackson, features 27 holes of golf: a Troon nine with rolling fairways and undulating greens; a Dunes nine with one of Florida's hardest par fours—an uphill 466-yard hole; and a Harbor nine, a traditional Florida combination of sand and water. The *Links Golf Course,* also designed by Tom Jackson, is a classic layout that uses the natural terrain of the land, with five holes along the Choctawhatchee Bay.

Sandestin also has the racket on tennis. Ranked as one of the "50 Greatest US Tennis Resorts" by *Tennis* magazine, there are 16 tennis courts with hard, clay, or grass court surfaces and plans to add seven more in the future. The courts and tennis pro shop are situated between the resort's spectacular white beaches and the calm waters of the Choctawhatchee Bay. Special packages are available for both tennis and golf.

**Sandestin Spa:** From the Hot Aromatherapy Body Wrap to the Glycolic Acid Facial, the *Salon and Day Spa* specializes in indulging guests from head to toe and all the nooks and crannies in between. Individual sessions, full-day packages, complimentary consultations, personal training, and wellness classes are but a few of the services provided.

**Seascape Resort & Conference Center** (100 Seascape Drive, Destin; 800-874-9106).

This 230-acre beach resort features an 18-hole championship golf course, five pools, and eight tennis courts. Both golf and beach villas are available, and there is a full-service restaurant on property.

**Sugar Beach Inn Bed and Breakfast** (3501 E. Hwy. 30A, Seagrove Beach; 850-231-1577).

With panoramic Gulf views, four fireplaces, and sweeping verandahs, Sugar Beach Bed and Breakfast is a perfect weekend getaway for a romantic rendezvous. The home is furnished with elegant yet comfortable wicker and antiques. Each room has a private bath. Sugar Beach Inn is only a short walk from Seaside.

**Tops'l Beach & Racquet Club** (9011 Hwy. 98W, Destin; 800-476-9222).

With 52 acres of hills and sand dunes, these Gulf-front and tennis villa accommodations are perfect for lounging away lazy summer days. There are 12 professional tennis courts, three pools (one indoor/outdoor), a complete fitness center, a 1.7-mile nature and fitness trail, and a full-service salon on site.

## Shopping

While the shopping in the Beaches of South Walton is limited, the selection still offers something for every pocketbook and in every style imaginable.

Interestingly enough, antiquing is a popular pastime. It's not Charleston or New Orleans, but there are enough antique shops dotting County Road 30A and Highway 98 to fill an afternoon. Here are a few for you to check out: **Fernleigh in Seaside** (850-231-5535); **This, That, & the Other** (850-267-3190); **Tea Tyme Antiques** (850-267-3827); and **Live Oak Antiques** (850-231-5121). For a complete list of all antique shops, call the South Walton Tourist Development Council.

Downtown Grayton Beach also has some fun shops to explore. There's **The Place Across the Street** (850-231-0200), a coffee shop; **Affinity** (850-231-0188), which features hand-painted recycled furnishings, art, antiques, and commercial displays; and the **Grayton Beach Market,** a general store with groceries, beer, and imported cigars (850-231-2994).

Seaside is all filled with unusual boutiques. For more information, refer to the Seaside section of this chapter.

**Clements Antiques** (Hwy. 98; 850-837-1473; open Monday–Saturday from 9:00 A.M. to 5:00 P.M.).

Clements specializes in estate quality antiques and 17th- and 18th-century Florida antiques.

**The Gourd Garden and Curiosity Shop** (CR 30A, Seagrove Beach; 850-231-2007; open Monday–Saturday from 10:00 A.M. to 5:00 P.M., Sunday from 12:00 P.M. to 5:00 P.M.).

Folk art is alive and well at the Gourd Garden, a small art gallery and curiosity shop located in Seagrove, just two miles east of Seaside on CR 30A. Gourds in every shape and size have been carved and painted by artisans to resemble anything from swizzle sticks and ukuleles to sea gulls and snakes. Outside, owner Randy Harelson has flats of flowers and potted herbs for sale.

**Magnolia House** (Magnolia Street, Grayton Beach; 850-231-5859; open Monday–Saturday from 10:00 A.M. to 5:00 P.M., Sunday from 1:00 P.M. to 5:00 P.M.).

Upscale gifts and accessories are standard fare at Magnolia House. Browse for that special knickknack through items like candles, clay-fired Christmas ornaments, potpourris, and antiques. Owner Nancy Veldman is also an accomplished pianist, and you can buy her CDs here.

**The Market at Sandestin** (Hwy. 98W at Sandestin Resort; 850-267-8092; open Monday–Saturday from 10:00 A.M. to 9:00 P.M., Sunday from 10:00 A.M. to 6:00 P.M.).

As part of Sandestin Resorts, the market is also convenient to folks passing by on Highway 98. There are 30 unique boutiques and eateries here, with designer fashions, exciting resort wear, fine jewelry, and foods like fresh seafood, homemade pizzas, and pastas.

**Monet, Monet** (100 E. Hwy. 30A, Grayton Beach; 850-231-5117; open Wednesday–Monday from 10:00 A.M. to 5:00 P.M.).

The color, composition, and artistry long admired in Impressionist painter Claude Monet's gardens have been transposed onto the gardens of Monet Monet, an intimate garden boutique located in Florida's Panhandle.

Inside, visitors discover one-of-a-kind planters made by local artists, wind chimes, raku and pottery, birdhouses, arches and trellises, a selection of seeds, and everything needed for self-contained water gardens. "All of our things are either my own design or are made locally and regionally," says owner Jonathan Quinn. Outside, Quinn has emulated the look of Monet's gardens by using plants hearty enough to survive the Florida climate.

**The Room at Lakewood** (Hwy. 30A, Seagrove Beach; 850-231-5141; open Tuesday–Saturday from 9:30 A.M. to 5:00 P.M.).

Browse this shop for original artwork including oils, acrylics, watercolors, sculpture, and pottery—most of which is made by local artists.

**Ruskin Place Artist Colony** (Ruskin Place, Seaside; 850-231-5424; open daily from 10:00 A.M. to 7:00 P.M., April–September, daily from 10:00 A.M. to 5:00 P.M., October–March).

Located in the heart of Seaside, Ruskin Place features a collection of unique and whimsical galleries with everything from tropical watercolors to contemporary crafts.

**Silver Sands Factory Stores** (10562 Emerald Coast Parkway on 98W, Destin; 800-510-6255, 850-864-9780; open Monday–Saturday from 10:00 A.M. to 9:00 P.M., Sundays from 10:00 A.M. to 6:00 P.M.).

As one of the Southeast's largest and most exclusive designer outlet shopping centers, Silver Sands has a hundred stores, from the Coach Factory Outlet and Clifford & Wills to G. H. Bass & Co., Anne Klein, and the Bose Factory Store. And don't forget about Morgan's, a food and entertainment complex for adults and children.

## Festivals and Special Events

*January*

### Emerald Coast Chef's Tasting

The finest culinary delights in the Beaches of South Walton compete for covered awards during this weekend of food and fun. Held at Sandestin Resort, all sales benefit the American Cancer Society. Call 800-277-0800 for more information.

### Great Southern Gumbo Cook-off

The area's finest restaurants showcase their gumbo in this cook-off. Three winners are chosen by a people's choice vote. This cooking extravaganza is also held at Sandestin. Call 800-277-0800 for more information.

*February*

### Seaside Coastal Gourmet Weekend

Sponsored by the Seaside Institute, this weekend-long class offers both novice and experienced chefs hands-on cooking and dining experiences with the region's most celebrated chefs. Call 850-231-2421 for more information.

*March*

### Camp Seaside Adventure Program

Make the most of spring break by participating in three days of nonstop activities at Camp Seaside. This program is appropriate for families, college students, and teens. Call 850-231-5424 for more information.

*April*

### Chautauqua Festival

Patterned after the Chautauqua camps of the 1920s, this one-day festival in DeFuniak Springs highlights local culture with arts and crafts, food, an antique and classic car show, a parade, a children's activities area, and live entertainment. Call 850-892-4300 for more information.

### Sandestin Wine Tasting

Spend a weekend sampling more than three hundred wines, listening to live music, and watching fashion shows—all at the market at Sandestin. Call 850-267-8092 for more information.

*May*

### Artsquest

Held each year during the second week of May, this week-long festival has grown into one of the region's most popular. Throughout the week, participate in lectures at local galleries and watch live entertainment at various venues in town. The festival culminates with a two-day fine arts show at Eden State Gardens. Artists from across the Southeast participate, from potters and painters to woodworkers and sculptors. Call 850-267-1691.

### Seaside Spring Wine Festival

Sponsored by the merchants of Seaside, this annual wine festival celebrates white wines with wine tastings, lectures, dinners, and music. Call 850-231-5425 for more information.

*August*

### Elephant Walk Triathlon and Baytowne Biathlon

Men and women from across the United States travel to the Beaches of South Walton to compete in this Grand Prix Series Event. Call 850-267-8135 for more information.

*October*

### Seaside's Annual Seeing Red Wine Festival

The first weekend in October marks the celebration of

Seaside's celebration of red wines. There are wine lectures, tastings, dinners, and music throughout the weekend. Call 850-231-5424 for more information.

**Seaside Institute Writer's Conference**

Both novice and professional writers will revel in this weekend of lectures, workshops, and readings with some of America's top writers as instructors. For more information, call the Seaside Institute at 850-231-2421.

*November*

**South Walton Sportsfest**

The annual USA Triathlon-sanctioned weekend features a triathlon, duathlon, half marathon, and 10K run. Other events include a beach-to-bay walk, bike race, century bike tour, and volkssport events. Held the first three weekends in November, the event is sponsored by the South Walton Tourist Development Council. Call 800-822-1216 for more information.

*December*

**Eden State Gardens Christmas Candlelight Open House**

Capture the holiday spirit by taking a candlelight tour at the Wesley Mansion. The tours generally run for two weeks in December. Call 850-231-4214 for more information.

# Seaside

With a nostalgic yet sensible approach to architecture and city planning, Seaside was born in 1982 when the first two houses were built and a master plan was developed. Among the guiding principles: each house must be constructed with indigenous materials, have a front porch, a picket fence, and native landscaping in lieu of grass. The plan also established the beach as community property.

Founder Robert Davis had wanted to create a traditional town influenced by the vernacular Cracker lifestyle, and one walk down the brick streets will convince you that he succeeded. Easter egg-colored houses reminiscent of turn-of-the-century Florida Cracker homes sit orderly behind white picket fences. Modeled

after regional styles like "Dog Trot" and "Shotgun," these contemporary classic cottages (360 in all) include architectural features such as widow's walks, towers, gazebos, piazzas, and cupolas.
So compelling was this concept of community that *Time* magazine named Seaside as its *Best Design of the Decade* in 1990.

The community's all-American appearance attracts catalog
shoots and movie productions, the most recent being Jim Carrey's *The Truman Show.* In fact, the Truman House, renamed
because Carrey stayed there during filming, is located on
Natchez Street.

Critics of Seaside argue that such strict architectural codes
have transformed the town into a quasi-Disneyesque community. On the surface, that might be true. Every house, every
street, every common area seems so perfect, so clean, so
planned. Yet it is also evident that without standard guidelines,
the community could easily turn into a hodge-podge of hokey
summer cottages built by people with more money than taste.

In reality, no two houses are alike in color or design, and it
is the tin roofs, indigenous landscaping, and picket fences
required by the code that give Seaside its character and conti-
nuity. Indeed, the nostalgic atmosphere evoked by these quaint,
picture-perfect homes has turned afternoons of ogling at the
houses into a unique Seaside pastime.

Another popular pastime is good old-fashioned visits on a
country porch. Many residents, both temporary and permanent,
hang out on the front porch to chat with newfound friends. Of
course, if privacy is a concern, they can retire to the cupola and
watch from a distance, but that might be missing the point.

The point is that Seaside was designed to encourage interaction among its residents. Perhaps the best example of this phi-
losophy is **Central Square,** located in the heart of town. Instead
of commuting into Destin or Panama City for the essentials of
daily life, guests can walk to **Dreamland Heights,** Seaside's ver-
sion of an upscale pedestrian strip mall. Here, they can find
stores stocking everything from home furnishings to fancy gourmet food items.

One such shop is the **Modica Market and Deli,** a darn good
replica of an old-fashioned grocery store. Shelves lined with cans,
bottles, and bags stretch from worn wooden floors to the lofty

*Shopping at the open-air market at Seaside is one of the community's most popular pastimes.* (Courtesy of the Beaches of South Walton.)

ceiling; some are accessible only by a sliding ladder. One suggestion for an afternoon hiatus from the sun is to grab a glass of fresh-squeezed lemonade and then sit outside and people watch—this spot is equivalent to 50-yard-line seats at a football game.

Directly in front of Dreamland Heights sits the **Post Office,** the community's most photographed building, and the **Amphitheater on the Green,** Seaside's equivalent to an Italian piazza. Annual wine festivals and concerts are held here, along with neighborhood movie events and classes for the Seaside Institute.

Across the street is **PER-SPI-CAS-ITY,** an open-air market that peddles unique clothing, jewelry, and beachwear. There is also a bookshop, an ice-cream stand, and a handful of boutiques with unique gift items. In time, two hotels will be added to the community, along with considerably more commercial development.

Additionally, Seaside has swim and tennis clubs, children's programs and family activities, three swimming pools, a world-class croquet lawn, bicycle rentals, shuffleboard, and nature walks.

Of course, the main reason people come to Seaside is the beach and its plethora of outdoor activities—jet skiing, snorkeling, and scuba diving. And then there's the all-time favorite pastime—lying limp in the sun on a cushy beach chair, only steps away from the crystal calm of the Gulf.

## Accommodations

Seaside offers a variety of accommodations available nightly, weekly, and for extended stays. In the cottages and townhomes, guests receive a bottle of wine upon arrival, fresh flowers, daily housekeeping, continental breakfast, newspaper delivery, evening turn-down service, Cabana Man beach chairs and umbrellas, and complimentary bike rentals.

### Classic Cottages

A group of select cottages, all privately owned, are available for rent throughout Seaside. Choose from spacious Gulf-front houses to smaller cottages tucked inside the heart of Seaside. Many of the houses feature secret walking paths through the scrub oaks surrounding them. Prices from $391 per night.

### Dreamland Heights

Accommodations atop Dreamland Heights feature one-bedroom metropolitan suites overlooking Central Square. Each suite has a living room, dining area, kitchen, and a view of both Seaside and the Gulf.

### Josephine's French Country Inn at Seaside (800-848-1840)

Josephine's is currently Seaside's only bed and breakfast. Beside a great location in the heart of Seaside, Josephine's also has a fabulous restaurant. Prices from $150 per night; suites from $195.

### The Motor Court

The most inexpensive of Seaside's accommodations, the Motor Court offers charming, 1950s-style studios for two people. There are theme rooms, including the Travel Room, Yesterday's Room, Nostalgia Room, Mom's Room, and the Caribbean Room. The Ivory Tower room has an observation loft. Prices from $135 per night.

### Ruskin Place Artist Colony

These New Orleans-style townhomes are located on the second floor in Ruskin Place. Many of the artists who have galleries on the ground floor live above their shops. Prices from $270 per night.

### Seahaven Penthouses

Atop 25 Central Square, these roomy penthouses include

access to a fitness center and terraces designed especially for viewing the sunset. Prices from $215 per night.

**Seaside** (800-591-8696; www.seasidefl.com).

This contact information is good for all of the above accommodations.

### Seaside Weddings

Since the early 1980s, Seaside has provided a romantic backdrop for hundreds of fairy-tale weddings. Obviously, most wedding couples are drawn to the beach, which is wide enough to accommodate a large wedding party. Another plus is that photographers like the contrast of sand and sea as a background for pictures, which means there's no need to invest in fancy flowers. When the sand is dry, it is soft and clean, so there's no risk of damaging the hem of your wedding gown. For informal ceremonies, consider asking both the wedding party and guests to leave their shoes behind.

The nine beach pavilions overlooking the Gulf are also popular wedding sites, and each has its own unique look. Because each is built at least 15 feet higher than the beach, the view of the ocean from the pavilions is spectacular.

Another charming location for a wedding is the gazebo in the center of town. Traffic is routed around the loop during the ceremony, which means you have the entire circular brick street to use for the wedding.

Small wedding parties can transform a cottage into a wedding wonderland. Front porches, towers, and spacious living areas work nicely as the setting for the ceremony.

Besides a breathtaking location, Seaside can take care of each and every detail associated with the wedding of a lifetime including hair stylists, bridal lunch, marriage license, officiant, chairs, rehearsal dinner, floral arrangements, horse-drawn carriage, photographer, videographer, musicians, and wedding cakes. Receptions for up to three hundred can also be arranged at Seaside.

At the close of your picture-perfect day, retire in style at one of Seaside's 12 honeymoon cottages along the beach. With a bedroom, living area, and small but fully equipped kitchen, these quaint cottages are just the right size for unwinding after the wedding. Each cottage also features a Jacuzzi on a private, screened back porch, complete with an intimate view of the ocean. Each cottage rental includes housekeeping, continental breakfast, newspaper delivery, evening turn-down service, Cabana Man beach chairs and umbrellas, and complimentary bike rentals.

## Day Trips

### DeFuniak Springs

DeFuniak Springs is a charming historic town in the northern part of Walton County. As the county seat, the town was incorporated in 1901 as a planned railroad community next to Lake DeFuniak for the Louisville & Nashville Railroad (L&N). When the railroad first began, it identified the stop as "Open Pond," which soon changed to DeFuniak in honor of Frederick deFuniak, chief engineer of the railroad. Springs was added to the name in reference to the almost perfectly round freshwater, spring-fed lake in the center of town. DeFuniak Springs also became home to the Winter Assembly of Chautauqua, an extension of the cultural and educational gatherings held each summer in New York.

If you like historic homes, then don't leave the area without taking a walking tour around *Circle Drive*. Most of the homes are private residences, but you can admire the exterior architectural features. Of note: the 1886 *Walton–Defuniak Library*, the oldest structure in Florida built as a library that is still used for its original purpose; the *Dream Cottage*, a Folk Victorian cottage that was once home to former U.S. consul to Scotland, Wallace Bruce; and the *Pansy Cottage*, home of Isabelle McDonald Alden, an author who penned more than one hundred books between 1890 and 1900.

In recent years, the assembly has been revived with a weekend festival featuring art workshops, plays, educational lectures, and exhibits. Call 850-892-4300 for more information.

**Chautauqua Vineyards** (I-10 at US 331, DeFuniak Springs; 850-892-5887; open Monday–Saturday from 9:00 A.M. to 5:00 P.M., Sunday from 12:00 P.M. to 5:00 P.M.; free).

A visit to this small winery north of the beaches is a relaxing way to spend an afternoon. Besides the free wine tastings, you'll get an inside look at how wine is made, from the grape vine to the bottle.

Operating since 1989, Chautauqua Vineyards uses muscadine grapes, a hybrid of native grapes, to make its wine. The grapes are grown in vineyards planted on the property in 1979. After the harvest in late August, they are crushed and processed mechanically. About two hundred tons are crushed each year at the winery.

Once the grapes are crushed, fermentation is started using select cultured wine yeast. Afterward, the wines are clarified and aged. Bottling usually occurs in the summer of the year following harvest.

Named for the Chautauqua Assembly from Chautauqua County, New York, which once met during the winter in DeFuniak Springs, the vineyards consistently produce award-winning wines. The blueberry wine is famous for capturing the flavor and fragrance of fresh blueberries, while the white wildflower wine, a new addition, is sweetened with wildflower honey. Chautauqua also offers home-brewed beer.

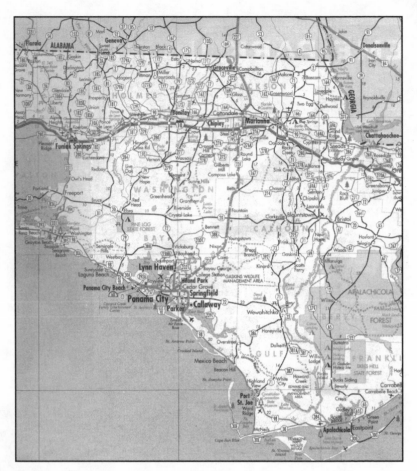

*Panama City area.*

# 6

## Panama City

### Introduction

Panama City has a split personality: in the spring, it's a mecca for college students on spring break. During the rest of the year, the city caters to its loyal family following.

It wasn't long ago that Panama City Beach was known as the "Redneck Riviera" because so many "good ole' boys and girls" from the Southern states vacationed along the Panhandle. Even today, the roads heading south to Panama City in the summertime are a four-laned lesson in local color. But "the times, they are a'changin'."

Today, the rest of the world is finally discovering what the "rednecks" have known all along: that Panama City, with its polished quartz sand and tourmaline-green waters, is perhaps the world's most beautiful beach. There are still plenty of mom-and-pop cinder-block motels, religious ministries and retreat camps, and oyster bars with sandy floors along the beaches, but there are also comfortable, upscale accommodations and eateries for the more sophisticated traveler. As one perennial visitor said, "Panama City means vacation with a capital V."

As for aesthetics, Dr. Beach (a.k.a. Stephen Leatherman, a former coastal geologist at the University of Maryland) ranked St. Andrews State Recreation Area in Panama City Beach as the number one beach in America in 1995, a distinction that retires the beach from competition for the next 10 years. Leatherman also recognized Panama City Beach as the number one sports beach in the country because of the jetskiiers, parasailers, fishermen, boaters, divers, and snorkelers who hang out on its shores.

While the scenery is more than enough to attract tourists to the area, the weather is another prime factor. The average year-round temperature is 68.8° F, with summer averages of 81.9° F, and there are approximately 320 days of sunshine.

It's hard to decide what time of year is best for a visit. Spring is no doubt the number one time for college students, families vacation here during the summer, and retirees and snowbirds have the beaches to themselves in the fall and winter months. The temperatures are the hottest during July and August, while the waters are their warmest during July, August, and September.

### History

St. Andrew, also called "Old Town," was the first settlement in this area, founded by pioneer James Watson. In 1838, Watson acquired large tracts of land and soon became the owner of a sawmill at the head of Watson Bayou. Another family, the Johnsons, moved to the area just before the Civil War, and their home at the foot of Harrison Street became the site of a small skirmish. St. Andrew supplied salt to the Confederacy at the beginning of the war, but the main plant was eventually destroyed by the Union. In 1940, an unexploded shell from a Federal gunboat was found by city street workers.

Real development began in 1888 with the "Cincinnati Land Boom," the sale of land by the St. Andrew Bay Railroad Land & Mining Company. The town was platted and several names were tried out, including "Floripolis," Park Resort," and "Harrison" (the name of its main street) before its present name stuck. Legend has it that George Mortimer West, a promoter from Chicago, vacationed in the area while the Panama Canal was being constructed. He noted that a line drawn from Chicago to the canal intersected the bay, and thus coined the name "Panama City." Others say the name came from developers who wanted to secure shipping contracts for Panamanian bananas.

Bay County was established in 1913 and took its name from St. Andrews Bay, which it fronts. When the bridges were constructed in the 1920s, legend has it that the 27-mile-long area along the beach became known as the "Miracle Strip," because of its velvety-soft white sand and clear waters. (Others attribute the name to the development boom in the 1950s, when land prices soared.) During the early part of the century, Panama City was a quiet coastal town, but activity increased during World War II, when Panama City became a major ship-building and war industry center and a temporary home for thousands of war workers. Today, Tyndall Air Force Base and Coastal Systems Center, a naval training center, play an important role in the economy of Bay County.

Another economic factor is the Port of Panama City. Established in 1967, the port has a Foreign Trade Zone and is home port to one of the Southeast's richest commercial fishing fleets. It is one of the most economical ports on the Gulf.

Bay County has eight municipalities: Lynn Haven, Callaway, Springfield, Mexico Beach, Parker, Cedar Grove, Panama City Beach, and Panama City, the county seat.

Lynn Haven was originally established in 1910 as a Civil War veterans' colony by Sen. W. H. Lynn. Lynn advertised his 7,400 lots in the *National Tribune*. Eventually, many veterans moved to the area, and as a consequence, the town has the only monument to Union soldiers in the South. The monument was built in 1920 by a group of retired Northerners who belonged to the Grand Army of the Republic.

Separated by Hathaway Bridge, Panama City has shopping malls, restaurants, and every other amenity you might find in a small Southern city, while Panama City Beach is a sprawling resort area with high-rise hotels, mega-nightclubs, and family attractions. Tourists drawn to the sun will likely spend most, if not all, of their time on Panama City Beach; indeed, there is little reason to cross the bridge since you'll find everything you need on the beach.

In the mid-19th century there were actually four islands running along the coastline in the Panama City Beach area: Sand, Hammock, Hurricane, and Crooked Islands. A major hurricane in 1868 destroyed Sand and Hammock Islands, but Crooked Island still exists and Hurricane Island remains as part of Shell Island.

Audubon Island, a tiny islet in St. Andrews Bay, was created during a dredging project in 1968. Within two years it had been colonized by laughing gulls and black skimmers, and today it is the only place between Mobile Bay and Cedar Key where brown pelicans breed and nest. About 150 pairs of pelicans produce 300 chicks each year. The island has since been designated as an Audubon Island Wilderness Preserve and is managed by the Audubon Society and the Florida Department of Natural Resources. Black mangrove seedlings were planted and nesting platforms were constructed in order to curb erosion and promote breeding.

## Contact Information

Tourism is Panama City Beach's number one industry, with the peak season extending from March through September. In the off season, "snowbirds" from Canada, Germany, and the northeastern United States flock to the beach for the mild winter.

When you are in town, visit the visitor information center at 12015 Front Beach Road, just across from the Miracle Strip Amusement Park for brochures, maps, coupon books, and a calendar of events. The center is open from 8:00 A.M. to 5:00 P.M. seven days a week.

**Panama City Beach Convention & Visitors Bureau** (P.O. Box 9473, Panama City Beach, FL 32417; 800-PC-BEACH, 850-233-5072; www.panamacitybeachfl.com).

The area also features a Computer Bulletin Board System (BBS) accessible via your home computer. Known as Florida ON-LINE, this 24-hour electronic magazine offers free up-to-date information on lodging, restaurants, and activities. To access, dial 850-234-2343 or 850-233-6503.

### Average Temperatures

| | |
|---|---|
| Spring | 76° |
| Summer | 87° |
| Fall | 81° |
| Winter | 65° |

## Transportation

Part of the allure of the Panhandle is the fact that it is only a day's drive away for visitors from most of the Southern states and some of the Midwestern states. U.S. Highway 231 and State Road 79 run directly north and south from Interstate 10.

For those who fly into Panama City/Bay County International Airport, there are several major carriers that connect through Atlanta, Nashville, or Charlotte. The airport is 10 miles from the beach. A taxi ride from the airport to the beach costs around $15.

**Affordable Limo Service** (850-233-1858)

**Ambassador Taxi and Limo Service** (850-747-9161)

**Amtrak** (101 S. 7th Street, Chipley; 800-USA-RAIL).

**Baytown Trolley** (850-769-0557)

The air-conditioned trolley offers a scenic ride along the beach from Monday to Friday for 50¢.

**Greyhound Bus Lines** (917 Harrison Avenue; 850-785-7861, 800-231-2222).

**Panama City–Bay County International Airport** (3173 Airport Road; 850-763-6751).

**Yellow Cab Company of Panama City** (850-763-4691)

*Rental Car Agencies*

All the major rental car agencies operate out of Panama City; many are located at the airport and do not deliver cars. Most require drivers to be 25 years of age; a few require drivers to be only 21 years of age.

**Avis** (3130 Lisenby Avenue; 850-769-1411).

**Budget** (3173 Lisenby Avenue; 850-769-8733).

**Enterprise** (669 West 23rd Street; 850-747-1110, 850-769-3369).

**Hertz** (3175 Lisenby Avenue; 850-763-6673).

**National** (3137 Lisenby Avenue; 850-769-2383).

**Snappy** (3704 West 23rd Street; 850-785-8808).

## The Beach

There are different names for different sections of the beach, but most folks refer to the entire strip of coastline as Panama City Beach.

One of the first comments tourists usually make concerns the whiteness of the sand. The grains are actually tiny quartz crystals which were washed down from the Appalachian

*Panama City Beach is known as the "World's Most Beautiful Beach."* (Courtesy of VISIT FLORIDA.)

Mountains tens of thousands of years ago and then broken down, bleached, polished, and deposited on the shore.

Before Hurricane Opal hit in 1995, Panama City Beach was protected by a two-sandbar system out in the water and large sand dunes on land covered with vegetation. The hurricane sheared off the second sandbar and damaged or destroyed the vital coastal dune system. Erosion occurred in the dry beach area and below the water, resulting in a loss of sand elevation and water depth.

To counter the hurricane damage and the normal loss by erosion of 60,000 to 70,000 cubic yards of sand each year, the largest beach nourishment project in Florida history was started in December, 1997. By the time it is finished in 1999, an estimated 8.2 million cubic yards of sand will have been added to replace what was lost following Hurricane Opal. The cost is estimated to be between $28.4 and $33.9 million.

The proposed 17½-mile project will add at least 50 feet to some parts of the beach and as much as 175 feet in other areas. To insure the sand color and texture is a perfect match with what is already in place, engineers will load their dredges 3,000–4,000 feet from the shoreline using sand that was washed out during the hurricane.

## Spring Break

Panama City Beach is where the boys are—and the girls, too. When Fort Lauderdale decided it no longer wanted the headache of hosting spring break for college students around the United States, Panama City gladly stepped in and offered its sandy shoreline as a backdrop for the world's largest party. More than 550,000 students flock to the beach during the spring months in search of sun, sex, booze, and rock 'n roll.

Few leave disappointed. Besides the incredible beaches, food and lodging are relatively inexpensive, especially when compared to other parts of Florida. The area also boasts some of the world's largest nightclubs that bring in top alternative, country, rock 'n roll, techno, and rap acts. And it certainly doesn't hurt that MTV has chosen to broadcast live from PCB (as it is often called) the last couple of spring breaks.

As long as you mind your own business and keep your hands to yourself, the authorities are pretty cool. After all, they want you to spend your money and have a good time so that in 10 years you'll bring your family back. Here are some spring break tidbits to keep in mind:

- Under Florida state law, you must be 21 years of age to purchase, consume, or possess alcoholic beverages. Open alcoholic containers inside a vehicle or on public property including streets, beaches, and sidewalks are not allowed.
- Glass containers are not allowed on the beach.
- Occupancy of guest rooms is limited to the number of people designated by the management. Violators risk losing their deposits and can be evicted from the property.
- No open fires are permitted on the beach.
- Thongs are allowed on the beach.

### Pelican Picks

**Cinnamon Twists from Thomas' Donuts** (19208 W. Hwy. 98; 850-234-8039; open daily from 5:00 A.M. to 3:00 P.M. except Wednesday).

There's nothing better than waking up to warm, soft cinnamon twists from Thomas' Donuts. The twists are a personal favorite; I've been told that the blueberry-filled and chocolate-covered donuts are just as good. Thomas' has over 30 kinds in all. This family-owned donut shop has been in business over thirty years.

**Camp Helen State Park** (off Hwy. 98 just W of the Phillips Inlet Bridge; 850-231-4210).

When plans are completed at Camp Helen, it is no doubt going to be one of the nicest state parks in Florida. But plans can't come to fruition until the state legislature makes decisions about funding. For now, it is open and about all you can do there is walk into it.

The 180-acre park is bordered by water on three sides: Phillips Inlet, Lake Powell, and the Gulf of Mexico. In partnership with Gulf Coast Community College, the Florida Parks and Recreation Department hopes to create an environmental education center on site. It will be the first joint venture of its kind between a community college and a Florida state park. The property will combine ecological and historical interpretation, preservation of habitats, education, recreation, and beach access.

Camp Helen has been designated one of the last remaining safe harbors in the area for birds migrating from Central America. It is also the largest unstabilized inlet providing undisturbed dunes, which are crucial to the nesting of threatened bird species.

The property is noted for regionally significant archeological sites and shows evidence of American Indian occupation.

There is a Craftsman Bungalow Lodge on site that was built in 1928 as a summer home for the family of Robert Hicks. It was later used as a summer vacation camp for employees of an Alabama manufacturing company and their families. Preserved in its original condition, the lodge is eligible for nomination to the National Register of Historic Places.

**Sunset Walks on the Beach**

If you're into the beach scene, you'll fit right in at Panama City Beach during the day. Hundreds of people hang out along the shore, sunbathing, swimming, listening to music, and pretty much having a good time doing a lot of nothing. Yet if you really want to discover the essence of the beach, head for the coast after everyone has packed up and gone home for the day. It's a completely differently experience. There's usually a breeze blowing, and if you sit for a while, you'll see birds scavenging in the dunes and sand crabs as they scurry along the beach. The sunsets are spectacular—glowing orange, pink, and red before melting into the horizon. Once the sun goes down, you can lie on your back and get a great view of the starry sky over the water.

## Attractions

What Panama City Beach lacks in high-tech theme parks it makes up for in cheesy, roadside amusement centers that feature good old-fashioned fun. No pseudo-sophistication here—what you'll find is literally dozens of go-cart tracks, bumper cars, and arcades. And make no mistake: this is the miniature golf capital of the world, with themes that range from jungle safaris to the seven wonders of the world.

Natural attractions also abound, from boating excursions to a plethora of state parks waiting to be explored.

**Coconut Creek Mini Golf, Gran Maze, and Bumper Boats** (9807 Front Beach Road; 850-234-2625; open Monday–Friday from 11:00 A.M. to 9:00 P.M., Saturday–Sunday from 10:00 A.M. to 9:00 P.M.; $14 for all activities, $6 for round of golf, $4 for bumper boats).

Deep in the Redneck Riviera, this human-size maze—the first of its kind in the United States—spans the length of a football field. In this lesson of logic, participants race against time by validating their tickets at various checkpoints before clocking

*Sunset walks along the beach are the best way to get acquainted with Panama City Beach.* (Courtesy of VISIT FLORIDA.)

out at the exit. There are also two 18-hole mini-golf courses through an African safari with native fish, plants, and waterfalls, and the beach's largest bumper boat lake.

**Cypress Springs** (Hwy. 79, Vernon; 850-535-2960; open weekdays from 9:00 A.M. to 6:00 P.M., weekends from 8:00 A.M. to 6:00 P.M.; $3 adults, $2 ages 11 and under).

These springs produce some of the purest and clearest water in the world. With a year-round temperature of 68° F, the water is perfect for underwater photography and spelunking, but you must be certified to enter the underwater cavern that is accessible through an oval-shaped vent. The flow of water is strong here so be sure to wear a weight belt. Once you're inside, the cave opens into a room about 40 feet wide with a ceiling that is 14 feet high. The spring pumps out about 80 million gallons of water a day, which empties into Holmes Creek in Vernon. Tubing and canoeing are also quite good in the springs.

**Ebro Greyhound Park** (Hwy. 20 and Hwy. 79, Ebro; 850-234-3943; nightly races begin at 7:00 P.M. from March thru September, satellite wagering from September thru February; general

*Ebro Greyhound Park is located 16 miles outside of Panama City Beach.* (Courtesy of VISIT FLORIDA.)

admission is $1, children get in free when accompanied by a parent).

If greyhound racing appeals to you, head to Ebro, about 16 miles outside of Panama City Beach, where you can catch live greyhound racing five or six nights a week, rain or shine. There are matinees of live racing on Wednesdays and Saturdays. Over a million dollars are paid out each week, and there is a greyhound adoption program on site.

Legend's Restaurant opens at 6:00 P.M. with trackside dining from a menu of prime rib, filet mignon, Gulf seafood, and pasta. Selected tables in the restaurant have private Tiny Time Betting Terminals.

The park also features Shuffle's Card Room with Seven Card Stud, Texas Holdem, Omaha Hi-Lo, and fast-action poker on blackjack-style tables. Simulcast betting on greyhound racing is also available with greyhound racing from the Jacksonville and Tampa Circuits and thoroughbred racing from Calder, Gulfstream, and Hialeah Park.

**Econfina Creek Canoe Trail** (four miles W of US Hwy. 231, S of Chipley; 850-487-4784; free; http://www.dep.state.fl.us/-parks/bigbend/econfina.html).

Beginning at Scotts Bridge, Econfina Creek Canoe Trail features steep-walled chutes of fast-moving water and tight curves. The lower sections of this 22-mile trail are more suitable for beginners. The high sand bluffs are covered with plants native to the Appalachian Mountains, and fern-covered limestone walls characterize the terrain surrounding Econfina Creek.

**Falling Waters State Recreation Area** (three miles S of Chipley off SR 77A; 850-638-6130; open 8:00 A.M. to sunset; $3.25 per vehicle; www.dep.state.fl.us/parks/northwest/falling.html).

The name says it all at this recreation area, where the 67-foot waterfall is considered to be one of Florida's most noted geological features. The cascade is created by a small stream flowing into and out of Falling Waters Sink, a 100-feet-deep, 20-feet-wide cylindrical pit. Although the water's final destination remains undetermined, it is known that the lower 30 feet of the sinkhole is filled with natural and pre-1900 industrial debris. The area also offers 945 feet of boardwalks traversing numerous dry sink holes, swimming, picnic areas, and nature trails that guide visitors through unique plant and geological formations in the park.

**Florida's Recreational Trail System** (850-487-4784)

Florida has 36 designated canoe trails, three of which are within close proximity to Panama City Beach. Beginning at Florida Caverns State Park, the 52-mile Chipola River Trail passes several caves and limestone bluffs and features small rapids and shoals. Holmes Creek is an excellent trail for novice canoers. The river is clear with high sandy banks and lush swamplands. Econfina Creek is a combination trail with over 20 miles of narrow, twisting, and swiftly flowing waters. With its natural springs, the lower section is ideal for novice paddlers, while the upper section is more challenging.

**Goofy Golf** (12209 Front Beach Road; 850-234-6403; open daily from 8:00 A.M. to midnight; $4 for 18 holes of golf, free for ages 4 and under).

Opened in 1959, Goofy Golf was the first putt-putt golf course built on the beach. Each hole has its own personality. There's one with an alligator that opens his mouth so you can putt the ball through and another with a Tiki head that kids can climb into. People who played golf here as children and had

*Goofy Golf is a Panama City landmark.* (Courtesy of Judy
Doherty.)

their picture made sitting in the monkey's hand come back with
their children to do the same.

**Gulf World** (15412 Front Beach Road; 850-234-5271; open
daily from 9:00 A.M. to 7:00 P.M. February–October, closed off
season; $14 adults, $8 for children ages 5–12, 4 and under free).

One of the Panhandle's top attractions, this marine park has
sea lions, sting rays, a shark tank, performing dolphins, and
underwater shows with fish and natural coral. Peacocks, flamin-
gos, and parrots live in the tropical gardens. Bordering on cheesi-
ness, the highlight of the Coral Reef Theater is a scuba diver who
swims around pointing to sharks, sting rays, giant sea turtles, and
barracuda. Kids love it, though, because it gives them the chance
to see these sea creatures up close and personal.

**Historic Martin Theatre** (409 Harrison Avenue; 850-763-
8900, 850-763-8080).

Originally called the Ritz, this theater hosted movies, vaudeville, and talent shows during the movie palace era. Built in 1936,
the Martin was renovated in the 1980s to its original splendor and
once again is the setting for musical reviews, dance performances,

and live entertainment. It is considered to be one of the finest small theaters in Florida. Call for schedule and price information.

**Holmes Creek Canoe Trail** (SR 79, Vernon; 850-487-4784).

Beginning at the wayside park in Vernon, the Holmes Creek Canoe Trail is known for clear, slow-moving water that winds through high, sandy banks and hardwood swamps.

**Junior Museum of Bay County** (1731 Jenks Avenue; 850-769-6128, 850-769-6168; open Tuesday–Friday from 9:00 A.M. to 4:30 P.M., Saturday 10:00 A.M. to 4:00 P.M.; free).

Native American tools, a life-size teepee, and a pioneer village complete with a reconstructed log cabin and cane mill are but a few of the artifacts on display at this living history museum. Chickens and ducks roam the village, and there are puppet shows and concerts, plus a nature trail to explore.

**Lagoon Cruise Lines—M/V Stardancer** (5325 N. Lagoon Drive at Passport Marina; 800-355-SHIP, 850-233-SHIP; sails nightly during season; cruises begin at $39.95 for six hours).

If you can't find enough excitement stateside, then set sail for international waters where you can gamble in Las Vegas style. Roulette, craps, oasis, video poker, and blackjack are but a few of the casino games awaiting. You can also enjoy live music, dancing, bingo, karaoke, and shipboard lotto. The cruise is all-inclusive and includes your meal, port charge, and tax.

**Miracle Strip Amusement Park** (12000 W. Front Beach Road, Panama City Beach, FL 32407; 800-538-7395, 850-234-5810; open weekends March–May, daily June–Labor Day, Sunday–Friday from 6:00 P.M. to 11:00 P.M., Saturdays from 1:00 P.M. to 11:30 P.M.; $15 for unlimited rides; http://www.miraclestrippark.com/).

More than 30 years old, Miracle Strip is a vacation tradition for families who visit Panama City Beach each year. There are more than 30 rides, including the Sea Dragon, a swinging Viking ship that rocks up to 70 feet in the air; the Abominable Snowman, a refrigerated ride that spins you around in the dark; and the Starliner; a rickety roller coaster with a wooden track with a 65-foot drop. This family-oriented park also has full food concessions, an arcade, and live musical revues.

**Museum of Man in the Sea** (17314 Back Beach Road; 850-235-4101; open daily from 9:00 A.M. to 5:00 P.M.; $4 for adults, $2 for children ages 6–16).

Owned by the Institute of Diving and managed by the Panama City Marine Institute, this museum is a tribute to the history of underwater exploration and archaeology. Exhibits include early scuba-diving gear and artifacts from shipwrecks that date back two centuries, including relics from the *Atocha* as well as the fleet that sank off Ft. Pierce in 1715. The Shipwrecks of Florida exhibit explains how 30 ships sank and describes the methods used to recover their treasures. The Two-legged Fish exhibit tells the story of experiments that led to man's ability to cruise through the water. Our Underwater Neighborhood exhibit highlights the fragile marine environment that lies on the floor of St. Andrews Bay. And the new Toucha-Quarium lets visitors interact with shallow-water creatures from the Gulf and St. Andrews Bay.

**Ocean Opry** (8400 Front Beach Road, two miles W of Hathaway Bridge; 850-234-5464; shows begin Monday–Saturday at 8:00 P.M.; $16.95 for adults, $8.45 for ages 5–11, ages 4 and under free).

This thousand-seat family theater showcases country, western, old-time rock 'n roll, blue grass, and gospel music entertainers. Occasionally, you can catch a big name entertainer like Randy Travis performing here. At other times the Rader family and a house cast of 18 performers fill the stage. The box office opens daily at 9:00 A.M.

**Pine Log State Forest** (Hwy. 79S, Ebro; 850-872-4175; open 7:00 A.M. to sunset; $8 per night for camping, electricity is additional $2).

Pine Log State Forest is one of Florida's first state forests. At the time it was purchased in 1936, the 6,911 acres were almost stripped of trees. Today, the land is covered with slash, sand, and longleaf pines. There are cypress trees growing along the shore of the larger lake; pine trees rim the smaller lake to the east. A pavilion with a stone fireplace and tables is ideal for picnicking, while the lakes provide excellent fishing for bluegills, largemouth bass, and catfish. Small boats with electric motors can be used, and swimming is allowed in the smaller lake. There are four designated hiking trails through the forest, including an eight-mile portion of the Florida National Scenic Trail and the four-mile Dutch Tiemann Trail that runs along Pine Log Creek.

Each campsite has its own bench, grill, and water, and all but one have electrical hookups. Though the forest seems remote, you'll be thrown back into civilization if you stay the night, when you'll be able to hear the track announcer calling the races from Ebro Greyhound Race Track, which is only a mile away.

**SEASCREAMER** (3605 Thomas Drive, Treasure Island Marina, Slip 41; 850-233-9107; cruises daily March–Labor Day; $8 for adults, $5 for ages 6-12, 6 and under free).

Take the ride of your life on this US Coast Guard-approved 73-foot, twin turbo-charged, V-12-powered vessel. Reputed to be the world's largest speedboat, the *Screamer* charges through open waters on the Gulf—wear your swimsuit because it's a given that you'll get wet. You'll cruise the Grand Lagoon, Shell Island, and Panama City's passageway before heading into the open waters of the Gulf. There are five cruises daily.

**Shell Island Cruise and Dolphin Watch** (5701 Hwy. 98 at the E end of Hathaway Bridge across from Gulf Coast College; 800-874-2415, 850-785-4878; cruises daily at 9:00 A.M. and 1:00 P.M.; $10 for adults, $6 for ages 6–11, 5 and under free).

This three-hour narrated harbor cruise of historic St. Andrews Bay lets visitors watch ships sailing from Port Panama City and the Navy base, view the birds on Audubon Island, then take a walk on Shell Island. Dolphins occasionally play in the wake of the boat. Reservations are required for the sunset dinner cruise.

**Shipwreck Island** (12000 Front Beach Road; 800-538-7395, 850-234-0368; open daily from 10:30 A.M. to 5:30 P.M. April through Labor Day; $18.50 for adults, $15 for people under 4'2"; http://www.shipwreckisland.com/).

The sister attraction to Miracle Strip Amusement Park, Shipwreck Island is a six-acre water park with all sorts of rides designed to soak you to the bones—not a bad concept in the sweltering Florida heat. There is a 35-mph speed slide, a lazy river that meanders throughout the park—the perfect ride for innertubers—a kiddie car wash, a tadpole hole for tots, a wave pool, and cascades along the Rapid River. Stand on the sunken wreck, the park's centerpiece, and swing on a rope off the deck and into the water. You'll also find sundecks, snack stands, and game areas throughout the park.

*Accessible only by boat, Shell Island offers over seven miles of pristine, undeveloped coastline.* (Courtesy of VISIT FLORIDA.)

**Smuggler's Cove** (17562 Front Beach Road; 850-234-7988; open daily from 10:00 A.M. to 11:00 P.M.; $4 for 36 holes of golf, $2.50 for 18 holes).

An arcade, bumper boats, and mini-golf make up the amusements at this small park.

**St. Andrews State Recreation Area** (three miles E of Panama City Beach off SR 392, 4415 Thomas Drive; 850-233-5140; open daily from 7:30 A.M. to sunset; $4 per vehicle, ferry to Shell Island is $7.50 for adults, $5.50 for children; www.dep.state.fl.us/parks/northwest/andrews.html).

In 1995, the beach at St. Andrews State Recreation Area was selected as the number one beach in America by Stephen Leatherman, better known as Dr. Beach. The rating was based on criteria such as the softness of the sand, water and air temperatures, the number of sunny days, the type of currents, and accessibility.

But the beach is only a small part of this 1,260-acre park. Surrounded by water on three sides, the park is one of Florida's most popular, with over 400,000 visitors each year. There are pine forests, marshes, flatwoods, and mountains of white sand dunes covered with sea oats. A nature trail leads through a number of plant communities where visitors can encounter an abundance of wildlife, including wading birds, alligators, raccoons, and opossums. The campground is clean and scenic; half of the 170 sites are waterfront and stretch down to the lagoon or the Gulf. If you want to camp out, be sure to make reservations in advance. Two fishing piers, saltwater and freshwater fishing, picnic sites, and boating also draw tourists to the area.

The park has remnants of its past on display, including an historic turpentine still once used by lumbermen to make turpentine and rosin, both important for caulking wooden ships. There are also cannon platforms from World War II when the park was part of a military reservation. One of the platforms is now a pavilion.

Across the beach is the Intracoastal Waterway and the jetties, a man-made channel that holds the sand in place. Beyond that is Shell Island, seven and a half miles of pristine, undeveloped coastline. Since it is accessible only by boat, a pontoon ferry leaves daily every 30 minutes from the parking lot in the park to transport visitors to and from the island. You can also catch other Shell Island cruises, but they don't offer the flexibility, nor do they allow you to bring your own drinks, food, and chairs. Dolphin encounters are common on the trip over to the island.

This barrier island, 80 percent of which is state or federally owned, offers some of the best shelling north of Sanibel Island (visitors are not encouraged to take the shells), and the grassy flat area on the back bay side of the island known as Spanish Shanty Cove is a great spot for snorkeling. If you choose to spend the day on the island, take along a cooler with plenty to drink and a pair of walking shoes. The island's interior is ideal for hiking and spotting wildlife.

**Super Speed Fun Park, Inc.** (9523 Front Beach Road; 850-234-1588; open daily from 9:00 A.M. to midnight; rides range from $4.00 to $6.75).

The 8HP thunder racers on the five tracks at the Super Speed Fun Park are billed as Florida's fastest. You'll also find an SR2 Simulate Ride, a sky coaster where you can plunge 137 feet through the air, bumper boats, and a haunted house.

**Tyndall Air Force Base** (10 miles SE of Panama City on Hwy. 98; 850-283-2641).

Named after Francis B. Tyndall, a World War II aviator, this active military base is situated just south of Panama City on a 29,000-acre peninsula. The 325th Fighter Wing is stationed here, along with headquarters for the 1st Air Force, the Southeast Air Defense Sector, the 475th Weapons Evaluation Group, and the United States Air Force Civil Engineer Support Agency. There is a beach, lakes, bayous, two nature trails, horseback riding, hiking, biking, and canoeing. Clark Gable was among the thousands of gunners who trained here during the war.

Today, the base is a major economic impact in the area, with 8,000 military and civilian personnel employed on base and facilities for more than 8,100 military retirees. Though it doesn't have an on-site museum, you can see several aircraft parked along Highway 231 as you approach, and you can take a tour of the base.

**US Navy Coastal Systems Station** (850-234-4803; open for group tours only; free).

Located on 648 acres along St. Andrews Bay, this research and development facility is responsible for coastal naval operations such as amphibious missions, swimmer operations, diving and salvage, and mine countermeasures. The Naval Diving and

Salvage Training Center is headquartered here, and more than a thousand divers train here each year. The systems station employs around 2,500 military and civilian personnel.

The coastal systems station operations are highly classified; therefore it does not conduct public tours, but it will consider group tours if the organization is related in some way to the station's mission.

**Visual Arts Center of Northwest Florida** (19 E. 4th Street; 850-769-4451; open Tuesday–Saturday 9:00 A.M. to 4:00 P.M., Sunday from 1:00 P.M. to 4:00 P.M., Thursday from 9:00 A.M. to 8:00 P.M.; free).

Located in the downtown arts district, this non-profit art gallery and art school features rotating exhibits throughout the year and has a permanent hands-on interactive gallery for children. The museum occupies the old city hall and jail and was founded to promote local artists.

**Zoo World Zoological and Botanical Park** (9008 W. Hwy. 98, Front Beach Road; 850-230-0096; open daily from 9:00 A.M. to sunset; $8.95 for adults, $6.50 for children ages 3–11, 3 and under free).

Established in 1980 by international zoological authorities, Zoo World is an active participant in the Species Survival Plan (SSP), a program that protects the world's most severely endangered animal species. More than 350 animals live here including rare and endangered species. Snakes and orangutans are part of the highlights at this park, along with the Gentle Jungle Petting Zoo, a walk-through aviary, a bat exhibit, and a giraffe exhibit with a platform that allows eye-to-eye contact and feeding opportunities. The largest captive alligator in Florida, "Mr. Bubba," lives in a simulated pine forest habitat on the premises.

### Fishing/Water Recreation

More than a quarter of a million people visit Panama City each year to fish for Spanish mackerel, redfish, flounder, sea trout, bonita, dolphin, sheepshead, bluefish, amberjack, marlin, sailfish and shark. And that's just the beginning! The bottom fishing for red snapper and grouper on the reef banks is legendary between Panama City and Pensacola.

Dating back to the late 1920s, this area is one of the oldest charter boat centers in Florida. The gulf water is consistently clear—so clear that anglers can sometimes see the fish approaching.

You can fish off the three piers in Panama City Beach; Dan Russell Municipal Pier is the longest at 1,642 feet. Party boats and charter boats are also plentiful, offering half-day, full-day, and weekend fishing trips.

Nonresidents are required to have a saltwater fishing license when fishing from either a boat or land. Florida residents may saltwater fish from land without a license but must have a license when fishing from a boat. Fishermen younger than 16 or older than 65 are exempt from having a saltwater license. Licenses can be purchased at the Bay County tax collector's offices or substations (850-784-4090). For saltwater fishing call the Florida Marine Patrol at (850-233-5150). If you charter a boat, make sure the captain has purchased a license for you.

**Adventure Sailing Cruise** (Treasure Island Marina; 850-233-5499, 850-832-1454).

This 51-foot ocean sailing yacht will take you out in the Gulf by the hour, by the day, or overnight.

**Bombay Sailing Charters** (located at Captain Anderson's Restaurant on Thomas Drive; 850-234-7794; leaves daily at 9:00 A.M. and 1:00 P.M.).

Snorkeling and sunset and moonlight cruises are available from Bombay. Kick back and relax or try your hand as a sailor by learning how to handle a sailing vessel from Captain Kinney.

**Captain Anderson's Marina** (Thomas Drive and N. Lagoon Drive; 850-234-3435).

Charter fishing boats, cruise boats, and a seafood market are found along Captain Anderson's Marina.

**Dan Russell Municipal Pier** (16101 Front Beach Road; 850-233-5080).

Jutting more than 1,600 feet over the Gulf, the Dan Russell Pier is a great place to fish or just hang out and see what the locals are catching.

**Destiny Sailing Charters** (8013 Thomas Drive; 850-234-5127).

This Morgan 41-foot ketch offers sunset and moonlight cruises. Snorkeling and fishing gear are provided; bring your own cooler.

**Fun Boat Rentals** (Thomas Drive at Grand Lagoon behind Hamilton's Restaurant; 850-233-7999).

Head for the open waters of the Gulf by renting a boat from Fun Boat Rentals. It has several different brand names and styles to choose from.

**The Glass Bottom Boat** (leaves from Treasure Island Marina; 3605 Thomas Drive; 850-234-8944).

This isn't your routine glass bottom boat ride. For starters, the boat features a sea school that allows for underwater viewing as you drift over the shallow flats of St. Andrews Bay. You'll cruise the Grand Lagoon and listen to a historical narration from the captain, and the crew will identify and explain the sea life caught in the shrimp net dragging from the boat.

**Great Adventure Water Sports** (6426 W. Hwy. 98; 850-234-0830).

On the beachside of Hathaway Bridge, this company specializes in water sports, from parasailing above the Gulf to waverunners and pontoon boat rentals.

**Island Waverunner Tours and Lagoon Rentals** (behind Hamilton's on Thomas Drive; 850-234-SAIL).

Besides renting waverunners, this outfitter conducts 20-mile tours around Shell Island. There is also a calmer one-hour tour offered.

**Marina Boat Rentals** (foot of the Hathaway Bridge next to Marina Grill; 850-230-0748).

Twelve-passenger pontoon boats and center-console fishing boats are available for rent.

**Panama City Beach Pier Tackle Shop** (Dan Russell Municipal Pier; 850-235-2576).

**Treasure Island Marina** (3605 Thomas Drive; 850-234-6533).

The area's largest boat dealer, here you can rent or purchase all types of sport boats, cruisers, and yachts.

*Charters*

**AR Holley** (850-265-2618, 850-832-1899)
**Barefoot** (850-230-8221, 850-234-2198)
**Bob Zale's Zodiac Charter Fleet** (850-763-7249)
**Capt. Sandy** (850-234-3610, 850-763-8327)
**Had Enuff** (850-230-2822)
**Kelly Girl** (850-763-5694, 850-872-0521)
**Nick Nack** (850-234-8246, 850-234-7604)

**Poseidon** (850-235-2564)
**Sure Catch** (850-230-9395, 850-832-7471)

*Marinas*

**Bay Point Yacht and Country Club** (100 Delwood Beach Road; 850-235-6911).
**Capt. Anderson Davis Marina** (5550 N. Lagoon Drive; 800-874-2415, 850-234-3435).
**Hathaway Marina** (6400 W. Hwy. 98; 850-234-0609).
**Panama City Marina** (1 Harrison Ave.; 850-872-7272).
**Port Lagoon Yacht Basin** (5201 N. Lagoon Drive; 850-234-0142).
**St. Andrews Marina** (3151 W. 10 Street; 850-785-2605).
**Treasure Island Marina** (3605 Thomas Drive; 850-234-6533).

*Diving*

While Panama City Beach has long been famous as the home of the "World's Most Beautiful Beaches," the area has also garnered a reputation for Northwest Florida's best diving spots. There are hundreds of natural reefs to explore, an abundance of freshwater springs, and more than 50 artificial reef sites, including Stage I, Stage II, ten barges, the City of Atlantic, the LOSS Project, and 15 160-feet-long and 35-feet-high bridge spans. Such success is due to the commitment of the community-coordinated Panama City Marine Institute. *Skin Diver* magazine calls Panama City the "wreck capital of the south" and in 1996, *Rodale's Scuba Diving* magazine chose Panama City Beach as one of the top two wreck diving destinations in the United States. The best time of year to dive in waters off Panama City Beach is between April and September.

Historical wrecks in the area include the:
- 465-foot *Empire Mica,* a 1942 World War II British tanker sunk by a German U-boat and the Gulf of Mexico's most famous wreck;
- 441-foot World War II liberty ship;
- 180-foot *B.J. Putnam,* a fish processing boat with three easily accessible deck houses;
- 220-foot World War II tug, *The Chippewa;*

*Panama City is regarded as one of the best diving destinations in the United States.* (Courtesy of VISIT FLORIDA.)

- 160-foot coastal freighter, S.S. *Tarpon*;
- 180-foot World War II mine sweeper, USS *Strength*;
- 110-foot tug, *Chickasaw*, covered with beaugregory, snapper, and blennies; and the
- 110-foot tug, *The Grey Ghost*.

The Gulf's warm water encourages rapid growth and is an excellent home and breeding ground for a variety of sea life.

If you prefer natural reefs, the Gulf has hundreds of reefs only a few miles offshore ranging in height from three to eight feet and in depth from 80 to 100 feet. Teeming with sea creatures, the area's prime activities are photography, spear fishing, lobstering, and shelling.

Snorkelers will also find a wealth of underwater attractions. St. Andrews State Park, where a rock jetty over one-quarter mile extends into the Gulf, is one of the best places to snorkel because there is no boat traffic. The Grass Flats, a local estuary in the bay behind Shell Island, is another local favorite.

The nearby Chipola River is an excellent location for divers. The river is exceptionally clear and has several springs with penetrable cave systems—for experienced divers only—and other springs with openings that are safe as long as divers remain in the natural sunlit opening. Some divers have discovered Civil War artifacts in the Chipola.

To deal with diving accidents, the Bay County Medical Center has a hyperbaric chamber available around the clock. This decompression chamber consists of a steel, double-lock chamber that can accommodate up to nine people at a time and is capable of treatments of 100 percent oxygen, nitrox, or heliox. Most treatments last between two and seven hours. Symptoms of physical problems produced by diving include joint pain, neurological injuries to the spinal cord, or arterial gas embolisms. Hyperbaric treatment has been used since the mid-1970s.

**Diver's Den** (3120 Thomas Drive; 850-234-8717).

**Emerald Coast Divers** (5021 Thomas Drive; 904-233-3355, 800-945-DIVE).

**Hydrospace Dive Shop** (Hathaway Marina, 6422 W. Hwy. 98; 800-874-DIVE, 850-234-3063).

**Hydrospace Dive Shop West** (3605-A Thomas Drive; 850-234-9463).

**Panama City Dive Center** (4823 Thomas Drive; 800-832-DIVE, 850-235-3390).

### Golf

Next to the beach, golf is perhaps the second favorite outdoor pastime in Panama City, and there are several courses to choose from.

**Holiday Golf & Racquet Club** (100 Fairway Blvd. on Back Beach Hwy. 98, one mile from the beach; 850-234-1800).

This semi-private, par-72 championship course features a lighted nine-hole executive par-3 course. Holiday is one of the area's oldest courses but is well maintained. Walking is permitted; call for tee times.

**Hombre Golf Club** (120 Coyote Pass; 850-234-3673).

As host of the annual Nike Panama City Beach Classic, this semi-private, 18-hole course is also a PGA Tour Qualifying School. The 11th hole is a replica of hole 16 at Augusta National. Water comes into play on 15 of the 18 holes, including an

*Next to the beaches, golf is a favorite pastime for visitors.*
(Courtesy of VISIT FLORIDA.)

island green on the seventh hole. There is a driving range and professional golf instruction.

**Marriott's Bay Point Resort** (100 Delwood Beach Road; 850-234-3307, 850-235-1922).

Bay Point's semi-private Lagoon Legend is said to be the most challenging championship level golf course in Florida. Water comes into play on 17 holes, including the dramatic double crossing on the 18th hole on the Grand Lagoon. A "shot maker's course," this is one of the highest rated and most challenging courses in the nation.

Long and narrow from the back tees but forgiving from the forward tees, Club Meadows at Bay Point is a perennial favorite. This classic, tree-lined championship course is a par 72.

There is a driving range and restaurant. Tee times are required.

**Signal Hill** (9615 N. Thomas Drive; 850-234-3218).

This public, par-71 course has 18 holes of golf, a golf shop, and a snack bar. Walking is permitted. The course is conveniently located on the beach and within minutes of area attractions.

**Sunny Hills Country Club** (1150 Country Club Blvd., on Hwy. 77 between I-10 and Hwy. 20 in Sunny Hills; 850-773-3619).

A little out of the way, Sunny Hills is an 18-hole public course worth the drive because of its affordable price and challenging layout.

### Tennis

**Marriott's Bay Point Resort** (100 Delwood Beach Road; 850-235-6910).

Twelve Har-Tru tennis courts are ready for play at the Marriott. Bay Point is the annual host of the Men's Collegiate Clay Court Classic.

### Restaurants and Nightlife

Touted as the "Seafood Capital of the World," Panama City Beach offers everything from amberjack, Florida lobster, and Apalachicola oysters to grouper, crawfish, and shrimp. Local dives as well as elegant eateries serve up fresh seafood nightly, and being this close to the ocean, there's no reason to settle for anything that has been frozen. In keeping with the beach's laid-back atmosphere, casual resort wear (meaning shorts, shoes, and shirt) is acceptable for most restaurants. Few places take reservations.

Across the bridge in Panama City, you'll be more apt to find good, old-fashioned Southern cooking in addition to fresh Gulf seafood and steaks.

If you came to the beach for the nightlife, you won't be disappointed. From movies and concerts to mega-bars and beachside breweries, you'll find plenty of places to spend your time—and your money. No trip to Panama Beach would be complete without cruising the strip, a long-standing Panama City Beach tradition.

It seems that anything goes, from lawn chairs in the back of lowrider pickup trucks to convertibles packed with bodies in various stages of dress or undress. It's also cool to walk along the road, where you can subject yourself to the leers and jeers of passing cars.

And then there's the nightclub scene. Many bars feature nightly entertainment, and if you're married or older than 25, you might want to call ahead and see what type of crowd hangs out at the bar you're planning to visit.

If you're interested in hanging out with the "sweet young things," head for the hangouts right on the beach. Two of the best known are Spinnaker and Club La Vela.

**Angelo's Steak Pit** (Alternate 98; 850-234-2531; open daily at 5:00 P.M., closed Sunday).

Ribs, seafood, and steaks are this Panama City landmark's specialties. Come early, bring your camera, and have your picture made with Big Gus, the larger-than-life Angus bull outside. Inside, there is a jewelry counter to browse while you're waiting.

**Billy's Steamed Seafood Restaurant, Oyster Bar and Crab House** (3000 Thomas Drive; 850-235-2349; open Sunday–Thursday from 11:00 A.M. to 9:30 P.M., Friday–Saturday from 11:00 A.M. to 10:00 P.M., off season daily from 11:00 A.M. to 9:00 P.M.)

Billy's is the place for the best steamed Florida blue crabs in town. Casual and low-key, this raw bar also is known for its shrimp, oysters, crabs, and lobster.

**Boar's Head** (17290 Front Beach Road; 850-234-6628; open daily from 4:30 P.M. to 10:00 P.M., closed Monday).

This Old English-style tavern features chargrilled and roasted steaks and seafood, prime rib, baby back pork ribs, fish and shellfish, pasta, and Cajun specialties such as crayfish meunière. It has an extensive wine list and cellar and is one of the few places on the beach that accepts reservations. Enjoy live music Thursday through Saturday.

**Captain Anderson's** (5551 N. Lagoon Drive; 850-234-2225; open Monday–Saturday at 4:00 P.M., closed November–January).

This restaurant has been named one of the top 200 restaurants in Florida by *Florida Trend* magazine, but in reality, the atmosphere is just as good as the food. A Panama City landmark since 1958, Captain Anderson's is located dockside at Grand Lagoon with a panoramic view of the fishing and sightseeing boats that dock only a few feet away; dine early to watch the boats come in. If you arrive during the peak dinner hour, expect up to a two-hour wait. The menu includes filet of scamp imperial, with fresh lump blue crabmeat, and grouper marguerey, a house specialty. The restaurant also offers steaks and pasta.

**Club la Vela** (8813 Thomas Drive, Panama City Beach; 850-234-3866; open daily from 10:00 A.M. to 4:00 A.M.; www.lavela.com).

By day, this beach club offers entertainment like parasailing and waverunners on the beach behind the bar. Inside, there is a five-thousand-square-foot pool surrounded by a massive deck, 17 bar stations, and a grill. This is the setting for La Vela's infamous contests: the Panama Jack Ms. La Vela Bikini Contest, the West and Wild Wet T-shirt Contest, Marco's Aerobics & Fitness Male Hardbody Contest, and the Ms. La Vela Bikinis Are Wee Contest.

By night, La Vela is actually eight clubs in one, which means there is something to suit whatever mood you might be in. La Vela is touted as the USA's largest nightclub.

**Hamilton's Restaurant and Lounge** (5711 N. Lagoon Drive; 850-234-1255; open daily from 4:00 P.M. to 10:00 P.M., off season daily from 5:00 P.M. to 9:00 P.M.)

Overlooking Grand Lagoon, Hamilton's serves mesquite-grilled steaks, ribs, and seafood, along with homemade sauces, soups, and desserts made from its own recipes. The vintage photographs of early life in Panama City are worth a look, and you can watch your meal being prepared through a large glass window. Outdoor seating is available on the covered deck; live jazz plays in the lounge each night.

**Lady Anderson Dining Yacht Cruises** (5550 N. Lagoon Drive at Captain Anderson's Marina; 800-874-2415, 850-234-5940; boards at 6:30 P.M. Monday–Saturday, sails from Memorial Day to Labor Day; $29.50 adults, $19.50 for children 11 and under, tips included).

This popular triple-decker dinner and dance cruise has served Panama City for over 40 years. Reservations are generally required well in advance, but it never hurts to call the day you'd like to sail to see if there are cancellations. After a buffet dinner, dance the night away under the stars. The boat often has special cruises such as the gospel music cruise.

**Pineapple Willy's Beachside Restaurant and Sports Bar** (9875 S. Thomas Drive; 850-235-0928; kitchen open daily from 11:00 A.M. to 9:00 P.M., bar from 7:30 P.M. to 11:00 P.M.)

Sports enthusiasts seek out Pineapple Willy's, which has nine satellite dishes and a 10-foot-screen television for watching all the college and pro games. The Jack Daniel's BBQ ribs are supposedly the best in the Panhandle according to the National

Barbecue Association; evidently others agree because the restaurant cooks over a thousand pounds of ribs daily. In the day, the restaurant caters to families; by night, it's the hangout for the 30-something set.

**Schooners** (5121 Gulf Drive at the E end of Thomas Drive; 850-235-3555; open daily from 11:00 A.M. to 1:00 A.M., closed from January to mid-February).

Advertised as the "last local beach club," Schooners is a favorite for locals and tourists who enjoy fresh seafood from the Gulf, specialty salads, and hearty homemade sandwiches. The open deck bar in the back is a great spot for bikini-watching on the beach.

**Shuckums Oyster Pub & Seafood Grill** (15641 Front Beach Road; 850-235-3214; open daily from 11:00 A.M. to 11:00 P.M.).

"We shuck 'em, you suck 'em." That's the motto at Shuckums, a laid-back pub and grill that serves up some of the best chargrilled seafood around. The pub is papered with dollar bills signed by patrons.

**Spinnaker** (8795 Thomas Drive; 850-234-7892; open daily from 11:00 A.M. to 4:00 A.M. during season; cover charge varies according to time of year and concerts; www.spinakerbeachclub.com).

This "World Famous Beach Club" comes alive each spring when thousands of college students descend upon Panama City Beach for a week of revelry in the sand and sun. Spinnaker doesn't disappoint. There are 12 levels to this beachside bar, and though you'll be entertained with live concerts, drink specials, and a swimming pool with water volleyball, the real reason most folks venture to Spinnaker is to see and be seen. There are volleyball contests, wet T-shirt contests, male and female revues, a Panama Jack Miss Spinnaker contest, and jet ski and Hobie Cat rentals.

**The Treasure Ship** (3605 Thomas Drive overlooking Grand Lagoon; 850-234-8881; open daily from 4:00 P.M. to 10:00 P.M.).

You can't beat the atmosphere at the Treasure Ship, where you eat aboard a replica of—you guessed it—a pirate ship. The restaurant serves steaks, seafood, and salads.

## Accommodations

Panama City and Panama City Beach have more than 18,000 hotel, motel, and condominium units as well as campgrounds and RV parks.

*Shaped like a pirate ship, the Treasure Ship restaurant is a Panama City landmark.* (Courtesy of Panama City Beach Convention and Visitors Bureau.)

**Edgewater Beach Resort** (11212 Front Beach Road; 800-239-GULF).

You can't miss Edgewater—it's the high-rise condo complex right on the beach. A pedestrian overpass leads across Front Beach Road to another section of condos and golf and tennis villas. There are one-, two- and three-bedroom condos and penthouses for rent. The 110-acre resort boasts its own nine-hole golf course, a Polynesian-style lagoon pool with waterfalls, reflecting ponds, footbridges, more than 20,000 species of tropical plants, tennis, shuffleboard, fishing, and moonlight strolls beside the Gulf. There is also a restaurant, beauty salon, spa, and arcade on the property.

**Flamingo Motel** (15525 Front Beach Road; 800-828-0400, 850-234-2232).

Family owned, this budget motel is clean, bright, and right in the thick of all the commotion on the beach. The rooms have kitchenettes; some units have showers instead of baths. The motel features a well-cared-for tropical garden, a heated pool, and a large sundeck overlooking the Gulf. The Dan Russell fishing pier is half a mile away.

**Marriott's Bay Point Resort** (100 Delwood Beach Road; 800-874-7105).

Rated among the nation's top 25 golf and tennis destinations, this 1,100-acre resort is nestled between St. Andrews Bay and Grand Lagoon. At this lush and tropical wildlife sanctuary, chances are you won't even notice that you're not on the Gulf—especially when you see the price for rooms. Here, they are substantially less than what you might pay elsewhere in the state.

The coral stucco hotel is surrounded by gardens filled with palms, oaks, and magnolias. Rooms are spacious and comfortable, with Queen Anne-style furnishings. There are several bars and restaurants on property: Fiddler's Green is the main restaurant serving breakfast, lunch, and dinner; Stormy's Golf Grill serves afternoon snacks; Teddy Tucker's Back Beach Club is the hangout for the pool party crowd; Circe's Sports Bar is an English-style pub; and in case you need another dose of sports, there's Dokker's Grill & Pub.

You have to meander through a residential area and around the golf courses to reach the resort, but with each mile, you realize that you're leaving behind the hustle-bustle found on the beach, and that makes it even more worthwhile.

There are 36 holes of golf here on a Bruce Devlin-designed Lagoon Legends and the Club Meadows golf courses. Both have clubhouses, putting greens, driving ranges, and private instruction. The tennis facility has 12 clay courts, four of which are lighted for night play.

The beach is nearby. A quick shuttle will take you over to St. Andrews State Park, the same St. Andrews beach that was ranked number one in Dr. Beach's survey. There are also plenty of water sports to try, from jet skiing to parasailing.

**Ocean Park RV Resort** (Hwy. 98, 15 miles E of Hwy. 331; 850-235-0306).

Adjacent to Lake Powell and just across the beach, this RV resort has a pool, laundry, games, pull-thru sites, and full hookups. It is conveniently located near restaurants, a golf course, fishing, and boating.

**Panama City Beach KOA** (three miles W of Hathaway Bridge at Hwy. 98 and SR 392; 850-234-5731).

Adjacent to Signal Hill Golf Course, this KOA site offers gasoline, LP gas, groceries, a swimming pool, cable TV, a game

*Marriott's Bay Point Resort has an on-site golf and resort shop.*
(Courtesy of VISIT FLORIDA.)

room, ice, bait, fishing and beach supplies. There are three hundred paved level sites and picnic tables.

**St. Andrews Bay Resort Management, Inc.** (726 Thomas Drive; 800-621-2464, 800-423-1889, 850-235-4075).

Whether you want to rent a one-bedroom condo for a night or a five-bedroom beach house for the week, this management company offers lots of selections in any price range.

## Shopping

**Alvin's Island Magic Mountain** (Front Beach Road next to Miracle Strip; 850-234-3048; open daily from 9:00 A.M. to 6:00 P.M.; free).

As one of America's top ten retail resort chains, Alvin's has animals mixed in with the merchandise. There are tropical birds, shark, and alligator feedings daily; in between feeding, you can shop around in 60,000 square feet of bikinis, beach towels, flip-flops, and all of that other stuff you buy on vacation that ends up in your top drawer. Alvin's has discount stores all over Panama City.

**Factory Stores of America** (950 Prim Avenue, Graceville; 850-263-3277; open Monday–Saturday from 9:00 A.M. to 8:00 P.M., Sunday from 12:00 P.M. to 6:00 P.M.)

A little out of the way, this outlet mall is worth the drive. You'll find name-brand stores here like the Corning Revere Factory store and the Black and Decker outlet.

**Panama City Mall** (Hwy. 231 and Route 77; 850-785-9587; open Monday–Saturday from 9:30 A.M. to 9:00 P.M., Sunday from 12:30 P.M. to 6:00 P.M.)

With more than a hundred franchise shops and national chain stores, Panama City Mall features Gayfers, JC Penney, Sears, Victoria's Secret, and Structure, to name a few stores.

**Shell Port Gift Shop** (9949 Thomas Drive, PCB; 850-234-7083; open daily from 9:00 A.M.).

This is Northwest Florida's largest outlet for seashells, plus gift items, T-shirts, jewelry, and airbrushing.

**Trader Rick's Surf Shop** (12208 Front Beach Road at the pier; 850-235-3243; open daily from 9:00 A.M. to 11:00 P.M. off season, from 8:00 A.M. to midnight during season).

This is your one-stop shop for everything you need for the beach, from beach gear and equipment to beach wear.

## Festivals and Special Events

*May*

### Gulf Coast Triathlon

As many as 1,500 athletes from around the world compete in this day-long event to test their individual endurance in a 1.2-mile swim in the Gulf, a 56-mile bicycle course around St. Andrews and North Bays, and a 13.2-mile marathon run around Panama City Beach. A $30,000 purse, trophies, and Ironman World Championship qualifications are among the prizes. Call 850-234-6575, 850-352-763-0720, or visit the website: www.gulf-coasttri.com.

### Human Powered Submarine Races

Sponsored by the Institute of Diving and the Museum of Man in the Sea, this event features competitors racing in a two-person, originally designed human-powered submarine around a four-hundred-meter oval course, 20 feet below the water. Call 850-235-4101, or visit the website: www.panamacity.com/subraces.

*July*

### Annual Shark Tournament

There are daily prizes and one grand prize for the person who catches the largest shark during this tournament. Call 850-234-2621.

### Bay Point Invitational Billfish Tournament

This is one of the largest invitational fishing tournaments on the Gulf Coast, with entries from all over the world. Held at the Bay Point Marina, its contestants vie for hundreds of thousands of dollars in cash prizes. Call 850-235-6911.

*September*

### Bay Art Show

Held at the Visual Arts Center of Northwest Florida, this is a mixed media competition open to artists who are residents of Northwest Florida counties. Call 850-769-4451.

### Treasure Island King Mackerel Tournament

Open to the public, this annual fishing tournament begins with a kick-off party on Friday evening. A barbecue is held on Saturday and a fish fry on Sunday. There is live entertainment throughout the weekend. Call 850-234-6533.

*October*

### Indian Summer Seafood Festival

For three days in mid-October, this annual festival at Aaron Z. Bessant Park across from Dan Russell Fishing Pier is the place to be in PCB. Fresh seafood, arts and crafts booths, and continuous musical entertainment are among the attractions. Dine on raw oysters, fried mullet, broiled shrimp, and shark-on-a-stick. Call 850-234-6575.

*November*

### Boat Parade of Lights

Sponsored by local marinas, this parade takes to the water with decorated fishing boats instead of floats. Call 850-785-2554.

## Day Trips

**Florida Caverns State Park** (3345 Caverns Road, three miles N of Marianna off SR 66; 850-482-9598, 850-482-9528, 850-482-8061; open 8:00 A.M. to sunset; $3.25 for vehicles, cavern admission is $4 for adults, $2 for children 3–12, free for ages 3 and under; http://www.dep.state.fl.us/parks/bigbend/caverns.html).

Spiky stalactites and stalagmites give these underground limestone caverns the look of a lunar landscape. As the state's only limestone caverns open to the public, Florida Caverns in Jackson County is a geologist's dream. This intriguing series of connecting cave clusters contain limestone outcroppings of stalactites, stalagmites, columns, rimstone pools, soda straws, flowstones, and draperies. These formations are composed of calcite which is dissolved from the limestone when surface water containing carbonic acid percolates through the rock and into the cave. It has taken thousands of years for the formations to build up, and they are still being created at a rate of about one inch every hundred years. New formations and caves are being discovered every year.

At one time, the caverns sheltered Indians from the Panhandle, and artifacts have been recovered dating back 1,100 years. The caverns were first discovered by the Spanish in 1693.

Some sections of the formations are named for what you see, such as the *Waterfall Room,* where waterfalls of rock appear fluid, and the *Wedding Room,* which has a wedding cake formation that has been the backdrop for several weddings. Others like *Tall Man's Torment* and *Fat Man's Squeeze* are named because of their size. The trails, passages, and lighting were all constructed by the Civilian Conservation Corps from 1938 to 1942. There is only one cave open to the public; a scientific research permit is necessary to enter any others. One-hour guided tours are given throughout the day beginning at 9:00 A.M., with the last one beginning at 3:45 P.M. A short orientation film before the tour explains how the formations were created.

Take care to wear non-skid shoes as the floors of the caverns are slippery, and don't touch the formations. They are brittle and can be easily stained and clogged by the oil in human skin. There is one spot you are allowed to touch, and there you'll realize how cold and slick these formations can be.

In addition to the caverns, there are 1,280 acres of freshwater marshes, lakes, rivers, springs, hardwood forests, swamps, hammocks, and floodplains to explore with plenty of opportunities for camping, fishing, hiking, picnicking, and swimming. The *Chipola River Canoe Trail* begins in the park and runs for 52 miles. Because of a hazardous log chute, canoeists should put in two miles downstream of the park. There are two horseback trails totaling more than seven miles; markers are provided at each junction, and there is a stable with covered stalls.

Swimming and snorkeling are popular in *Blue Hole Springs,* where a small sliver of a white sand beach rims the water. The springs are clear most of the year, and diving is allowed but not recommended since the cave is silty and plummets to a depth of 85 feet—conditions considered dangerous for all but the most experienced divers.

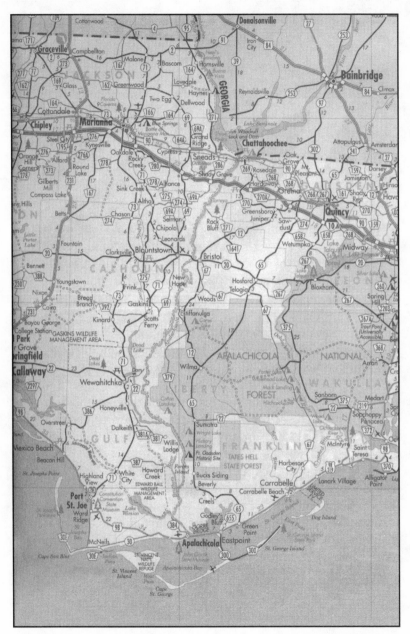

*Apalachicola area.*

# 7

## Apalachicola

### Introduction

In the violet hour at dusk, I sit on the deck at the Rainbow Inn and Marina on Apalachicola Bay and take in the night. Shades of purple paint the water and sky. An occasional boat sputters by. Hot bugs buzz in the stifling heat of Florida twilight, almost drowning out the laughter and clanking of beer bottles that slip through the screen door from the bar behind me. In this sea village hugging the Gulf Coast, worries seem as far away as lighted buoys bobbing in the distance. I expected to find a quiet, seaside town with a smattering of T-shirt and tackle shops and fewer diversions than other Panhandle destinations, but here, along the "Forgotten Coast," I ended up stumbling across paradise.

I hesitate to tell you about Apalachicola for fear that this treasured place will soon go the way of full-service gas stations and neighborhood ice cream trucks. A model for award-winning planned, small-town communities like Seaside and Celebration in Orlando, Apalachicola's quaint charm is in jeopardy of the rapid development sweeping across the Panhandle. Indeed, the recent construction of a one-stop convenience store and gas station built in the town's historic district seems a harbinger, as does the doctor's clinic out on St. George Island, where a

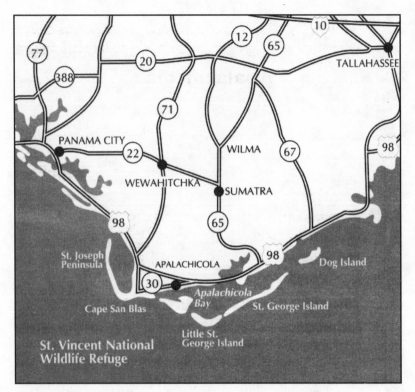

*Apalachicola.* (Courtesy of the Apalachicola Chamber of Commerce.)

physician is now performing state-of-the-art breast implants through the navel.

Locals themselves are in a quandary over what to do with the onslaught of tourists and new developments. Some welcome the economic boost, having spent most of their lives scrounging around for money. Others share the sentiment expressed on a popular local bumper sticker, "Stop and linger in Apalachicola. Spend your money, then get the hell out."

Yet paradise is different things to different people. Within the city limits—the county lines for that matter—there are no swanky resorts, no shopping malls, no theme parks.

What you will find is an uncontrived taste of the "real Florida," a kick back to the days before coastal living was tainted by million-dollar "Cracker" homes built by Bohemian wannabes.

## History

Apalachicola, an Indian word that means "land beyond" or "those people living over there," was inhabited for thousands of years by Native Americans who recognized the natural harbor along the river estuary as an ideal transportation network stretching from the Gulf to inland points. As many as 40,000 Native Americans lived here before Europeans discovered the area, leaving behind elaborate burial sites, exquisite pottery shards, arrowheads, medicine man stones, and shell mounds—traces of the bay's first seafood industry.

In 1655, Franciscan friars from Spain began to establish missions in the area. A fierce fur trade developed in the early years of European settlement, with Spain, France, and England jockeying for control of the industry and the land. William Augustus Bowles, a pirate captain, led the Creek Indians in defense against the Spanish and French, but was shipwrecked after attacking the fort at St. Marks. The Spanish picked him up and held him captive in a Cuban dungeon, where he died. Legend has it that Bowles buried a fabulous treasure somewhere on St. George Island.

The Indians, manipulated by both sides, were eventually driven west by Andrew Jackson, and settlers moved into the Chattahoochee and Flint River areas to establish homesteads. In 1821, the area between Cape Florida and the Apalachicola River was declared a customs district with St. Marks as the port of entry, and a customs house was moved here in 1823. The district officially became the city of Apalachicola in 1831. Nearby Wewahitchka was the area's earliest permanent settlement.

Laid out on the plan of Philadelphia, Apalachicola was ruled by cotton in the early 1800s, and the great plantations of Alabama and Georgia brought a steady flow of cotton merchants, riverboat hands, and sailors to town. By 1860, Apalachicola had grown to become the third largest port on the Gulf. Even today, you can see the brick warehouses and walk the broad streets that were built along the waterfront to accommodate the storage, loading, and unloading of cotton. Yankees blockaded the river during the Civil War and put an end to Apalachicola's boom period.

In the late 19th and early 20th centuries, lumbering and sponge fishing enjoyed a brief heyday, but by the 1920s Apalachicola once again turned to the sea for its livelihood. Mullet, pompano, mackerel, blue fish, trout, oysters, and shrimp were plentiful. The oysters were canned, the fish either canned or salted, and the processing plants grew in number, once again lining the waterfront with commercial businesses.

Today, fishing and oystering continue to have strongholds on the area's economy. Shrimping is a viable industry and though the Gulf of Mexico as a whole has shown a decreasing trend in shrimp harvest in the past few decades, the Apalachicola Bay catches have remained relatively stable. This is mainly due to the protection of the state-owned salt marsh nursery grounds in nearby East Bay.

There are three major types of shrimp harvested from waters in and around Apalachicola Bay; white, brown, and pink shrimp. Inshore shrimpers generally use a small bay boat, less than 38 feet long. They shrimp day or night depending on the time of year and the habits of the species sought. Offshore shrimpers use larger boats, 72 to 90 feet long; the shrimp are flash frozen since the boats may be out for 10 days or longer. In all, Apalachicola Bay shrimpers average more than a million pounds of shrimp per year, nearly 20 percent of the state's shrimp supply.

### Apalachicola Oysters

But oysters are the county's prime catch. Ninety percent of the state's oyster production is harvested in Apalachicola, and more than half of Florida's shellfish output comes from the town. It is said that nine out of every ten oysters eaten in Florida are harvested from Apalachicola Bay.

Oysters, mollusks with a soft body protected by two connecting shells called valves (hence the nickname "bivalves"), flourish here because nutrient-rich fresh water from the Apalachicola River—a vital component in the bay's natural productivity—empties into a saltwater bay that is guarded by several islands. The 210-square-mile estuary is wide and shallow; depths average only six to nine feet at low tide. In this ideal environment, oysters grow rapidly—faster than anywhere else in the country—and reach marketable size in less than two years.

Harvesting oysters is extremely hard work. Oystermen, or tongers, stand on the edge of small wooden boats and use specially designed tongs resembling two rakes hinged together like scissors to scrape the bottom and lift the oysters from the beds. Cullers accompany the tongers to separate marketable oysters from those too small to harvest. Out on the bay, the oysters are stored in burlap sacks and shaded until they are brought to shore. At the seafood houses, they are passed on to shuckers who shuck, wash, and package them.

Oystermen harvest oysters from more than 7,000 acres of public and 650 acres of private leased oyster "bars" in the bay. With names like Cat Point, East Hole, Hotel Bar, and St. Vincent's Bar, these beds have a hard, rocky, and sandy bottom which causes oysters to grow a thick deep cup just right for oysters on the half-shell. In some areas, the water is so shallow during low tide that the oysters can actually be scooped up from the bay's floor by hand. Appropriately, this is called "hogging."

To open an oyster, a shucker grinds the small end of it against a spinning blade, inserts a shucking knife between the two shells and pries them apart in order to cut away the meat. The shucking room is kept refrigerator cold at all times to keep the oysters fresh, and a dusty haze fills the room when the shuckers are grinding shells. Ironically, most shuckers are women. "Men don't seem to have the patience for it," says Grady Leavins, owner of Leavins Seafood, Inc., one of the largest oyster houses in Apalachicola. Before shipment, all oysters are tagged so that they can be traced back to the oyster house, the oysterman, and the day and place they were caught.

The Gulf Coast oyster industry is based on the highly preferred "American" or "Eastern" oyster, also known by its scientific name, *Crassostrea virginica*. Often considered the best oysters in the world, Apalachicola oysters are naturally salty, fat, and creamy. Many people swallow them whole, but oyster connoisseurs like Leavins insist that you must bite into an oyster to capture its full flavor.

According to Leavins, the taste changes with the seasons. "The best time of year to eat an oyster is from December to March, when they're creamier and fatter," he says. Why is this?

Many outside factors have an effect on Apalachicola Bay. Perhaps the most pressing is the growing demand for water by Florida, Georgia, and Alabama. Unditched, undiked, and undammed, the free-flowing Apalachicola River is considered one of the cleanest, most productive river systems in North America. Decreases in the amount of water coming from upstream would be detrimental to the bay's seafood industry.

Another concern is recent years is *Vibrio vulnificus,* a naturally occurring marine bacterium that thrives in warm waters. While the bay relies on fresh waters from the river, too much fresh water reduces the salinity and allows bacteria to grow. That's why the bay closes and oystering is halted after flooding and torrential rains. "The bay is an environmentally sensitive area," says Leavins. "The least little thing can upset the ecology. All of us have become environmentalists after living here."

Carriers of the microscopic bacteria like raw shellfish are no threat to normally healthy people, but people with chronic illnesses of the liver, stomach, or blood, those with prolonged steroid use (as for asthma and arthritis), or those who have immune disorders are at greater risk for serious illness, and some have even died from the bacteria. These at-risk people should eat only fully-cooked shellfish and avoid swimming in the ocean and bay where the bacteria live—just as many at-risk people have died from swimming in the bacteria as from eating them in shellfish. "I'd much rather gamble with eating oysters than playing golf in Florida," says Leavins, referring to the state's high rate of lightning strikes and related deaths.

Though health concerns have scared away some, oyster lovers are hard-pressed to give up the briny freshness of a hand-shucked oyster on the half-shell. One of nature's richest sources of iron and zinc, oysters have very high amounts of calcium and vitamin A and are low in calories. And of course, they do have their lusty reputation as being aphrodisiacs. As the old saying goes:

*Eat fish and live longer. Eat oysters and love longer.*

## Contact Information

**Chamber of Commerce Visitor Center** (99 Market Street, Apalachicola, FL 32320-1776; 850-653-9419; www.homtown.-com/apalachicola; email:chamber1@digitalexp.com).

The Apalachicola Chamber of Commerce Visitor Center is conveniently located downtown between the Apalachicola State Bank and the Old Fashioned Soda Fountain. Stop by to pick up free brochures and a town map Monday through Friday from 9:00 A.M. to 4:00 P.M. and on Saturday from 10:00 A.M. to 3:00 P.M.

Note: Apalachicola is on Eastern Standard Time, which makes it one hour ahead of the rest of the Panhandle.

**Gulf County Chamber of Commerce** (P.O. Box 964, Port St. Joe, FL 32456; 850-227-1223).

### Average Temperatures

| | |
|---|---|
| Spring | 66° |
| Summer | 81° |
| Fall | 70° |
| Winter | 55° |

## Transportation

If you have your own plane, you can fly into the Apalachicola Airport which has a 5,200-foot lighted runway. There is also an airport in St. George Plantation on the island with a 3,800-foot unlighted runway. If you're flying a commercial airline, the closest airports are in Panama City and Tallahassee.

Driving is the most practical way to get to Apalachicola. Greyhound Bus Lines provides transportation to the area. You can rent cars at the Apalachicola Airport or at Gulf Ford, or call the local taxi or bus service.

**Amtrak** (918½ Railroad Ave., Tallahassee; 800-872-7245, 850-224-2779).

**Apalachicola Airport** (850-653-2222)

**Crooms Transportation** (850-653-8132)

**Greyhound Bus Lines** (112 W. Tennessee St., Tallahassee; 800-231-2222, 850-222-4240).

**Gulf Ford Car Rentals** (850-653-9765)

**Panama City–Bay County International Airport** (3173 Airport Road, 52 miles west/one-hour drive; 850-763-6751).

**St. George Plantation** (850-927-2072)

**Tallahassee Regional Airport** (3300 Capital Circle SW, 72 miles/hour-and-a-half drive; 800-610-1995, 850-891-7800).

## Beaches

Because Apalachicola sits on the bay, there are no beaches in the town. However, nearby barrier islands and other Franklin County locales feature plenty of the sugar-white sand synonymous with the Gulf Coast.

### Cape San Blas

Cape San Blas, west of Apalachicola, sits at the bend of a long, skinny piece of land attached to the mainland between the cape and Indian Pass. There are few amenities in the area, but the pristine beaches—named as some of the best in the nation—make the isolation well worth the trip.

Salinas Park Beach, a recent development, has beachfront picnic areas, boardwalks, a playground, restrooms, and an octagonal gazebo that sits atop a high sand dune. One mile south of the park is an historic marker for the Confederate Saltworks, now the site of the Old Saltworks Cabins and Store.

The lighthouse at the Coast Guard station is worth visiting, but you can't go inside the tower. Supposedly, the German-made Fresnel lens in the light was cracked by musket fire from Confederate soldiers. The lighthouse was in continuous operation until it closed in 1996.

### Dog Island

Dog Island is the smallest inhabited island of the chain. A single sand road leads from the dock and meanders around the island. There is an eight-room Pelican Inn and about a hundred vacation homes on the three-square-mile island, most of which is a nature preserve. A small airstrip allows access for small, private aircraft, while a ferry service to the island is available in Carrabelle and through tour operators.

### Indian Pass

There's not much around this solitary stretch of beach, and that suits most folks just fine. West of Apalachicola, Indian Pass has a few homes for rent, and the new Turtle Beach Inn has

*St. George Island is the largest barrier island in Franklin County.*
(Courtesy of VISIT FLORIDA.)

rooms and a guest cottage. There is also a secluded camp-ground, a boat ramp, and an oyster bar. Closer to Cape San Blas, if you have a permit, you can drive your car on a strip of beach right up to the water.

### Little St. George Island

This island was once a part of the larger St. George Island, but in 1957 the U.S. Army Corp of Engineers opened a permanent pass to shorten the time required for fishing boats to get from Apalachicola Bay to the open Gulf. Almost three square miles in area, the island bends like a half-stretched arm in the water.

The Cape St. George lighthouse sits at the elbow. Built in 1852, it is fully operational but closed to the public. There have been rumors that the Coast Guard may abandon the structure since erosion and violent weather have repeatedly reduced the beach until the lighthouse sits only a few yards away from the water.

Accessible only by private boat and through transportation provided by some tour operators, Little St. George Island is owned by the state of Florida and operated by the Department of Natural Resources as part of St. George Island State Park.

Camping is allowed, but campers must notify the state when they plan to stay overnight. Dove and duck hunting are also permissible with appropriate permits.

## St. George Island

The largest barrier island in Franklin County and the main protector of the Apalachicola Bay, St. George Island is about 28 miles long and one-fourth to one mile wide. At its peak, the island measures a full 12 feet above sea level. Although over 50 percent of the land is state owned, there are about five hundred full-time residents and many vacation homes that are available for rent. As in other parts of the Panhandle, real estate has skyrocketed in recent years. Today, homes on St. George sell for as much as a million dollars, and vacation rentals can easily cost three thousand dollars per week.

The east end of the island is occupied by Dr. Julian G. Bruce St. George Island State Park, with stretches of uncrowded beaches for sunning and pristine marsh and wooded areas ideal for nature lovers and bird watchers. A motel, an inn, several restaurants, lounges, convenience stores, and art galleries are located on St. George. The island is connected to the mainland by a bridge and causeway.

## St. Vincent Island

An atypical coastal barrier island, St. Vincent is triangular in shape, gradually forming a narrow point at the west end. The 12,358-acre undeveloped island is a National Wildlife Refuge managed by the U.S. Department of the Interior, with offices at the end of Market Street in Apalachicola.

Accessible only by boat, St. Vincent's 14 miles of primitive beaches are open to daytime public use throughout the year.

### Pelican Picks

**Tupelo Honey/LL Lanier and Son** (850-639-2371)
Wewahitchka, northwest of Apalachicola, is the place to go for pure tupelo honey. Made from May blossoms of the rare white tupelo tree, the honey is special because it doesn't granulate or become rancid. More than half a million pounds of honey are

*St. Vincent Island is a National Wildlife Refuge managed by the U.S. Department of the Interior.* (Courtesy of the Apalachicola Chamber of Commerce.)

produced annually, making Florida the third largest honey-producing state in the nation. You'll see signs on the roadside advertising honey for sale, but if you're a movie buff, then make sure you head for LL Lanier and Son's on Lake Grove Road by the water tank. Lanier was the inspiration for Peter Fonda's character in the 1997 production of *Ulee's Gold,* and the film was shot in his backyard. Lanier's father started the business in 1898; LL, his son, still helps out at the store, but if he isn't around, you'll probably get to meet his son Ben. Call 850-639-2371 for more information.

### Dog Cafés

It's no secret that dogs are well liked in Apalachicola. Indeed, many shops, restaurants, and hotels welcome these four-legged friends. But the dog cafés around town are true testimony to the city's affections. One is located just past downtown on Market Street, catercornered to Magnolia Hall. With aluminum slanted roofs, these crude, whitewashed troughs have signs above them proclaiming,

God Is Love

Dog Café

Free Eats

Always Open

The troughs also feature clear plastic flaps on the front to protect the food from birds, but no matter: they seem to find their way in anyway. No one is certain who replenishes the troughs each day, but if you pass by several times during your stay, you're bound to see birds, possums, raccoons, cats, and of course, the dogs who reap the benefits.

**Old Time Soda Fountain and Luncheonette** (93 Market Street; 850-653-2606).

Located next to the Chamber of Commerce, the Old Time Soda Fountain was once the town's drugstore. Today, it sells kitschy souvenirs like snow globes filled with sand and rubber alligators, but the main attraction is the fountain. After wandering around downtown, there's nothing better than plopping down on one of the bar stools at the counter and sipping fresh-squeezed lemonade or an old-fashioned chocolate malt made with hand-dipped ice cream.

**Going Solo in the Kitchen** (N end of Market Street; 850-653-8848).

Take a culinary vacation under the direction of Jane Doerfer, a transplanted Yankee who also happens to be a noted cooking teacher and author of *The Victory Garden Cookbook* and *Going Solo in the Kitchen*. As the only established cooking school devoted solely to teaching cooking for one, the establishment offers both weekend courses and in-depth full-week curriculums. All participatory classes are held in the spacious kitchen of a 19th-century cypress and heart-pine plantation house overlooking the shrimp boats on the Apalachicola River Basin. Students stay at nearby Pelican Inn on Dog Island. Classes are held sporadically throughout the year; call ahead for a schedule and prices.

## Attractions

**Apalachicola Bluffs and Ravines Preserve** (Hwy. 12 outside of Bristol, 40 miles SW of Tallahassee; 850-643-2756; open daily from daylight to sunset; free; www.tnc.org).

The Apalachicola Bluffs and Ravines Preserve is one of eight preserves managed by the Nature Conservancy in the Northwest Florida program. As the name suggests, the bluffs are spectacular—they're the largest geological site in Florida where you can actually see *outcroppings*, the layers of soil. The preserve encompasses several habitats: sandhills, an upland mixed forest, bluffs, a slope forest, bayheads, and a floodplain forest and swamp. These habitats are home to all types of plant and animal life including several endangered species such as the torreya tree. The preserve is currently involved in upland restoration and just planted its one-millionth tree. If you visit, you can pick up a self-guided tour brochure at the Nature Conservancy Field Office.

**Apalachicola Historic District**

The Apalachicola Historic District lies in less than a two-square-mile area near downtown, only a short walk from Market Street. You can pick up a map and self-guided tour brochure from the Chamber of Commerce. Many homes, churches, and businesses have architectural value as well as interesting stories dotting their history.

An example of Greek Revival style, the *Raney House* was built by commission merchant David G. Raney in 1838. Dating to the beginning of the city, the house barely escaped destruction in the Civil War. Today the house is on the National Register of Historical Places.

The *Coombs House Inn*, built in 1905, was once the most elegant home in Apalachicola. In 1900, its owner, James Coombs, turned down his party's nomination for governor of Florida, and in 1908, he was considered a possible candidate for the vice presidency. Today the house is a popular inn.

With twin ionic columns and tall, narrow windows, the Greek Revival *Trinity Episcopal Church* dates to 1836, making it the third oldest Episcopal church in the state. It was one of the first pre-fabricated buildings constructed in Florida, with sections shipped by schooner from New York and assembled with wooden pegs.

In 1942, a British oil tanker was torpedoed by a German submarine near Cape San Blas, 40 miles southwest of Apalachicola. Locals took their own boats out to look for survivors, recovering only 14 of the 47 crewmen. The hull of the *Sea Dream,* one of the boats used in the recovery, is on display near the waterfront.

In 1895, between 80 and 120 men were employed by the sponge trade in Apalachicola, and the city had two warehouses. Though the harvesting never reached the magnitude of Key West's, it was ranked third in the state at one time. The *Sponge Exchange,* circa 1840, is one of the structures still standing.

The private *Marks–Bruce House* was built at St. Joseph in 1804, but was abandoned during the yellow fever epidemic of the early 1840s through the 1850s. The house was then moved by barge to Apalachicola and located at its present site in 1954.

Confederate soldiers as well as victims of a yellow fever epidemic are buried at the *Chestnut Street Graveyard.*

**Apalachicola Maritime Museum** (268 Water Street; 850-653-8708; open Tuesday through Friday from 8:30 A.M. to noon; free).

A labor of love for several salty dogs in Apalach (as it is sometimes called), this privately funded museum features exhibits on the history of shrimping and oystering in Apalachicola Bay. There are examples of sailor knots, lanterns, antique motors, and a valuable historic binnacle, commonly known as a case for a ship's compass. The museum is also home to a small boat factory which you can walk through to see how wooden boats are crafted. Upstairs, learn how canvas sails are made.

The museum owns the *Governor Stone,* the oldest vessel still sailing the Gulf Coast. Not to be confused with a Biloxi schooner, the

*Trinity Episcopal Church in the Apalachicola Historic District is the third oldest Episcopal church in the state.* (Courtesy of the Apalachicola Chamber of Commerce.)

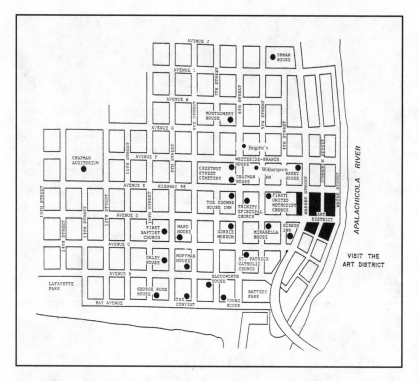

*Apalachicola Historic District.* (Courtesy of the Apalachicola Historic District.)

*Governor Stone* is a National Historic Landmark and the last Northern gaff-rigged schooner in existence. The 63-foot vessel is made entirely of wood, has over five thousand square feet of canvas sails, and weighs 14 tons. Volunteers maintain the boat, which costs more than $50,000 per year just to keep afloat.

The Ships Chandlery and Cof-A-Cuppee, located downstairs, is a coffeehouse and ship shop that sells supplies for private boats, gifts for sailors, pet lifejackets, and items with an environmental edge.

**Apalachicola National Estuarine Research Reserve** (7th Street at N end of Market Street near Scipio Creek; 850-653-8063; open Monday through Friday from 8:00 A.M. to 5:00 P.M.; free).

The largest of 21 federally monitored research estuaries, the Apalachicola National Estuarine Research Reserve (ANERR) encompasses a large section of the Apalachicola River and

*Private residences in the city's historic district are excellent examples of early Florida architecture.* (Courtesy of the Apalachicola Chamber of Commerce.)

adjoining flood plains, all or portions of three barrier islands, Apalachicola Bay, and associated sounds. The intent of designating this area as a research reserve is to protect the fragile wetlands, bay area, and coastal uplands that fall within its boundaries.

Research activities include long-term monitoring of physical, chemical, and biological parameters important to the estuarine's productivity, marsh restoration, and threatened sea turtle and migratory bird nest protection and monitoring programs.

The reserve is one of the most important bird habitats in the southeastern United States, with more than 315 species. There are also more than 360 species of marine mollusks found in the reserve, many of which are endangered, along with 180 species of fish and 1,300 species of plants. The highest species diversity of amphibians and reptiles north of Mexico is found in the basin, including 10 species considered threatened, endangered, or of special concern.

Off 7th street, ANERR has an educational and research center that houses exhibits representative of the coastal ecosystem.

There are all sorts of skeletons, shells, and stuffed animals collected from the area on display as well as the Estuarine Walk, an educational exhibit highlighting the different water habitats in the area, complete with the live plants and animals that inhabit them.

**Apalachicola National Forest** (SW of Tallahassee; 850-942-9300; recreation areas are open daily from 8:00 A.M. to sunset; fees begin at $2 for day use of recreation areas, camping fees begin at $4; www.fs.fed.us/recreation/forest_descr/fl_r8_florida.html).

The largest in Florida, the Apalachicola National Forest covers more than one-half million acres and is home to animals like black bears and wild pigs. Contrary to belief, the forest does not border the coast, but is situated inland between Apalachicola and Tallahassee.

Part of the *Florida National Scenic Trail* crosses through the forest. It begins on Highway 12 about 10 miles south of Bristol and runs east to Porter Lake Recreation Area near the Ochlockonee River, passes through Bradwell Bay Wilderness, and exits at Highway 319 at Medart. The main trailhead is at Camel Lake Recreation Area, but several access points are available along the entire route. Additional trails include *Munson Hills* for off-road bicycles and *Vinzant Trail* for equestrian use.

Camping is allowed in most areas of the forest except during general gun-hunting season. During this time camping is allowed only in developed recreation areas and designated seasonal hunt camps. Camping stays are limited to 14 days except during hunting season at designated hunt camps.

For a leisurely drive, follow the *Apalachee Savannahs Scenic Byway,* a pleasant drive through some of Florida's most scenic landscapes. Take Highway 12 to Highway 379, then head south on Highway 65 at the Sumatra community.

Canoeing and boating opportunities are abundant in the Apalachicola National Forest. The *Sopchoppy River* is awaiting designation by Congress as a Wild and Scenic River and is a popular destination for canoers who prefer calm, downstream floating. The *Ochlockonee River* has been designated for study as a Wild and Scenic River and is another favorite corridor for boating and fishing. *New River* is to be studied for Wild and Scenic designation. Located inside the Mud Swamp/New River Wilderness, it requires experienced canoers as it involves some portaging to navigate it successfully.

**Constitution Convention State Museum** (200 Allen Memorial Pkwy., Port St. Joe; 850-229-8029; open Thursday through Monday from 9:00 A.M. to noon and from 1:00 P.M. to 5:00 P.M.; $1 for adults and children 6 and older; www.dep.state.fl.us/parks/northwest/constitutional.html).

Once upon a time, St. Joseph was a booming port town that exported cotton to world-wide destinations. Known as the most wicked city in the Southeast, the town was the sixth most populated in Florida and, in 1838, was the site where Florida's first state constitution was drafted. The boom was halted by a devastating hurricane and an epidemic of yellow fever that wiped out three-fourths of the population. As a result, real estate values plunged, so folks literally packed up their belongings and dismantled their homes and shipped them by barge to Apalachicola. The museum tells the story of the town and the convention and has many interesting exhibits on early Florida history.

**Dead Lakes State Recreation Area** (one mile N of Wewahitchka off SR 71; 850-639-2702; open daily from 8:00 A.M. to sunset; $3.25 per vehicle; www.dep.state.fl.us/parks/northwest/dead.html).

The name is somewhat deceiving. Instead of finding dead lakes, you'll find thousands of dead trees at this state recreation area. The lakes are thought to have been formed when sandbars created by the current of the Apalachicola River blocked the Chipola River. The ensuing high water killed thousands of trees in the floodplain. The dead trees make for an eerie photograph, but you'll also want to take in the natural uplands that feature an abundance of sweetbay, magnolia, cypress, and longleaf pine trees, along with diverse wildlife. Be sure to look for the white tupelo gum tree. It grows only in the swampy waters of Dead Lakes. There is fishing, boating, camping, and a boat ramp in the park.

**Dixie Theatre** (Avenue E; 850-927-2708).

With seating for over three hundred, the Dixie Theatre is a labor of love for Rex Partington and Cleo Holladay, who bought the dilapidated structure in 1994. After four years of refurbishment, the non-profit theater now showcases professional acting troupes, film festivals, dances, and other evening events.

Originally constructed in 1912, the building has an auditorium with a balcony and a proscenium arch stage with a 30-feet-high opening. Flexible seating allows for dances, cabarets, banquets, meetings and conventions, live stage performances, concerts, recitals, and motion pictures. Call ahead for show times and schedules.

**Fort Gadsden Historical Area** (Hwy. 65, 30 miles from Apalachicola; 850-643-2282, 850-926-7095; open daily until sunset; free).

Located on the banks of the Apalachicola River, Fort Gadsden is the site of one of Florida's most violent military battles. During the War of 1812, the fort was a British recruitment center for Seminole Indians and blacks; later, it was inhabited by escaped slaves who felt they'd been left in charge by the British. Feeling threatened, the United States ordered the fort destroyed, and all but 30 of the three hundred people inside— including women and children—were killed. Two years later, it was rebuilt as a supply depot under the order of Andrew Jackson. Confederate forces occupied the fort briefly during the Civil War.

Today, all that remains of the fort are ruins. The site also includes picnic areas, nature trails along the Apalachicola River, a cemetery, a visitor center with artifacts, a replica of the fort, and interpretive displays that trace the fort's history.

**Governor Stone** (268 Water Street; 850-653-8700; $20 for adults, $10 for ages 10 and under).

Take a starlight sail on an historic 1877 Gulf Coast schooner, completely restored by the volunteers at the Maritime Museum, Inc. The *Governor Stone* hosts group charters and special events and provides sail training, small boat building, safe boating, and navigation classes.

The *Governor Stone* is the oldest vessel still sailing the Gulf Coast. Built for the bay's shallow waters, the boat has been used for various jobs including U.S. Merchant Marine training, oyster buying, freighting, and "rum-running."

**John Gorrie State Museum** (6th Street off US 98; 850-653-9347; open Thursday through Monday from 9:00 A.M. to 5:00 P.M.; $5 for adults, $1 for children, under 6 are free; http://-www.dep.state.fl.us/parks/bigbend/gorrie.html).

When Dr. John Gorrie created a method to cool the rooms of his patients with yellow fever, little did he realize the impact such an invention would have on modern America—and Florida, in particular. His discoveries laid the groundwork for modern refrigeration and air-conditioning, necessities in the heat of Florida summers. Gorrie was from Apalachicola, and a replica of his refrigeration machine is on display in the museum that bears his name.

**Jubilee Paddle Wheeler** (departs from 79 Market Street; 850-653-2084, 850-653-9502).

First he built the boat; now Capt. Daniel Blake takes visitors on it for picturesque tours of the Apalachicola River. Blake started building the *Julibee* in 1996; he finished in July 1998. The Blakes also own Chesnut Street Antiques in town. Call ahead for the daily schedule of the paddle wheeler.

**Ochlockonee River State Park** (four miles S of Sopchoppy on Hwy. 319; 850-962-2771; open daily from 8:00 A.M. to sunset; $3.25 per vehicle; http://www.dep.state.fl.us/parks/bigbend/-ochlockonee.html).

Only 10 miles from the Gulf Coast, the pine flatwoods, bayheads, and oak thickets create a diverse habitat for the deer, bobcats, foxes, and birds that live in this 392-acre park. There are riverside campgrounds for camping and plenty of places to fish and picnic.

**St. George Island State Park** (Hwy. 98, 10 miles SE of Eastpoint, St. George Island; 850-927-2111; open daily from 8:00 A.M. to sunset; $4 per vehicle; http://www.dep.state.fl.us/-parks/bigbend/stgeorge.html).

Open to the public in 1980, St. George Island State Park is one of the best examples of Florida's Gulf Coast barrier islands. You'll find extensive beaches and dunes, forests of slash pines, sandy coves, salt marshes, and live oak hammocks. The ocean and bay support an abundance of marine life, while freshwater ponds and sloughs provide a limited aquatic habitat. These conditions limit the number and type of resident animal life. Osprey frequently fish the waters, and their nests can be seen at the tops of living or dead pine trees in the park. Raccoons, ghost crabs, salt-marsh snakes, and diamondback terrapins are common residents. Birds such as the snowy plover, least tern, black skimmer, willet, and many species of shorebirds nest along the park's sandy shores and glass flats.

During the early and mid-1900s, the island's pine forests were turpentined; many scars are still visible on the largest slash pines. The island was also used during World War II for numerous training exercises. In 1942 a British oil tanker was torpedoed by a German submarine just off Cape San Blas. Volunteers rushed out in their own boats to pick up survivors, rescuing 14 of the 47 who had been aboard. The hull of the *Sea Dream,* one of the boats used in the rescue, is on display at the waterfront in town.

The white beaches in the park are among the best in the area. There are also camping facilities, observation decks, and nature trails. Swimming and sunbathing are popular on the beaches, but no lifeguards are provided.

**St. Joseph Peninsula State Park** (15 miles SW of Port St. Joe on CR 30E; 850-227-1327; open daily from 8:00 A.M. to sunset; $3.25 per vehicle; www.dep.state.fl.us/parks/northwest/joseph.-html).

Named as one of the top ten beaches in America, the 2,516-acre T.H. Stone Memorial St. Joseph Peninsula State Park is surrounded by water on three sides by St. Joe Bay and the Gulf of Mexico. Miles of white sand beaches and tall dunes fringe the park, which resembles a long, narrow finger of land. The northern part of the park is a 1,650-acre wilderness preserve; hike into the primitive area by following the beach or a central sand road in the island's interior. Noted as an excellent birding area, it is a premier location in the eastern United States for observing hawks during fall migration. Many species can be seen including the endangered peregrine falcon. The Monarch butterfly rests here in autumn during its migratory journey from Northern states to Mexico. Currently, the park boasts sightings of 209 bird species.

Camping, fishing, cabins, a boat ramp, hiking trails, and miles of natural beach are among the features of the park.

**St. Vincent National Wildlife Refuge** (N end of Market Street near Scipio Creek; 850-653-8808; free; www.fws.gov/~r4eao/nwrsvn.html).

Located in Franklin County about nine miles offshore from Apalachicola, this refuge offers stunning examples of Florida habitats, from rolling sand dunes, scrub oak-live oak ridges, pine flatwoods, and cabbage palm and magnolia hammocks to tidal marshes and freshwater lakes and swamps.

Indians inhabited the island at one time, and pottery shards have been found dating back to the year 240 AD. In 1868, George Hatch bought St. Vincent at an auction for three thousand dollars; he was later buried here. In 1908, a Dr. Pierce purchased the island and spent $60,000 importing Old World game animals. The Loomis brothers added to the collection in 1948, bringing zebras, elands, black bucks, ring-necked pheasants, and Asian jungle fowl. In 1968, the Nature Conservancy bought the island. The U.S. Fish and Wildlife Service repaid the conservancy with money from the sale of federal duck stamps, and the island was established as a National Wildlife Refuge.

All the zebra and eland were removed before the refuge was established, but the sambur deer, a large deer native to Asia, became acclimatized, and a small herd still thrives. Black buck also remain in small numbers but are rarely seen.

The refuge was initially established for waterfowl, but its mission has been broadened to include the protection of a number of federal and state endangered and threatened species. Bald eagles nest in pine trees near the freshwater lakes and marshes, loggerhead sea turtles nest on the sandy beaches, indigo snakes inhabit gopher tortoise burrows in the inner dunes. Woodstorks and peregrine falcons stop during migrations. The refuge is also one of several Southeastern coastal islands where endangered red wolves are bred prior to their release at mainland release sites.

The refuge offers transportation once a year in October during National Wildlife Refuge Week. Sign up is on a first-come, first-served basis, and only five groups of 28 people, one group per day, are allowed. During the remainder of the year, tour operators can drop you off, or you can take your own boat.

*The beaches at St. Vincent Island are unspoiled.* (Courtesy of the Apalachicola Chamber of Commerce.)

Freshwater fishing is permitted; managed hunts for deer and hogs are held annually.

The refuge visitor center at the end of Market Street exhibits dioramas with examples of wildlife found on the island and provides free maps and brochures. Ask for Charlotte Chumney; she's always happy to answer questions about the refuge and other area attractions.

**Tate's Hell Swamp State Forest** (off Hwy. 98; 850-265-3676; open 24 hours a day; free).

Adjacent to the national forest, Tate's Hell is rough, undeveloped swamp land supposedly infested with water moccasins. Legend has it that it was named after an early settler who disappeared after chasing a panther into the swamp.

The forest takes up most of Franklin County, with its western boundary next to State Road 65 and its eastern boundary extending to State Road 67 and the Ochlockonee River. If you decide to visit, you'll find a raw, outdoor wilderness experience with few amenities. There are long-range plans to develop day-use facilities like boat ramps and camping, but nothing in the near future.

**Three Rivers State Recreation Area** (Hwy. 271 two miles N of Sneads; 850-482-9006; open 24 hours a day; free).

This state recreation area is named for the three rivers that run through the park: the Chattahoochee, Flint, and Apalachicola. Hills covered by hardwood hammocks and pine forests are home to whitetail deer, gray foxes, and a variety of birds, and they make great hiking terrain. You can also boat, fish, camp, and picnic throughout the area.

**Torreya State Park** (CR 1641, 13 miles N of Bristol; 850-643-2674; open daily from 8:00 A.M. to sunset; $2 per vehicle, house tours are $1 for adults, 50¢ for children; http://www.dep.state.-fl.us/parks/bigbend/torreya.html).

Because much of Florida is so flat, the 150-feet-high wooded bluffs above the Apalachicola River are an unexpected sight. The land in this park is more reminiscent of the Appalachians than is most of the state; indeed, many of the hardwood trees and plants in the park are commonly found in Northern Georgia. The park is home to the only native habitat of one species of evergreen, the torreya, also known as stinking cedar trees for the smell they release when bruised. You'll also find the Florida yew, the US champion winged yew, and unusual plants like the pitcher plant, which drowns bugs and eats them.

Torreya State Park is also the site of the *Gregory House,* a yellow pine and cypress plantation home open for tours. The house was originally built by Jason Gregory in 1849 at Ocheesee Landing on the Apalachicola River. In 1935, it was given to the state and subsequently dismantled and moved over the next three years by the Civilian Conservation Corps to its present site. House tours are given Monday–Friday at 10:00 A.M. and Saturday–Sunday at 10:00 A.M. and 2:00 P.M.

Civil War buffs should check out *Battery Point,* where the remains of Confederate earthworks guard a splendid view over the river basin.

A variety of recreational activities, including camping, primitive camping, and hiking on a seven-mile loop trail, are

*Apalachicola offers superb fishing without the crowds.* (Courtesy of VISIT FLORIDA.)

available. Ranger-guide tours of the restored Gregory House are given daily.

### Fishing/Water Recreation

Equivalent to Key West as it was in the 1960s, Apalachicola offers superb fishing without the crowds and fancy footwork that are now status quo at many of the world's hot spots. Here, you can simply hang out and rediscover the reason you fell in love with fishing in the first place. The flats are home to tarpon, redfish, speckled trout, and pompano. Controversial net bans and conservation measures have restored the redfish to healthy numbers; king mackerel, cobia, snapper, amberjack, and grouper are also abundant. Bass and bream thrive in the Apalachicola River.

**Apalachicola River Tours** (317 Water Street; 850-653-2593; $20 per adult, $10 for children under 12).

This leisurely cruise aboard the *Osprey,* a Coast Guard-certified, 32-passenger, all-weather tour boat, traces the role that the river and bay have played in Apalachicola history. Following the harbor tour, the *Osprey* turns upriver to explore various ecosystems, from marshes to tupelo and cypress swamps.

**Benign Boat Works, Inc.** (317 Water Street; 850-653-8214; open daily from 8:00 A.M. to 6:00 P.M.; cost ranges from $7.50 for a one- or two-man pedal boat to $65 an hour for a 24-foot canopied boat for eight).

In an effort to cut down on pollution caused by boating in Apalachicola Bay, Benign Tours offers a twist on tradition: ecological adventures aboard silent electric boats. Electric boats are much quieter than motor boats, allowing for tranquil opportunities to view and photograph birds, alligators, and other wildlife in the area. Benign Boat Works will supply you with a map of the area; you can also hire a captain for guided tours.

**Broke-A-Toe's Adventures** (location changes, call for daily launch sites; 850-229-WAVE; www.capesanblas.com/broke-a-toes).

Broke-A-Toe's specializes in all sorts of water adventures for both the novice and experienced. There are kayak and canoe rentals with maps and directions to Indian camp sites, a whale dune, cypress swamps, bayous, Gulf and bay islands, and other natural and historical sites. You can take guided kayak and canoe trips as well, along with photography outings, birding excursions, Tupelo honey tours, and gator treks. Talk to Broke-A-Toe and he can also set up shrimping expeditions with Apalachicola shrimpers and overnight fishing excursions.

**Captain Black's Marine** (Hwy. 98, Port St. Joe and at Captain Black's Beachside in St. Joseph State Park; 850-229-6330).

From snorkeling, scalloping, and dolphin watching to all-day fishing trips and diving, Captain Black can show you the bay and its inhabitants like no other captain in town. Boat over to the remote eastern tip of St. Joseph's Peninsula and learn about the habits of bottlenose dolphins or snorkel St. Joe Bay and learn how to find, catch, clean, and cook your own scallops. Call for prices and schedules. Captain Black also has a full-service dive shop at his Port St. Joe location.

**Captain Parrothead's Dog Island Adventure** (Hwy. 98, Carrabelle; 850-697-3847; open daily; $15 per person for sunset sail, $25 per person for half-day Dog Island excursion).

Get ready for adventure on the high seas with Captain Jack at the helm. As you explore islands that once teemed with pirates and buccaneers he'll spin yarns about bygone days. On the Dog Island cruises, you can get out and wade in shallow, clear water or comb the beaches. The sunset sails are best for kicking back and enjoying the cool Gulf breezes while watching for dolphins playing in the boat's wake.

**Captain Tom's Adventures in Paradise** (launch sites: Apalachicola, St. George Island, Indian Pass, and St. Joe Bay; 850-653-8463; cost varies according to tour and length).

A former biology teacher, shrimper, and commercial fisherman, Captain Tom is an expert on the waters surrounding Apalachicola. Besides his barrier island trips and canoe adventures on the lakes in the area, he offers sailing lessons, biking tours of St. Vincent, sunset sails, and Gulf cruises. Two of his more interesting classes are the Baybottom University, where you'll learn to drag a shrimp trawl, tong oysters, pull crab pots, and throw a cast net, and the Bay Shallows by Night, where you'll wade in knee-deep water and look for baybottom critters by the light of a lantern.

**Captain Tony Charters** (850-653-3560)

Captain Tony Thompson can take individuals or groups

fishing in the bay and Gulf, spearfishing and diving, and on sightseeing trips along the river, to the islands, or to the St. George lighthouse. If you have a specific destination in mind, he can get you there. Call for loading and price information.

**Jeanni's Journeys, Inc.** (320 Patton Street, St. George Island; 850-927-3259; open March 1 through December 30).

Jeanni's Journeys is a one-stop shop for travelers who want to experience more than the beach and bars dotting the coast in and around Apalachicola. Jeanni McMillan, the owner, has been a jill-of-all-trades—a special education instructor in Singapore, an environmental planner, a waitress, a public school teacher—plus, she has spent almost 30 years camping and exploring the Panhandle. Jeanni approaches her tours with an educational bent.

Her trips include sails on her 20-foot Keywest or 23-foot Aqua Sport around local barrier islands, kayaking and canoeing on Owl Creek, St. Vincent, and Little St. George Island, marine experiences where you can snorkel and scallop, overnight camping on a deserted island, sunset bay cruises, castnetting and sand sculpture classes, and just about anything else you can dream up to do in or near the water.

Jeanni's Journeys offers guided tours and daily rentals of sailboats, canoes, surfboards, kayaks, and boogie boards.

**Robinson Brothers Guide Service** (94 Market Street; 850-653-9669; $300 per boat, maximum two anglers per boat).

As the two most famous flats guides in town, Tommy and Chris Robinson know all the secrets about fishing the shallow flats, bays, rivers, and lakes in the area. Depending on the time of year, they'll take you to pompano and redfish on the flats, tarpon that hang out in the creek mouths, and to bluefish and Spanish mackerel around the edges of the flats. The Robinson brothers are also the authorized Orvis dealer in town and have a store right on Market. Check there for schedules and fishing gear.

*Marinas*

**Deep Water Marina** (Water Street; 850-653-8801).
**Miller Marina** (Water Street; 850-653-9521).
**Rainbow Marina** (Water Street; 850-653-8139).

## Golf

**St. Joseph's Bay Country Club** (Route C-30 S., Port St. Joe; 850-227-1751).

This course features an 18-hole, par-72 course.

## Restaurants and Nightlife

**Boss Oysters** (125 Water Street; 850-653-9364).

Overlooking the river, Boss Oysters serves famous Apalachicola oysters 30 ways, from oysters Monterey to oysters Diana. Entrées begin at $9.

**Harry A's** (Bay Shore, St. George Island; 850-927-9810).

This St. George Island tavern and package store—supposedly the oldest on the island—may be casual in style, but the food is anything but. Fresh local fish, shrimp, crab, and oysters are served with a South American flair. Harry A's serves lunch and dinner and has happy hour specials.

**Indian Pass Trading Post and Raw Bar** (Hwy. 98 W of Apalachicola; 850-227-1670).

An oasis along the hot, humid, and sticky Florida Gulf Coast, Indian Pass Trading Post and Raw Bar is the place to stop and sit a spell. Nothing beats a cold brew and fresh oysters on the half-shell from the McNeill family oyster lease. They serve lots of local seafood, and you can also buy refreshments, ice, sunscreen, and anything else you might need for a day at the beach.

**Java Joe's** (86 Commerce Street; 850-653-2608).

This is the place to get the best pressed Cuban sandwiches outside of Miami. As the name says, Joe's also serves good coffee.

**Magnolia Grill** (Avenue E at Hwy. 98 and 11th Street; 850-653-8000).

Folks drive from as far away as Tallahassee to sample Chef Eddie Cass's interpretations of local favorites. Among the most popular entrées: oak-grilled pork tenderloin with sauce Béarnaise, seafood Ponchartrain, and black beans and scallops. Cass is also known for his rich desserts like espresso cake and white chocolate crème brûlée.

The Magnolia Grill is one of the most romantic restaurants in town, but you can still dine in casual attire. Entrées begin at $11.95.

Here are a couple of recipes to try at home:

*Magnolia Grill Escalloped Apalachicola Oysters*

> 2/3 sleeve saltine crackers, crumbled
> 2 dozen freshly shucked Apalachicola oysters
> 1 cup heavy cream
> 1/8 lb. sweet butter
> 2 tbsps. chopped garlic
> 1 tbsp. Worcestershire sauce
> Paprika

In a saucepan, melt the butter, reserving a small amount to drizzle on top before baking. Add the oysters and garlic and cook on medium until outside of oyster starts to curl. Add Worcestershire and cream and bring to a simmer. Add crackers and toss lightly, then place in a buttered casserole dish. Drizzle melted butter and top with two or three dashes of paprika. Place in preheated 350-degree oven until golden brown, 5 to 8 minutes.

Makes four appetizer portions or two entrée portions.

*Boss Oyster's Oysters Monterey*

> 1 dozen oysters on half-shell
> Cooking sherry
> Garlic powder
> 12 ozs. crabmeat
> Monterey Jack cheese
> Black pepper
> Chopped parsley
> Melted butter

Splash cooking sherry on each oyster. Sprinkle with dash of garlic powder, then top each with 1 ounce of crabmeat. Sprinkle Monterey Jack cheese over crabmeat; add dash of black pepper and chopped parsley to each. Top with a splash of butter.

Bake in 350-degree oven or microwave just until cooked through—5 minutes or less.

## Accommodations

**Anchor Realty** (HCR Box 222, St. George Island; 850-927-2735, 800-824-0416).

This realty company offers an assortment of accommodations for rent in the area.

**Cape San Blas Camping Resort** (off CR 30, 20 miles W of Apalachicola; 850-229-6800; www.capesanblas.com/capecamp).

Though it is hardly a resort, this facility offers accommodations that are secluded, modest, and inexpensive. It features six cottages as well as tent and RV pitches. There is a pool, and the camp is located right on the beach.

**Coombs House Inn** (80th 6th Avenue; 850-653-9199).

Built by a lumber baron who saved the finest black cypress from his mills for paneling, this handsome Victorian home was described in a 1905 account as the most elegant home in town. Almost a hundred years later, the description is still accurate. As the town's first bed and breakfast, the home had fallen into disrepair until acclaimed interior designed Lynn Wilson restored it to its original grandeur in the early 1990s.

The 10 rooms are furnished with Victorian reproductions, and each features a modern bathroom with a whirlpool tub. There is an annex half a block away with eight more rooms, and though they are still quite comfortable, they're not as lavish as those in the main house.

There are perks to staying at the Coombs House. If you arrive in Apalachicola by water, the friendly innkeepers, Pamela Barnes and Anthony Erario, will meet you and pick up your bags. Bikes are also free to guests.

**Gibson Inn** (51 Avenue C; 850-653-2191).

When you come into town from the east, the first thing you'll see once you cross the bay is the Gibson Inn, a big blue dollhouse that sits smack in the middle of downtown. This 1907 Victorian-era inn has 31 moderately priced rooms, each with a full bath and television. Tin-roofed verandahs surround both the first and second floors.

The Gibson is also the place to be on Friday night, when the locals head to the restaurant, rated as one of the best in town.

**Magnolia Hall Guest House** (177 5th Street; 850-653-2431).

If you like cozy B&Bs where you can sit around and chat with the owners, then Magnolia Hall is your kind of place. To ensure personal attention, only two rooms are rented out each night.

Built in 1838 by Thomas Orman, a federal land agent, this stately mansion overlooks the bay from a hilltop. Inside, owners Douglas and Anna Gaidry, who bought the home from descendants of Orman, have lovingly restored the house to its original grandeur. The rooms, which are filled with period antique furniture, have telephones and televisions, and each has its own modern private bathroom.

**Pelican Inn** (located on Dog Island; 800-451-5294).

The only way to reach this quaint inn is by small plane or boat. The ferry leaves daily from Carrabelle at 11:00 A.M.

**The Prudential** (123 Gulf Beach Drive W, St. George Island; 850-927-2666, 800-332-5196).

Call for information about condos, townhomes, and hotel rooms for rent in the area.

**Sportsman's Lodge Motel & Marina** (five minutes from Apalachicola, Eastpoint; 850-670-8423).

The Sportsman's Lodge Motel & Marina is nothing fancy, which makes it an ideal spot for sportsmen who are interested in only fishing or hunting. The lodge sits right on Apalachicola Bay. Besides sparse motel-style rooms with equipped kitchenettes, it also offers hook ups for RVs or campers on the property.

**Turtle Beach Inn** (140 Painted Pony Road on Indian Pass; 850-229-9366; turtlebeach@digitalexp.com).

As Gulf County's only beachfront bed and breakfast, Turtle Beach Inn offers spacious guest rooms and a separate guest cottage for rent. Resident owner/manager Trish Petrie prepares fabulous breakfasts, while the Indian Pass Raw Bar is only a short walk away.

## Shopping

Shopaholics will be pleasantly surprised by the quality of boutiques in Apalachicola. You won't find a mall or even a Wal-Mart, but there are plenty of specialty shops in the downtown area to keep your wallet hot. Most of the store owners are artists or experienced retailers who fell in love with the area and moved to town, bringing their eclectic tastes with them. Be forewarned, however, that shop owners cater to tourists and people who have second homes on the island, so you'll find few items at bargain prices.

**George Griffin Pottery** (1 SunCat's Ridge, Sopchoppy; 850-962-9311; open Tuesday–Saturday from 9:00 A.M. to 6:00 P.M.).

Here's your chance to pick up some fabulous pottery from the creator himself. Look for the 15-foot sign off Hwy. 319, then take the dirt road right beside it. George does spontaneous sculptures and individualized functional stoneware. You can order dinnerware, but otherwise he doesn't do special orders. "I've got too many unrealized ideas to get into that," he says.

**Island Adventures** (115 E. Gulf Beach Drive, St. George Island; 850-927-3655).

You'll find everything you need for island life at this tropical boutique. It has hand-carved wooden benches and screens, handmade pottery, an excellent selection of name-brand fishing rods, reels, and accessories, and lots of clothing for ladies. You can also buy or rent bicycles built for two—perfect for a bike ride around the island.

**Riverlily** (82 Commerce Street; 850-653-2441).

If shopping is a major pastime for you while on vacation, then you won't want to miss Riverlily. Exquisite jewelry, candles, ladies' clothing, bath salts, greeting cards—these are just a few of the special little treasures you'll stumble across.

**Sunflowers** (14 Avenue D; 850-653-9144; open Monday–Saturday from 10:00 A.M. to 6:00 P.M., Sunday from 12:00 P.M. to 4:00 P.M.).

This kitchen boutique has everything you need to equip a gourmet kitchen, from glassware and silverware to table linens, pots and pans, and gourmet food. It also has cookbook and grill sections.

**Wefings** (252 Water Street; 850-653-9218; open Monday–Friday from 8:00 A.M. to 4:30 P.M.).

Paint, lights, parts—anything you may need for a boat you'll find at Wefings. An Apalachicola landmark, this Water Street boating supply will order anything it doesn't have in stock for overnight delivery.

## Festivals and Special Events

*March*

### St. George Island Charity Chili Cookoff & Auction

Rain or shine, the first Saturday in March is the day of the St. George Island Charity Chili Cookoff & Auction, the largest regional chili cookoff in the United States. Competition spots are booked a year in advance, and more than 50 cooks compete annually for an opportunity to advance to the nationals. The event raises more than $250,000 a year, with proceeds benefiting the St. George Island volunteer fire department and first responders. Call 850-653-9419 for more information.

*May*

### Historic Tour of Homes

Every first Saturday in May, members of Trinity Episcopal Church in Apalachicola sponsor an historic home tour in downtown Apalachicola. Many of the homes are within walking distance of the church, and the tour is the only time during the year that some of them are open to the public. Call 850-653-9419 for more information.

*June*

### Big Bend Saltwater Classic and Carrabelle Waterfront Festival

Created by the Organization for Artificial Reefs (OAR), this saltwater fishing tournament is the largest non-profit saltwater fishing event in the Florida Panhandle. Over five hundred men, women, and children compete for thousands of dollars in prizes during the three-day Father's Day weekend event held at the Moorings Marina in Carrabelle.

In conjunction with the fishing tournament, the Carrabelle Waterfront Festival held on Marine Street, just off Highway 98, features arts and crafts booths, food vendors, a gumbo cookoff,

*The Seafood Festival is the oldest and largest annual marine and seafood event in Florida.* (Courtesy of the Apalachicola Chamber of Commerce.)

rides aboard the historic *Governor Stone,* and balloon and aircraft rides. Call 850-697-2585 for more information.

*October*

### St. George Island Music Festival

Held the first weekend of the month, the festival features arts and crafts and all sorts of music, from blues to zydeco. There is a different theme each year. The festival is held in the center of St. George Island. Call 850-653-9419.

### St. Vincent Island National Wildlife Refuge Week

The first week in October, the refuge offers transportation on a first-come, first-served basis to the island, and only five groups of 28 people, one group per day, are allowed. The groups are led by a knowledgeable ranger. Call 850-653-8808 for more information.

*November*

### Florida Seafood Festival

The state's oldest and largest annual marine and seafood

event is held the first Saturday in November in Apalachicola. Vendors set up in Battery Park, selling everything from world-famous Apalachicola oysters on the half-shell to mullet-on-a-stick. There are oyster-shucking and oyster-eating contests, the 3.1-mile Red Fish Run, blue crab races for children, educational booths, live musical entertainment, and a blessing of the fleet. King Retsyo (oyster spelled backwards), who reigns over the entire event, arrives at Battery Park aboard the historic *Governor Stone* accompanied by his queen, Miss Florida Seafood. On Sundays after the festival, gospel groups from across the South perform in the park. Call 850-653-9419 for more information.

## Day Trips

**Carrabelle** (Carrabelle Chamber of Commerce; P.O. Drawer DD, Carrabelle, FL 32322; 850-697-2585).

Though Carrabelle is only a short drive east of Apalachicola, the two towns have very distinct personalities and are often considered rivals in everything from high school football to bragging rights on the bay's best oysters. Founded in the late 1800s, Carrabelle's railroads and port made it easy to ship lumber, turpentine, and seafood to other parks of the country. In 1898 a hurricane almost destroyed the town. It rebuilt slowly, buoyed by World War II, when the entire area was used as a training area for the European invasion force. Numerous soldiers came through the area (including Eddie Arnold) and were stationed at Camp Gordon Johnston.

Today, locals like to joke that there's a "great deal of nothing" going on here—no pollution, no traffic, no crime. That's fine for those who like the town's calm, settled way of life, but others are itching to get in on Florida's booming tourist business. Slowly, modern condos and townhouses are popping up along the harbor, replacing the dilapidated oyster houses and warehouses that once occupied waterfront property. Still, it's not hard to discover the small-town charm in this seaside village. Old rusty boats sit around the waterfront like trashed junk cars. In town, death announcements are posted on the door of the post office; outside, the latest local news—everything from yard sales to lost dogs—is stapled to the telephone pole.

If you have time to linger in Carrabelle, visit the Chamber of Commerce or the Carrabelle Realty next to the police station for brochures and information about what's happening in town.

Nicknamed the "Pearl of the Panhandle," Carrabelle's claim to fame is its *police station,* touted as the world's smallest. Once a phone on the wall of a building in the center of town, the station has upgraded to a telephone booth painted in patriotic colors. Calls come in from all over the world, and the former police chief was even a guest on Johnny Carson's *Tonight Show.* Kids often like to steal the station for pranks.

Also downtown is the *Riverwalk,* where Carrabelle's Waterfront Festival is held each June. The *Moorings Marina* is the site of the nationally acclaimed Big Bend Saltwater Classic. The ferry to Dog Island also leaves from the Marina.

For a quick beach break, stop at *Carrabelle Beach* on Highway 98. The sand is white, the water is calm, and you'll find restrooms and picnic tables; but if you decide to lie out, you'll be able to hear the highway traffic behind you. Locals go to the beach on Gulf Beach Drive.

Carrabelle has a lighthouse outside of town that's barely visible from the road. The *Crooked River Lighthouse* is about one-half mile west of town on the right side of Highway 98. You can take the dirt road all the way to the bottom of the lighthouse, but you can't go inside and there's not much to see. At one time, there were two houses next to the lighthouse. These have been moved, and now one sits about two miles away along Highway 98, just past the Tate's Hell Forest sign.

*Lanark Village* east of Carrabelle is now a modest retirement village but was once the home of Camp Gordon, a WWII training camp that Walter Winchell called the "Alcatraz of the Army." There's a six-hole, par-three golf course and Chillas Hall, where you can buy a light breakfast of toast and coffee and chitchat with the locals. Lanark Village looks the same as any other neighborhood, but if you're a war buff, you'll be fascinated at how the old barracks and living quarters have been converted into duplexes and single-family homes.

For eats and entertainment, check out *Hobo's Ice Cream Parlor,* which also has poetry readings. *Julia Mae's* is a down-home

Southern-style restaurant known for its tasty pies. *Shorty's BBQ* next to the ballfield is considered the best in town.

Carrabelle also has a few motels and condos. The pink cinderblock *Beachside Motel* is a perfect example of how the Panhandle looked 30 years ago. It's clean, close to the beach, and as the sign out front says, it's "American-owned." For information on vacation home and condo rentals, call the Chamber of Commerce.

**Gulf County** (P.O. Box 964, Port. St. Joe, FL 32456; 850-227-1223).

Gulf County lies between Apalachicola and Panama City and includes the small villages of Port St. Joe, Wewahitchka, Mexico Beach, Cape San Blas, and Indian Pass. This area has all the characteristics of the North Florida coast—sugar-sand beaches and emerald waters—but tourism has yet to take a strong hold on the region. That means uncrowded beaches but fewer activities for tourists. Here, honey, cattle, a fishery, and a paper mill are the major economic resources. The area was hard hit when the St. Joe Paper Mill closed in 1996.

There are several motels, hotels, and rental cottages available; call the Chamber of Commerce for rental information. Fishing is also good in Gulf County. Try your luck at deep-sea trolling, surf-casting, wading into the grass flats, or fishing the freshwater lakes and ponds. Charter boats leave Mexico Beach and Port St. Joe daily.

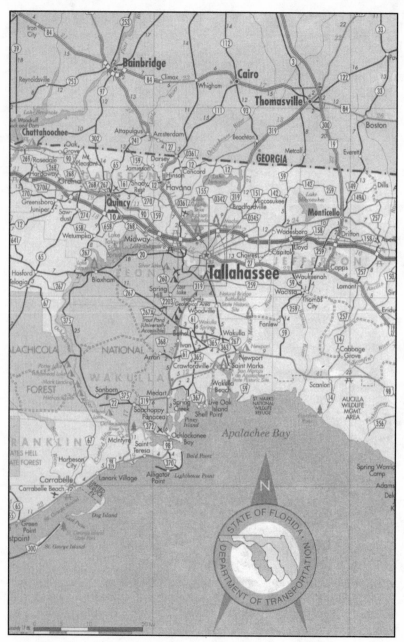

*Tallahassee area.*

# 8

# Tallahassee

## Introduction

There's something rather odd about seeing Tallahassee emblazoned across the front of a touristy T-shirt. Unlike her neon neighbors, the city has no swanky resorts, no sprawling theme parks, and no streets lined with souvenir shops. Closer to Atlanta than Miami, this land-locked, Southern city appears to be at a disadvantage in a state driven by tourism.

In fact, most folks—native Floridians included—think Tallahassee offers little more than college football, state government, and a string of exits along a desolate stretch of Interstate 10.

In reality, it is Tallahassee's lack of tourist hype that is quickly becoming her strong suit. This is what's left of the "old Florida," a rare pocket of natural beauty where patriarch oaks take the place of imposing, high-rise hotels along the sun-dappled skyline.

## History

Geologically speaking, Tallahassee's red hills originally came from Georgia and the Appalachian foothills. The Big Bend area, like the rest of Florida, spent most of its early days under water. Over time, layers of sand and other sediments carried by Northern streams collected on the limestone foundation of the ocean floor, and when the seas subsided, the red

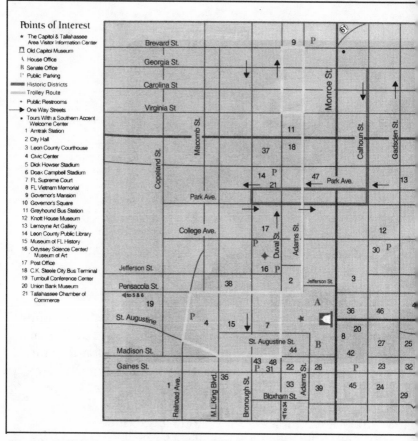

*Downtown Tallahassee.*

clay hills of Tallahassee and the flat, sandy plains of the coastal lowlands slowly emerged.

Much later, nomadic Indian tribes from the north and west migrated to Florida, living temporarily in one location, then moving to another when the area's food supply was depleted. Their descendants, the Apalachees, also hunted and fished, but they eventually became farmers, planting and harvesting domesticated crops such as corn, beans, and squash. Farming supplemented their diet, yet more importantly, it was instrumental in the Apalachees' transition from a nomadic to a more sedentary lifestyle.

Prosperous years followed, and the Apalachees evolved into a highly advanced civilization, with trade routes stretching the entire continent. Goods were traded with tribes as far north as

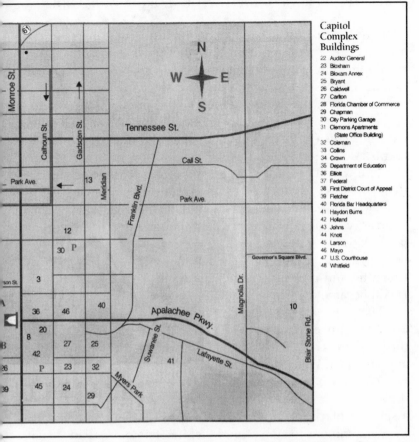

(Courtesy of the Tallahassee Area Convention and Visitors Bureau.)

Minnesota and as far south, as some archaeologists believe, as South America. Consequently, Tallahassee quickly became a regional center for the area's commerce, and social, political, and economic systems grew increasingly complex.

Early explorers visited Apalachee territory as early as 1528, but it wasn't until 1539 that Hernando de Soto led six hundred men to the area in search of purported riches. De Soto's winter camp has long been thought to be the site of the first Christmas Mass in North America, a theory supported by the 1987 discovery of brass chain mail, coins, pig bones, and pottery shards dating the present-day site to that particular time period.

Sometime before 1656, two Franciscan missions were established in Tallahassee by missionaries from the Spanish settlement at Saint Augustine. At the time, relations between the two groups were strained, but the missions continued to grow, and the population of both Spaniards and Christianized Indians had steadily increased by the end of the 17th century.

In the 1700s, however, the Apalachee population was virtually wiped out when Governor James Moore of South Carolina led an English military expedition against the mission settlements. Moore's troops destroyed the missions, and those Indians who weren't murdered were captured, sold into slavery in the Carolinas, or relocated on the Oconee River in Georgia.

It was more than a hundred years later before Florida became a territory of the newly formed United States. In 1821 President James Monroe appointed Andrew Jackson the provisional or military governor of Florida, a position he held for 80 days before resigning and returning to his Tennessee home. William Pope DuVal became the first territorial governor in 1822.

The cities of Saint Augustine and Pensacola were flourishing, but the distance between the two made it increasingly difficult for the legislative council to meet. As a compromise, Governor DuVal appointed Dr. William H. Simmons of Saint Augustine and John Lee Williams of Pensacola to set out on horseback and explore the area between the Ochlockonee and Suwannee Rivers to find a suitable place for a permanent capital. Williams finally persuaded Simmons to agree upon the site of an old Indian village, Tallahassee, meaning "old town" or "old fields."

Just as the Indians who came centuries before, settlers from across the Southeast soon arrived, attracted by Tallahassee's rich, fertile soils and abundant wildlife and vegetation. Still, it's hard to imagine the difficulties those first pioneers confronted in settling the city. Ralph Waldo Emerson disliked his 1827 visit so much that he described Tallahassee as "a grotesque place ... rapidly settled by public officers, land speculators, and desperadoes."

Yet the wild and spirited character of early Tallahassee continued to attract settlers. By 1845, when Florida became a state and Tallahassee the official state capital, Leon county had a population of 11,500. The prime meridian marker in the heart of town marks the spot from which all Florida land surveys are calculated.

In 1861 on the eve of the Civil War, Tallahassee hosted the secession convention in which Florida became the third state to secede from the Union. As the state capital, Tallahassee was the base for all of Florida's wartime activity, and the state as a whole provided vital support to the Confederate cause. Even so, Florida was not considered a major threat in the war, and the closest combat to Tallahassee was the Battle of Natural Bridge near St. Marks. When the Confederate armies were finally defeated, Tallahassee was the only state capital east of the Mississippi that had not fallen to the Union during the war.

At the turn of the century, the extensive plantation system spreading across Leon County and into south Georgia was revived—not by Southerners—but by Northerners who turned the land into winter "hunting lodges" or "shooting plantations" for quail. More original plantations now remain in and around Tallahassee than anyplace else in the country; there are 71 plantations covering 300,000 acres.

Once an agricultural hot spot, today Tallahassee's economy is driven by government and education. It is the site of two universities: Florida State University (FSU), once a women's college, and Florida A&M University (FAMU), one of the preeminent black universities in the nation. Over 250,000 people call the Tallahassee Metropolitan Area home, and that number swells by more than 50,000 each August, when college students return to town. One poll ranked Tallahassee as the 15th fastest-growing city in America. Over an 18-year period, Leon County grew from 149,000 to 233,000. In 1998, *Money* magazine named Tallahassee as one of the best cities in the country to live in.

Over the years, several attempts were made to move the capital from Tallahassee to Orlando. All failed, and in the 1990s there has been expansion of the state buildings to the outlying areas of town. Visitors should keep in mind that the legislature meets for 60 days beginning in March of each year; this makes it especially hard to find accommodations or make reservations at area restaurants.

### Contact Information

The visitor's center at the capitol building has lots of brochures on Tallahassee sites and information about the free downtown trolley, which you can catch at the corner of College

Street and Adams every 15 minutes. You can also visit the Talla-hassee Area Convention and Visitors Bureau down the street. The bureau is open Monday–Friday from 8:00 A.M. to 5:00 P.M. and Saturday–Sunday from 9:00 A.M. to 3:00 P.M.

Note: Tallahassee is on Eastern Standard Time, which makes it one hour ahead of the rest of the Panhandle.

**Tallahassee Area Convention and Visitors Bureau** (200 West College Avenue, Tallahassee, FL, 32301; 800-628-2866, 850-413-9200; www.co.leon.fl.us/visitors/index.htm).

### Average Temperatures

| | |
|---|---|
| Spring | 80° |
| Summer | 91° |
| Fall | 81° |
| Winter | 65° |

### Transportation

**Amtrak** (918½ Railroad Avenue; 800-872-7245, 850-224-2779).

Connecting in Tallahassee, Amtrak offers east-west service aboard the transcontinental *Sunset Limited* with stops in Los Angeles, New Orleans, Jacksonville, Orlando, and Miami.

**Annett Bus Lines** (800-282-3655; 850-877-2163)

Annett provides an airport shuttle for individuals and groups to downtown, hotels, and other attractions in and out of town.

**Budget Rent a Car** (800-527-0700, 850-575-9191)

This rental agency offers mini-vans, passenger vans and cars, free mileage, and no drop fees in some areas. There are three locations in town: 1415 Capital Circle SW, 3300 Capital Circle SW at the airport, and 628 N. Monroe Street.

**Dollar Rent a Car** (800-800-4000, 850-575-4255)

Dollar offers mini-vans, passenger vans and cars, and free mileage in Florida and surrounding states. It is located at 1900 Capital Circle SW.

**Greyhound Bus Lines** (112 W. Tennessee Street; 800-231-2222, 850-222-4240).

Bus line with routes throughout the United States.

**Tallahassee Regional Airport** (3300 Capital Circle SW; 800-610-1995, 850-891-7800).

*The downtown trolley is a fast and fun way to visit the sites in the capitol complex area.* (Courtesy of the Tallahassee Area Convention and Visitors Bureau.)

US Airways, Delta, and Continental are the current carriers flying out of Tallahassee.

**Taltran City Bus** (850-891-5200)

This is an extensive public-transit system with a modern transfer facility, the C.K. Steele Plaza, located near FSU.

**Trolley Tours** (departs from the plaza level of the New Capitol; 850-413-9200; operates Monday–Friday from 7:00 A.M. to 6:00 P.M., Saturday–Sunday from 9:00 A.M. to 3:00 P.M.; free).

Wooden slatted seats, brass handrails, and a cable car gong make this streetcar replica a fun way to see downtown sites. Trolley route maps are available at the visitor information center at the capitol.

**V.I.P. Star & Tours Limo Service** (850-681-6062, 850-298-2198)

Guided limo tours let you see Tallahassee in style. Call ahead to make an appointment.

**Yellow Cab** (850-575-1653)

Yellow provides cabs and shuttle van services around Tallahassee.

**Pelican Picks**

**Leon County's Canopy Roads**

Taking a leisurely drive down one of Tallahassee's canopy roads is like stepping into a scene from *Forrest Gump*. Majestic live oak trees dripping with Spanish moss line the roads; their branches intermingle above to form a dappled green tunnel. Throughout Tallahassee, you'll find spots where the road is indeed canopied by tree limbs, but these roads—the best and longest examples—are designated canopy roads, which means that efforts are being made to respect the roads' scenic, cultural, historic, and archaeological character. I'd suggest taking a drive as soon as possible. While the roads are protected for now, their fate is uncertain in the path of progress.

Along *Old Bainbridge Road,* archaeologists have found remains of Native American villages and Spanish rancheros. The massive trees here are protected, and new development within a hundred feet of the road is monitored. *Old St. Augustine Road,* once known as Royal Road, dates back to at least the 1600s when it linked the Spanish missions of Leon County to St. Augustine. This road also served as the foundation for Florida's first American road, the Pensacola–St. Augustine Highway. A designated canopy road, *Miccosukee Road* began as an Indian footpath leading to the Native American village of Mikasuki. Historic *Centerville Road* is one of the most picturesque in Leon County. It leads to *Moccasin Gap Road* and *Magnolia Road,* two of the oldest in the county. Magnolia Road, now a narrow dirt road, once led to the antebellum port of Magnolia on the St. Marks River. When the St. Marks Railroad linked Tallahassee to St. Marks in the 1830s, Magnolia swiftly fell into decline and all but vanished. *Meridian Road,* another designated canopy road, was created in 1824 when federal surveyor Benjamin Clements laid lengths of chain through the

Tallahassee woods to establish the prime meridian as the point of beginning for all land surveys in the state of Florida.

**A Taste of Italy** (850-878-9738)

Ariella Monti-Graziadei brings the tastes of her childhood in Northern Italy to life in cooking classes that explore the nuances of northern Italian cuisine. You'll master general principles and specific techniques, preparing authentic dishes, menus, and variations for individual tastes. Register for individual classes on baking, cooking with fish, breads and soups, and the basics, or gather a group together for a Sotto Chef Dinner Party, where you'll learn to prepare your favorite dishes and then enjoy a full-course dinner.

**O'Toole's Herb Farm** (Rocky Ford Road, Madison; 850-973-3629; open Monday–Friday from 9:00 A.M. to 6:00 P.M., Saturday from 9:00 A.M. to 4:00 P.M., Sunday by appointment; free, costs for workshops vary).

Spend a day in the country at O'Toole's Herb Farm, where you can walk amid acres of organically grown herbs, purchase a few items to take home from the greenhouse, or attend one of the many workshops on gardening, cooking, and aromatherapy—all with herbs, of course—that are held throughout the year.

This farm is a labor of love for owners, Jim and Betty, and they'll be happy to show you around or answer any of your gardening questions.

**Seven Hills to the Sea Bicycle Tour** (Office of Greenways and Trails, Mail Station 795, 3900 Commonwealth Boulevard, Tallahassee, FL 32399-3000; 850-488-3701; www.dep.state.fl.us/gwt).

A 283-mile loop around the Panhandle, this bicycle tour starts at Wakulla Springs State Park and continues through coastal areas and the red clay hills of the Piedmont. In all, the tour links six state parks.

Named for the seven hills of Tallahassee, the tour is divided into five day trips and is fairly easy to follow. Call and request a map of the tour.

**Blackberry Patch** (5773 Veteran's Memorial Drive; 850-893-3163).

There's nothing better than biscuits sopping with homemade blackberry jam. For a taste of the South, visit Geraldine Rudd at the Blackberry Patch, a cottage industry that specializes in homemade jams, jellies, flavored honeys, vinegars, syrups, and biscuit and pancake mix. "We're not real fancy," says Rudd, "but people are more than welcome to drive out and visit our kitchen and retail outlet." You'll see jams and jellies being made, packaged, and packed for shipment. Rudd says they are always working during the weekend, but if you want to visit over a weekend, call ahead and make an appointment. Blackberry Patch products—all made from old-fashioned family recipes—are sold throughout the United States in specialty stores and gourmet food shops.

### Attractions

**Alfred B. Maclay State Gardens** (3540 Thomasville Road; 850-487-4556; open daily from 8:00 A.M. to sunset; $3.25 per vehicle; http://www.dep.state.fl.us/parks/bigbend/maclay.html).

About 100 varieties of camellias and more than 50 varieties of azaleas are the show stoppers in this state park, but there are also more than 160 other species of exotic and native plants on display. Situated on a hillside overlooking pristine Lake Hall, the property was once a hunting lodge and home to New York financier Alfred B. Maclay. Mrs. Maclay donated the property to the state in 1953.

The 1930's house on the grounds is surrounded by ornamental gardens that capitalize on each season's blooming beauties. Spring is the best time to see blossoming trees, flowers, and shrubs, but something will be in bloom no matter what time of the year you visit. In addition to the more than two hundred

*The reflecting pond at Alfred B. Maclay State Gardens is one of the many attractions within this state park.* (Courtesy of the Tallahassee Area Convention and Visitors Bureau.)

floral varieties including azaleas, dogwoods, and camellias, native animals such as birds, deer, bobcat, fox, alligators, turtles, and fish make the gardens their home.

Lake Hall, a natural freshwater lake on the property, has a sandy beach, nature trails, picnic tables, grills, fishing, swimming, boating, and a lifeguard during the summer season. Guided garden tours are conducted on Saturdays and Sundays during the peak bloom, around mid-March. Call ahead for dates and times. The home, which is furnished as it appeared when the Maclay family lived there, is open January through April. Tours are self-guided.

**Apalachicola National Forest** (SW of Tallahassee; 850-942-9300; recreation areas open daily from 8:00 A.M. to sunset; $2 for day use of recreation areas, camping fees begin at $4).

The largest of Florida's national forests, the Apalachicola National Forest covers more than one-half million acres and is home to animals like black bears and wild pigs. Contrary to belief, the forest does not border the coast, but is situated inland between Apalachicola and Tallahassee.

The *Florida National Scenic Trail* crosses both districts on the Apalachicola. It begins on Highway 12 about 10 miles south of Bristol and runs east to Porter Lake Recreation Area near the Ochlockonee River, through Bradwell Bay Wilderness and exits at Highway 319 at Medart. The main trailhead is at Camel Lake Recreation Area, but several access points are available along the entire route. Additional trails include *Munson Hills* for off-road bicycles and *Vinzant Trail* for equestrian use.

The *Leon Sinks Geological Area* just off Highway 319 in Crawfordville has several prominent geological features. There are wet sinkholes, numerous depressions, a natural bridge, and a disappearing stream, all created by rain and groundwater that have dissolved underlying limestone bedrock, thereby causing the ground to cave in, or sink. The Leon Sinks lie in the Woodville Karst Plain that extends from Tallahassee southward to the Gulf of Mexico. An observation platform at Big Dismal Sink offers a view of more than 75 different plants cascading down the sink's steep walls.

For a leisurely drive, follow the *Apalachee Savannahs Scenic Byway*, a pleasant drive through some of Florida's most scenic landscapes. Take Highway 12 to Hwy. 379, then head south on Highway 65 at the Sumatra community.

Camping is allowed in most areas of the forest except during general gun-hunting season. During this time camping is allowed only in developed recreation areas and designated seasonal hunt camps. Camping stays are limited to 14 days except during hunting season at designated hunt camps.

Canoeing and boating opportunities are abundant in the Apalachicola Forest. The *Sopchoppy River* is awaiting designation by Congress as a Wild and Scenic River and is a popular destination for canoers who prefer calm, downstream floating. The *Ochlockonee River* has been designated for study as a Wild and Scenic River and is another favorite corridor for boating and fishing. *New River* is to be studied for Wild and Scenic designation. Located inside the Mud Swamp/New River Wilderness, it requires experienced canoers to navigate successfully.

**Birdsong Nature Center** (20 miles N of Tallahassee, four miles N of the Florida/Georgia border on Meridian Road; 912-377-4408; open Wednesday and Friday from 9:00 A.M. to noon, Saturday from 9:00 A.M. to 2:00 P.M., Sunday from 1:00 P.M. to 5:00 P.M.; $5 for adults, $2.50 for children under 12).

The 565 acres of lush fields, wooded forests, and undisturbed swamp of this nature preserve offer a pristine haven for birds and other native wildlife.

Betty and Ed Komarek, both dedicated naturalists, purchased the land in 1938 and used controlled burning and other land management techniques to transform this Georgia farm into a haven for wildlife. They began Birdsong in 1981, and it is now a non-profit preserve.

While visiting, hike the Bluebird Trail, where a series of 30 nest boxes are maintained and monitored throughout the year for activity and nesting success. Also take time to look through the Bird Window, where you can learn to identify and observe the center's feathered friends. Nature programs are offered year round.

**Black Archives Research Center and Museum** (Historic Carnegie Library on the FAMU campus at Martin Luther King Boulevard and Gamble Street; 850-599-3020; open Monday–Friday from 9:00 A.M. to 4:00 P.M.; free).

The Black Archives Research Center and Museum is one of the most extensive archives and artifacts collections of African-American history in the Southeast. While many other museums of its kind are now popping up throughout the country, this established research facility has been in existence almost 30 years.

The museum and archives were started from the personal collection of FAMU professor James N. Eaton and is located in the restored Carnegie Library building on the FAMU campus. There is a branch of the museum downtown in the Union Bank Building that houses a history of Florida's African-Americans. Donations of memorabilia, artifacts, and papers from faculty and community members led to the museum's growth.

According to archivist Murell Dawson, the museum provides visitors with a first-hand look at the lives and experiences of African-Americans and people of color throughout the world. A 500-piece Ethiopian cross collection, slave irons from pre-Civil War times, and African tribal masks are among the many exhibits.

In the archives section, more than half a million papers, including rare books, newspapers, photographs, maps, and personal manuscripts, are used as cross-reference points and are available as research materials. "Our motto is 'Afro-American history is the history of America,'" says Dawson. "We have been here in all the major eras, and we have contributed to this country's history. The archives and museum simply provide examples of our contributions."

**Calhoun Street Historic District**

Listed on the National Register of Historic Places, Calhoun Street was once known as "Gold Dust Street" because of the many prominent planters, merchants, lawyers, and governors who lived here. There are several residences of note:

The *Bowen House,* a Greek Revival-style home built in 1830, is the oldest in the district and one of the first examples of a pre-fab house. The New England pine was cut, numbered, tagged, mortised, and pegged, then sent South for instant construction. The build-by-number markings can still be seen on the window shutters.

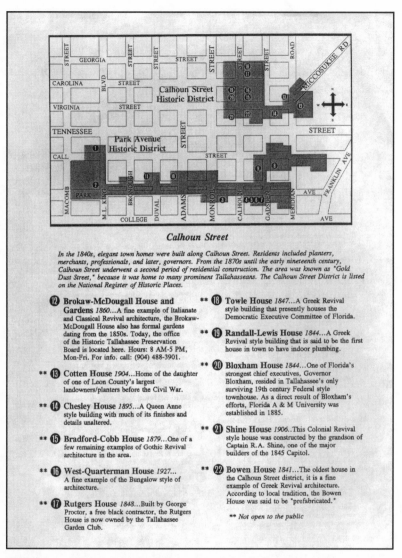

## Calhoun Street

*In the 1840s, elegant town homes were built along Calhoun Street. Residents included planters, merchants, professionals, and later, governors. From the 1870s until the early nineteenth century, Calhoun Street underwent a second period of residential construction. The area was known as "Gold Dust Street," because it was home to many prominent Tallahasseans. The Calhoun Street District is listed on the National Register of Historic Places.*

**⑫ Brokaw-McDougall House and Gardens** *1860*...A fine example of Italianate and Classical Revival architecture, the Brokaw-McDougall House also has formal gardens dating from the 1850s. Today, the office of the Historic Tallahassee Preservation Board is located here. Hours: 8 AM-5 PM, Mon-Fri. For info. call: (904) 488-3901.

** **⑬ Cotten House** *1904*...Home of the daughter of one of Leon County's largest landowners/planters before the Civil War.

** **⑭ Chesley House** *1895*...A Queen Anne style building with much of its finishes and details unaltered.

** **⑮ Bradford-Cobb House** *1879*...One of a few remaining examples of Gothic Revival architecture in the area.

** **⑯ West-Quarterman House** *1927*... A fine example of the Bungalow style of architecture.

** **⑰ Rutgers House** *1848*...Built by George Proctor, a free black contractor, the Rutgers House is now owned by the Tallahassee Garden Club.

** **⑱ Towle House** *1847*...A Greek Revival style building that presently houses the Democratic Executive Committee of Florida.

** **⑲ Randall-Lewis House** *1844*...A Greek Revival style building that is said to be the first house in town to have indoor plumbing.

** **⑳ Bloxham House** *1844*...One of Florida's strongest chief executives, Governor Bloxham, resided in Tallahassee's only surviving 19th century Federal style townhouse. As a direct result of Bloxham's efforts, Florida A & M University was established in 1885.

** **㉑ Shine House** *1906*..This Colonial Revival style house was constructed by the grandson of Captain R.A. Shine, one of the major builders of the 1845 Capitol.

** **㉒ Bowen House** *1841*...The oldest house in the Calhoun Street district, it is a fine example of Greek Revival architecture. According to local tradition, the Bowen House was said to be "prefabricated."

*\*\* Not open to the public*

*Tallahassee Historic District.* (Courtesy of the Tallahassee Area Convention and Visitors Bureau.)

The 1860 *Brokaw–McDougall House* (850-488-3901) is a two-story, Italianate and Classical Revival construction with formal gardens dating from the 1850s. Today, it houses the Historic Tallahassee Preservation Board, where you can pick up maps of the downtown historic districts.

The *Rutgers House,* circa 1848, was built by George Proctor, a free black contractor. The house is now the home of the Tallahassee Garden Club.

**De Soto State Historic Site** (1022 De Soto Park Drive off Lafayette Street; 850-922-6007; free).

Before the discovery of this historic site, archaeologists and historians could only speculate about the location of De Soto's encampment during his first winter in Florida. When physical evidence was uncovered, the proof was overwhelming. Among the 40,000 artifacts recovered were Spanish and Indian pottery dating to the 16th century, as well as glass trade beads, links of chain mail armor, coins from the early 1500s, and the jaw of a pig, all of which were unknown to the New World.

Currently, the site is the only confirmed De Soto camp in North America, and it is located less than a mile from the state capitol building. Artifacts, along with the knowledge that De Soto camped here during the winter, give credibility to Tallahassee's claim that this was the site of the first Christmas celebrated in North America. An annual Winter Encampment is held each January. Call for information on tours.

**Florida State Capitol—Both Old and New** (Monroe Street at Apalachee Parkway; 850-487-1902; open Monday through Friday from 9:00 A.M. to 4:30 P.M., Saturday from 10:00 A.M. to 4:30 P.M., Sunday from noon to 4:30 P.M.; free).

Perched atop one of Tallahassee's highest hills, the close proximity of the Old Capitol and the New Capitol is a nice contrast between the "old" and "new" Florida.

The New Capitol was completed in 1977 and from its 22nd floor you can see all the way to the Gulf Coast on a clear day. The governor's office is on the plaza level; the secretary of state, members of the governor's cabinet, legislative offices, and the Tallahassee Area Visitor Information Center are also housed in the building, which buzzes with activity from March through May during the legislative session. It sits only a few hundred feet

*Florida has two capitols; the Old Capitol, restored to its 1902 grandeur, and the New Capitol, completed in 1977.* (Courtesy of the Tallahassee Area Convention and Visitors Bureau.)

behind the Old Capitol because original plans called for the old building to be destroyed.

With its red candy-striped awnings, stained-glass dome, glass rotunda, and historically accurate House and Senate chambers, the Old Capitol is a pre-Civil War structure completed in 1845 that served as the first Florida state capitol building. Although additional wings were added over time, these were removed during the reconstruction process that restored the building to its 1902 simplicity. Much of the renovation was done as a massive treasure hunt. Few documents were kept on the original decor, so vintage photos, postcards, broken bits of glass found between the walls, and paint analyses were used in the building's restoration. Today, the Old Capitol is part of the Museum of Florida History and offers exhibits on the state's political and social development. Both self-guided tours and guided tours are available.

**Florida Supreme Court** (500 S. Duval Street; 850-922-5270; free).

The court is in session the first full week of each month. Sessions generally begin around 9:00 A.M. and continue until they finish, usually around noon. The court sessions are open to the public; call ahead for times and to see which cases are being heard.

**Foster Tanner Fine Arts Gallery** (Florida A&M University; 850-599-3161; open Monday–Friday from 9:00 A.M. to 5:00 P.M.; free).

Described as "a little jewel sitting in the middle of the FAMU campus," the Foster Tanner Fine Arts Gallery predominantly features local, regional, and national African-American artists working in all types of media, although the exhibitions are not exclusive to African-American art.

"Anyone interested in the arts should visit the gallery," says Yvonne Tucker, an artist and professor at FAMU in the Department of Visual Arts, Humanities, and Theatre. "With its cozy, intimate feeling and the high quality of the exhibitions, they'll really be in for a treat."

**FSU "Flying High" Circus** (Chieftain Way on the FSU campus; 850-644-4874; performs in April; http://mailer.fsu.edu/-~mpeters/fsucircus.html).

Florida State may be the only university in the nation to give credits for clowning around. Composed of amateur students turned circus performers, this big-top circus offers a stage and aerial presentation rivaling any professional circus, without the use of animals. Tightrope walkers, jugglers, clowns, and gymnasts are among the performers in the show's 18 to 22 acts—all performed under a big-top circus tent.

The circus was started in 1947 by Jack Haskin, who was looking for a coed activity for the women on campus and the men who were just returning from the war. Today, the circus performs at FSU, as well as throughout the Southeast, and participates in a summer recreational program at Callaway Gardens in Georgia.

Cost varies; call for prices for matinees and evening performances.

**FSU Museum of Fine Arts** (corner of Copeland Street and Park Avenue; 850-644-6836; open Monday–Friday from 10:00 A.M. to 4:00 P.M., Saturday–Sunday from 1:00 P.M. to 4:00 P.M.; free).

A small university museum, this gallery features contemporary and traditional rotating exhibits of regional artists, as well as works from FSU students.

**FSU School of Dance** (located at the corner of Copeland Street and College Avenue; 850-644-1023).

Ranked second in the nation, this university dance school offers a full season of performances at Ruby Diamond Auditorium. Ticket prices and schedules vary; call for more information.

**Fun Station, Inc.** (located at 2821 Sharer Road; 850-383-0788; open Monday–Thursday from 10:00 A.M. to 11:00 P.M., Friday from 10:00 A.M. to midnight, Saturday from 9:00 A.M. to midnight, Sunday from 11:00 A.M. to 11:00 P.M.).

While putt-putt golf and amusement parks such as these are common in Panama City and Pensacola, Fun Station is one of the few in Tallahassee. This park features 36 holes of miniature golf, a 20,000-square-foot arcade, bumper boats, batting cages, a pizza kitchen, and Actual Reality Laser Tag direct from Edmonton, Canada.

**Goodwood Plantation** (Miccosukee Road and Medical Drive; 850-877-4202; open Monday–Friday from 8:00 A.M. to 5:00 P.M.; free).

*The governor's mansion is located a mile from the capitol.*
(Courtesy of the Tallahassee Area Convention and Visitors
Bureau.)

The grounds and gardens of one of Tallahassee's most significant antebellum plantations are currently under restoration, with completion scheduled for the end of 1999. The barn will be converted into a state-of-the-art conference center, and the skating rink will become an amphitheater. In the meantime, you can stop by the office and pick up information, then tour the grounds. Be sure to walk around the swimming pool, where you'll see a door leading underneath it. This is the entrance to the old coal furnace, which heated the pool during the winter months.

**Governor's Mansion** (700 North Adams Street; 850-488-4661; tours offered only March through May; free).

If it weren't for the massive wrought-iron fence surrounding the property, no one would guess that the Florida governor's mansion lies nestled behind the shady magnolias on the grounds. Built in 1956, the Georgian-style Southern mansion features a portico designed similarly to that of Andrew Jackson's Tennessee home, the Hermitage. Inside, the interior is furnished with 18th- and 19th-century collectibles, with state rooms displaying gifts from foreign dignitaries. Located as it is only a mile from the capitol, the governor could easily walk to and from work.

**Gulf Specimen Marine Lab** (Hwy. 98 in Panacea; 850-984-5297; open Monday–Friday from 9:00 A.M. to 5:00 P.M., Saturday from 10:00 A.M. to 4:00 P.M., Sunday from noon to 4:00 P.M.; $4 for adults, $2 for children under 12; www.adsul.com/-gulfspecimen/).

Discover the wonder of marine biology through interactive touch aquariums featuring native marine life and education and demonstration programs. Unlike the popular city aquariums that emphasize large marine animals, this laboratory focuses on sea horses, hermit crabs, spiny box fish, and other small creatures of the sea. Pick up sea squirts and starfish or watch as biologists pack flaming red sponges and sea horses for shipment to schools and research centers. Group tours are available.

**Historic Tallahassee Tours** (850-222-4143; cost ranges from $6 for adults and $4 for students for walking and driving tours to $15 per person for carriage rides; www.christopher.org/tallahassee/tours).

Experience the history of Tallahassee with three exciting walking tours led by Maynard Jackson. Explore historic downtown with a leisurely walking tour, enjoy a 45-minute horse-drawn carriage tour complete with costumed guide, or take a 90-minute driving tour throughout the area. Reservations are suggested but not required.

**Lake Jackson State Archaeological Site** (Hwy. 27 at Crowder Road; 850-922-6007, 850-562-0042; open daily from 8:00 A.M. to sunset; $2 per vehicle; http://www.dep.state.fl.us/parks/big-bend/jackson.html).

Three earth temple mounds serve as a reminder of the complex Native American civilization located here from the 1200s through the 1500s. Considered one of the most important archaeological sites in North Florida, the Lake Jackson Mounds represent what is known as the Fort Walton period.

There are six temple mounds and a burial mound, the largest of which is 36 feet high and more than 78 feet long. Some of the artifacts excavated from here are astounding, particularly a copper breastplate showing a dancing falcon figure that is now on display at the Museum of Florida History. Kiosks provide background information on the history of the site, and interpretative programs and guided tours are given upon advance request. You can climb to the top of the mounds or hike a one-fourth mile nature trail past the ruins of a grist mill dam and earthen dike. Also on the property are the ruins of an early 19th-century plantation built by Col. Robert Butler, adjutant to Gen. Andrew Jackson. The site has a picnic area.

**Lake Talquin State Recreation Area** (Vause Road; 850-922-6007; open daily from 8:00 A.M. to sunset; $3.25 per vehicle; http://www.dep.state.fl.us/parks/bigbend/talquin.html).

Picnic sites, fishing, boating, and nature walks among rolling hills, deep ravines and thick forests of pine and hardwoods await visitors. This park is also home to osprey, bald eagles, and wild turkeys.

**Legislative Sessions** (begin in April and last into June; call 488-6167 for information).

The Florida legislature convenes each spring for 60 days. If you're interested in seeing these lawmakers in action, you can sit in on both the House and Senate. Call ahead for times and a schedule of what will be debated.

**Lemoyne Art Foundation** (125 N. Gadsden Street; 850-222-8800; open Tuesday–Saturday from 10:00 A.M. to 5:00 P.M., Sunday from 1:00 P.M. to 5:00 P.M.; $1 for adults and children ages 12 and up, free on Sunday).

Incorporated in 1963, LeMoyne Art Foundation is the city's oldest art gallery. Both permanent and traveling exhibits by local, regional, and national visual artists are routinely featured in the gallery. In addition, the magnificent gardens laid out in the back of the gallery offer an elegant backdrop for the sculpture displayed on the grounds and the art openings sponsored by the museum.

LeMoyne is a supporter of community arts and offers a variety of classes and workshops on various art topics for both adults and children throughout the year. Since 1968, LeMoyne has been housed in the historic Meginniss–Munroe antebellum home.

The foundation is named in honor of Jacques LeMoyne, an amateur artist and explorer who came to Florida in the 1500s. His primary responsibility was mapping Florida's sea coast, towns, and rivers, and portraying the dwellings of the area's natives.

**Museum of Art/Tallahassee** (Capital Cultural Center at Kleman Plaza on S. Duval Street; 850-671-5001).

Housed in a new downtown building along with the Odyssey Science Center, the Museum of Art/Tallahassee was opened in January 1999. The museum features both permanent and temporary exhibitions. Call for prices and information.

**Museum of Florida History** (500 S. Bronough Street behind the capitol; 850-488-1484; open Monday–Friday from 9:00 A.M. to 4:30 P.M., Saturday from 10:00 A.M. to 4:30 P.M., Sunday and holidays from noon to 4:30 P.M.; free).

This state of Florida museum is one of the perks of being a capital city. With exhibits ranging from the prehistoric to the present, the museum is a visual timeline of the people and events who shaped the Sunshine State.

Buckskin clothing embellished with elaborate beadwork, and 14-foot canoes, each carved from a single tree, offer visitors a glimpse of the lifestyles of Florida's first inhabitants, the Indians. Treasures from old Spanish galleons provide insight to the explorers who tried to claim Florida as their own.

Pioneer homesteads resembling those described by Marjorie Keenan Rawlings exemplify the simplicity and hardship of pioneer life. And above it all, a nine-foot mastodon skeleton, assembled from bones cast from a mastodon discovered at nearby Wakulla Springs, serves as a towering reminder of Florida's earliest days. Permanent exhibits such as these are enhanced by traveling tours, special events, and educational programs that frequently feature Florida's various cultures and environments.

**National High Magnetic Field Laboratory** (1800 E. Paul Dirac Drive in Innovation Park; 850-644-0311, 850-644-2943; group tours available by appointment Monday–Friday; free).

This high-tech laboratory for scientific research and engineering conducts experiments critical to modern technologies such as magnetic resonance imaging, semiconductors, and high temperature superconductors. The annual open house features hands-on activities, demonstrations, displays, tours, and more.

**Natural Bridge Springs & Natural Bridge State Historic Site**
(CR 363, Woodville; 850-922-6007, 850-925-6216; open daily
from 8:00 A.M. to sunset; free; http://www.dep.state.fl.us/-
parks/bigbend/bridge.html).

Just southeast of Tallahassee, the Natural Bridge Springs are
a popular watering hole for locals who like to snorkel, scuba-dive,
and fish; they are also a good place to hike and picnic.

Nearby is the Natural Bridge State Historic Site, a rural park
that was the site of a major Civil War battle where Confederate
soldiers stood firm against a Yankee advance on St. Marks.

**Odyssey Science Center** (Capital Cultural Center at Kleman
Plaza on S. Duval; 850-671-5001; www.odysseysciencecenter.org).

Opened in October 1998, Odyssey is the first interactive,
hands-on science center in Tallahassee. The center is housed
along with the Museum of Art in a new building downtown
behind the capitol. Call for prices and information.

**Park Avenue Historic District**

Originally the northern boundary of the city, Park Avenue was
a two-hundred-foot clearing that protected the city from Indian
attack. Parks were established in the clearing around the turn of
the century. In 1905 Mrs. Mary Frances Chittenden petitioned
the city to name the street Park Avenue instead of its former
McCarthy Street so that she could print a "more sophisticated"
street name on her son's wedding invitations. The Park Avenue
Historic District is listed on the National Register of Historic
Places, and includes:

The *Chittenden House,* built in 1841. Originally bought with
Louisiana Lottery winnings totaling a whopping two thousand
dollars, the home has been a hospital, boarding house, and popular dining spot for Tallahassee legislators.

*Old City Cemetery.* Dating to 1829, the cemetery is the final
resting place for pioneers, slaves, and members from both the
Confederate and Federal armies. Napoleon's nephew, Achille
Murat, Prince of Naples, is buried here.

The *Meginnis–Munroe House.* Once a hospital for wounded sol-
ders, this 1854 home is now the home of the LeMoyne Art Foundation, which hosts permanent and traveling art exhibitions.

*First Presbyterian Church.* This 1838 church is the only one in
the city that dates from territorial days.

*Owner LuElla Knott wrote poems about the furniture and accessories in her home, which is now a local museum.* (Courtesy of the Tallahassee Area Convention and Visitors Bureau.)

The *Knott House Museum.*
"I'm just an old, old home,
And you are welcome here;
Listen and look, and find in me
Spirit and atmosphere."

There's more rhyme and reason to this museum than just a display of fine antiques and turn-of-the-century memorabilia. Rather, this carefully restored home at 301 Park Avenue depicts life as it existed in the 1930s, from the yellowed pieces of mail and vintage magazines scattered on top of Mr. Knott's desk to the hand-cut and pieced French wallpaper flanking the stairs.

Yet perhaps the most important piece of history preserved is the memory of the eccentric personality of the home's last mistress, LuElla Knott. An author, poet, and musician, LuElla was so inspired by her unique collection of Victorian furnishings that she wrote a poem about each piece and attached it to the furniture with a satin ribbon. Full of clever wit and an occasional moral, these poems earned the Knott House its nickname, "The House That Rhymed."

*Pebble Hill Plantation is a fine example of the many hunting plantations in and around Tallahassee.* (Courtesy of the Tallahassee Area Convention and Visitors Bureau.)

A guided one-hour tour through the house is included in the admission price of $7 for families, $3 for adults, $1.50 for children under 18. The home is open Wednesday–Friday from 1:00 P.M. to 4:00 P.M., Saturday from 10:00 A.M. to 4:00 P.M. Call 850-922-2459.

**Pebble Hill Plantation** (Hwy. 319, five miles N of state line; 912-226-2344; open Tuesday–Saturday from 10:00 A.M. to 5:00 P.M., Sunday from 1:00 P.M. to 5:00 P.M., closed from Labor Day to October 1; admission to the grounds is $2 per person, admission to the main house is $5 for adults, $2.50 for children).

Just off Highway 319 between Tallahassee and Thomasville sits a large brick house only a few feet from the road. The sign posted in the yard reads "Pebble Hill Plantation," but from the looks of the building, it's hard to believe that this was ever a grand plantation at all—that is, until you realize that the brick structure is only the gate house to the more than three thousand acres that make up the complex.

For many years, Pebble Hill was the winter home of the Hannas from Cleveland. With over 65,000 square feet in the main house and an overflow cottage for additional guests, the Hannas could easily entertain their friends and family, as well as business associates, politicians, and royalty such as the Duke and Duchess of Windsor. Stables, kennels, a schoolhouse, servants' quarters, a carpenter shop, and a dog hospital were some of the other structures located on the property.

Elisabeth Ireland Poe, better known as "Miss Pansy," was the last of the Hanna heirs, and an avid sportswoman. Throughout the house, the collection of Audubon prints and carvings and sculptures of her dogs and horses command as much attention as the prime antiques, crystal, and porcelain.

When Miss Pansy died, she willed that the house be opened to the public and provided ample funding to ensure that her wishes were carried out.

**Riley House Museum of African American History & Culture** (419 E. Jefferson Street; 850-681-7881; open Monday, Wednesday, and Friday from 10:00 A.M. to 4:00 P.M. or by appointment; free).

Built in 1890, this was once the home of John Gilmore Riley, who educated himself in spite of the law and became principal of Tallahassee's first public high school for blacks, Lincoln High Academy, later Lincoln High School. The house is the last visible evidence of the middle-class black community that once existed in downtown Tallahassee. Inside, the museum is a repository of African-American history from Reconstruction through the Civil Rights movement.

**San Luis Archaeological and Historic Site** (2020 Mission Road; 850-487-3711; open Monday–Friday from 9:00 A.M. to 4:30 P.M., Saturday from 10:00 A.M. to 4:30 P.M., Sunday from noon to 4:30 P.M.; guided tours are given weekdays at noon, on Saturday at 11:00 A.M. and 3:00 P.M., and on Sunday at 2:00 P.M.; free).

This site is a digs-in-progress of the ruins of San Luis de Talimali, once the largest of the 16 Franciscan missions in the Apalachee Indian province. According to a 1655 census, San Luis was the capital of the province; another census in 1675 lists 1,400 Indians and Spaniards living at the mission. In 1696, a fort was built to protect the mission from English and Creek raiders. As a result, the marauders never attacked San Luis, but wreaked such havoc elsewhere that Spanish authorities ordered the mission abandoned and razed in 1704.

Exhibits feature renderings of the mission's buildings, and there are living history demonstrations and on-going excavations. Tours on Spanish colonial life, archaeology, and Apalachee Indians are held each Saturday; call ahead for the schedule.

**San Marcos de Apalache State Museum** (South of Tallahassee on Route 363, St. Marks; 850-925-6216; open Thursday–Monday from 9:00 A.M. to 5:00 P.M.; grounds are free, museum costs $1 for ages 6 and up; http://www.dep.state.fl.us/parks/-bigbend/sanmarcos.html).

This site marks the spot where Panfilo de Narvaez arrived with three hundred men in 1528. Impressed with the confluence of the Wakulla and St. Marks Rivers, they built and launched the first ships made by white men in the New World.

In 1679, the Spanish governor of Florida constructed the first fort at the site, which subsequently was burned and looted by pirates. Other forts followed with Spanish, British, and U.S. control. In 1821, Florida was ceded to the United States, and troops were sent to occupy the fort. The final confrontation at San Marcos occurred in 1861 when the Confederates took the fort and renamed it Fort Ward.

Today, stonework from a subsequent third fort can still be seen on the site, along with a Confederate magazine. The museum contains relics of the colonial and Civil War eras as well as artifacts excavated from the site that date back to the 1500s.

**St. Marks Lighthouse and National Wildlife Refuge** (CR 59, three miles south of Hwy. 98 at Newport; 850-925-6121; refuge is open daily during daylight hours, the visitor center is open Monday–Friday from 8:00 A.M. to 4:15 P.M., Saturday–Sunday from 10:00 A.M. to 5:00 P.M.; $4 per vehicle; http://www.dep.-state.fl.us/parks/bigbend/stmarks.html).

The 65,000 acres preserved in the St. Marks National Wildlife Refuge show Florida at its best. Throughout the year, about 300 bird species, 50 types of reptiles and amphibians, and over 40 kinds of mammals live in the refuge. In the winter, the wetlands, palm hammocks, and scrubby forests become nesting grounds for migrating birds—making this the

*Riding the St. Marks Trail is a popular weekend pastime for Tallahasseans.* (Courtesy of the Tallahassee Area Convention and Visitors Bureau.)

home of more species of birds than anyplace else in Florida except the everglades.

Lighthouse Road, the main access into the refuge, leads to its namesake, a registered historic site that overlooks the St. Marks River. Visible from the top of the capitol on a clear day, the lighthouse was built in 1831 with stones salvaged from Fort San Marcos de Apalache, which was built nearby in 1639.

The trails are one of the main reasons visitors come to St. Marks. As Florida's first designated state trail, it follows the abandoned railbed of the historic Tallahassee–St. Marks Railroad.

The Tallahassee–St. Marks was the first railroad under construction in Florida and the first in the nation to receive a federal land grant. Completed in 1837, the 20-mile line connected the territorial capital with the Gulf port of St. Marks. In 1984, the Florida Department of Transportation purchased 16 miles of the corridor to preserve the right-of-way. The recreational trail was subsequently constructed.

In all, there are more than 75 miles of marked trails through the refuge, winding through diverse habitats such as the Florida National Scenic Trail that continues for 41 miles throughout the refuge, the Headquarters Pond Trail, a ¼-mile trial that leads to a wooden deck for observing wading birds, ducks, and wood storks, and the St. Marks Primitive Walking Trails that follow an old logging road.

Daily bike and in-line skate rentals and sales are available at the head of the trail at About Bikes.

**Tallahassee Antique Car Museum** (3550 A Mahan Drive; 850-942-0137; open Monday–Saturday from 10:00 A.M. to 5:00 P.M., Sunday from noon to 5:00 P.M.; $7.50 for adults, $4 for children ages 6–10, under 6 years free; www.tacm.com).

This impressive showroom features 70 different types of automobiles, including award-winning Chevys, a one-of-a-kind Ford roadster, 1913 Car-Nation Tourer, 1931 Duesenberg Lagrand Phaeton, 1948 Tucker, 1953 Cadillac Eldorado convertible coupe, 1956 T-Bird, a Delorean, Corvettes and more.

**Tallahassee Ballet** (218 E. Third Avenue; 850-222-1287).

The ballet performs three annual concerts throughout the year using both local and national talent. Call for a schedule, ticket prices, and information on performance sites.

*The Tallahassee Museum of History and Natural Science is an ideal attraction for families.* (Courtesy of VISIT FLORIDA.)

**Tallahassee Little Theatre** (1861 Thomasville Road; 850-224-8474).
This small theater showcases outstanding community productions of plays, musicals, and concerts from popular Broadway shows to modern avant-garde works. Ticket prices and schedules vary; call for more information.

**Tallahassee Museum of History and Natural Science** (3945 Museum Drive near Lake Bradford; 850-575-8684, 850-576-1636; open Monday–Saturday from 9:00 A.M. to 5:00 P.M., Sunday from 12:30 P.M. to 5:00 P.M.; $6 for adults, $5.50 seniors, $4 for kids ages 4–15, under 4 years free; www.freenet.tlh.fl.us/Tal).

A massive Florida black bear lies snoring against the shaded side of a large rotting log. From the wooden boardwalk that zigzags above his fenced-in habitat, he appears to be the perfect cuddly companion for one of Tallahassee's nippy winter nights. Just next door, a bobcat is pacing between the trees and underbrush, growling softly in the afternoon sun.

Although these are only two of the many native animals on display, the Tallahassee Museum of History and Natural Science is more than just a zoo. By combining native wildlife and early vernacular architecture in an unspoiled natural setting, the museum attempts to preserve endangered pieces of our region's cultural and natural heritage from a common predator: progress. Birds and animals injured and unable to survive in the wild can find a home at the museum, while its endangered animals, the Florida panthers and the red wolves, are participants in state and federal breeding and repopulation programs.

In addition to the animal habitats, historical buildings are rescued from destruction and brought to the museum's grounds for restoration. These include a plantation home, a single-pen Cracker house, a rural African-American church, and a one-room schoolhouse.

One of the homes, a simple one-and-a-half story vernacular cottage named Bellevue, was home to George Washington's great-grandniece, Princess Catherine Murat, between 1854 and 1867. She married Achille Murat, Prince of Naples and nephew of Napoleon, in 1826 over the objections of her relatives. He later became a postmaster and mayor of Tallahassee. After his death in 1847, she received recognition as a princess of France from Napoleon III and a sum of money that allowed her to purchase Bellevue. The cottage is restored and furnished with antebellum antiques.

Founded in 1957, the museum exemplifies the intricate relationship that exists between people and their environment. Traditional woodworking, quilting and sewing, syrup-making, and farming are a few of the on-going living history programs that attract more than 125,000 annual visitors. Diverse exhibits—both permanent and rotating—also illustrate the interwoven connection between humans and their surroundings.

**Tallahassee Symphony Orchestra** (performances are held at FSU's Ruby Diamond Auditorium; 850-224-0461, 850-644-6500; season runs from October to April; www.fsu.edu/musicsp/~tso).

The Tallahassee Symphony Orchestra, founded in 1979 by Nicholas Harsanyi, is a professional symphony orchestra that performs symphonic and classical music in concert and chamber settings. Under the direction of David Hoose, the orchestra is made up of a hundred artists, including music faculty from FSU and FAMU, professional musicians from the Tallahassee community, and talented students from area colleges. Call for a schedule and ticket prices.

**Tours With a Southern Accent** (209 E. Brevard Street at the corner of N. Monroe Street; 888-756-0045, 850-513-1000; $20 for basic two-hour driving tour).

Tours with a Southern Accent offers a general overview of the area with a two-hour Taste of Tallahassee tour, but if you really want the down and dirty, opt for the Duels and Lynchings tour, which exposes the rough and sordid side of Tallahassee's past. The company also offers several other themed tours: the Gates of Heaven, which highlights historic churches; the Old South, a look at the old Southern towns surrounding Tallahassee; and the Plantation Crescent, where you can visit several of the working plantations in the area. Both walking and driving tours are available. Tours depart twice a day from the office; call ahead for reservations.

**Union Bank** (across from the Old Capitol on Apalachee Parkway; 850-487-3803; open Monday–Friday from 9:00 A.M. to 4:00 P.M., Saturday and Sunday by appointment; free).

Built in 1841, the Union Bank is one of the few buildings to survive a fire that destroyed downtown Tallahassee in 1843. It prospered by financing local cotton plantations when the state was still a territory, but later failed because of frozen crops, the Seminole War, and poor financial planning. Before its restoration in 1984, the building had served as a freedman's bank for emancipated slaves, a church, a shoe factory, a dance studio, a beauty shop, and a bakery.

This charming structure appears to be created from blue stone, but it is actually a brick building stuccoed on the outside and then scored to look like big blocks of masonry. Once located on Adams Street, the building was moved in 1971 to its present location on the corner of Apalachee Parkway and Calhoun Street. Today, it houses a branch of the FAMU Black Archives Research Center and Museum with exhibits focusing on Florida's African-American history.

**Vietnam Era Veterans' Memorial** (across from the Old Capitol on S. Monroe Street; accessible year-round, 24 hours a day).

Dedicated on Veteran's Day 1985, Florida's Vietnam Era Veterans' Memorial honors the state's 1,942 known Vietnam casualties and the 83 soldiers missing in action. Each of these soldiers' names is inscribed in the monument's black marble. During its

*Wakulla Springs offers visitors a taste of the real Florida.*
(Courtesy of the Tallahassee Area Convention and Visitors Bureau.)

construction, veterans placed meaningful objects inside the 40-foot columns, including items such as purple heart and bronze star metals, a P-38 can opener, and a chunk of granite representing the toughness of a unit that suffered heavy casualties. These not only symbolized the heroism of the veterans, but also the realities of life in the service during the war. The 28' x 15' flag was carried by veterans on an 83-day journey around Florida before being hoisted between the two columns.

**Wakulla Springs Lodge and Conference Center** (Hwy. 267 at Hwy. 61, 14 miles S of Tallahassee; 850-922-3633; open daily from 8:00 A.M. to sunset, boat tours are daily from 9:15 A.M. to 4:30 P.M. during the spring and from 9:45 A.M. to 5:00 P.M. in the summer, conditions permitting; $3.25 per vehicle, glass-bottom and jungle boat cruises are $4.50 per adult, $2.25 for children; park website: http://-www.dep.state.fl.us/parks/bigbend/wakulla.html, lodge website: http://www.dep.state.fl.us/parks/bigbend/lodge.html).

Look for alligators—and lots of them. Wakulla Springs may be touted for the simple sophistication of its Spanish-style inn, the crystal clear water found in its 185-feet-deep spring opening, and the abundance of birds and wildlife that call the park home, but it's the alligators that people distinctly remember. In all, about four hundred of these bathing beauties, ranging in size from three inches to 14 feet, live within the boundaries of the 2,860-acre state park. Most are spotted lying lazily along the banks of the springs, oblivious to the covered pontoon tour boats floating by and the rhythmic chanting of the park guide. Amid squeamish squeals from the tourists on board, one will occasionally swim by, gliding silently between the grasses that sway in the underwater current.

The Indians captured the beauty of Wakulla Springs with its original Indian name, *Tah-ille-ya-aha-n,* which means "where the water flows upward like the rays of heavenly light out of the shadow of the hill." Later, the name was changed to *Wah-kola,* meaning "loon," and eventually to its present name, which means "mysteries of the water." A treasure chest of Native American history, the park has within it 54 sites that have been identified by archaeologists as areas used by Indians ranging from Stone Age hunters to 19th-century Seminoles.

Indians relied on the spring—one of the world's deepest—for medicinal purposes; when Ponce de Leon and Spanish explorers stumbled upon it, they first thought it was the coveted Fountain of Youth. Yet neither of these early inhabitants realized the true mysteries buried within its depths. Dating back 35 million years, the area's limestone foundation is a maze of underground rivers and caves, and geologists are still unable to pinpoint the origin of the spring. Almost directly under the lodge, a grand cavern tall enough to enclose a 16-story building was discovered by divers, while scattered throughout the bottom of the spring are exotic living crustaceans and fossilized bones of prehistoric mastodons. The complete remains of one mastodon skeleton is now on display at the Florida Museum of Natural History. The remains of two others were lost in a shipwreck off Cape Hatteras while en route to a Philadelphia Museum and now lie at the bottom of the Atlantic Ocean.

The late financier Edward Ball bought the undeveloped land in 1933, and two years later began construction on a 27-

room lodge open to the public. Glass-bottom and jungle cruise boat tours went into commission, a restaurant serving regional cuisine was opened, and because the spring water is a constant 70° F. year round, a swimming area featuring a three-tiered diving platform was created. As a weekend getaway for Ball, who had his own three-room suite on the second floor, the lodge soon became the stomping grounds for up-and-coming politicians, business tycoons, and even military leaders such as U.S. general George Patton and French colonel Charles de Gaulle.

Although the state purchased the pristine wilderness area in 1986, the park almost mirrors its image of 50 years ago. A dip of ice cream at the marble soda fountain or a walk along the park's nature trails remain popular as afternoon excursions. And under the blanket of a night unbroken by neon signs and flashing billboards, the lonesome wail of the loon echoing across the spring still lulls lodge guests to sleep.

## Sports

Whether sunshine or rain, Tallahassee is paradise for the avid sportsman. In the local vicinity alone, there are 60 bowling lanes, 1,800 acres in the 55 public parks for tennis, racquetball, picnicking, basketball, baseball, and walking, and several quality golf courses to choose from.

Not only are the area's parks enjoyed by the locals, but they're also a drawing card in attracting sports events to the Capital City. These include the Sunshine State Games, the Law Enforcement Olympics, and the Florida State Junior Olympics. The abundant parks, as well as athletic facilities at local universities, also contributed to the decision made by the British Olympic Association to select Tallahassee as the training site for the 1996 Olympic Games in Atlanta.

Because the temperature averages 65° in the winter and 90° in the summer, Tallahassee is also host to other outdoor activities such as cycling and hiking. For cycling enthusiasts, the shaded canopy roads are perfect escapes for pedaling pleasures. Hikers find that the city and nearby state parks provide excellent trails, such as the Florida National Scenic Trail, which is the only U.S. trail of eight that can be hiked from end to end during the winter.

*A Seminole warrior mounted on his horse, Renegade, rides around the FSU football stadium before games.* (Courtesy of the Tallahassee Area Convention and Visitors Bureau.)

*FAMU's Marching 100 band are world famous for their sassy music and moves.* (Courtesy of the Tallahassee Area Convention and Visitors Bureau.)

For Tallahasseans, the most anticipated season of the year begins around Labor Day and ends on New Year's Day. In the Deep South, college football is more than just a Saturday afternoon outing. Children are taught the principles of pigskin along with their ABCs; Thanksgiving and Christmas dinners, more often than not, center around the football game on television. Actors Burt Reynolds and Robert Urich played football for the Seminoles, while pro volleyball star and model Gabrielle Reese played volleyball for FSU. At FAMU football games, the renowned Marching 100 entertains crowds during halftime.

And fans aren't disappointed. The FAMU Rattlers compete in 17 collegiate sports and have captured 11 national titles to date. The FSU Seminoles compete in 18 collegiate sports and have five national titles, including their reign as the collegiate football national champions in 1993.

Tallahassee has recently acquired several semi-professional and professional sports teams that fill the calendar during other parts of the year.

**Florida A&M University Sports** (850-599-3230)

**Florida State University Sports** (850-644-1830)

**Tallahassee Scorpions** (850-222-0400; tickets start at $12).

Part of the Eastern Indoor Soccer League, the Tallahassee Scorpions play in June and August at the Leon County Civic Center.

**Tallahassee Tempests** (850-942-7142; $6 for adults, $5 for students, $4 for ages 11 and under).

Tallahassee's pro soccer team kicks it up at Corey Field in Quincy. The Tempests are an A-League (Division II Professional) team affiliated with the Tampa Bay Mutiny.

**Tallahassee Tiger Sharks** (850-222-0400; tickets start at $6).

Tallahassee's first professional sports team plays hockey from October to March in the Leon County Civic Center.

### Fishing/Water Recreation

Fishing and boating on the numerous lakes and rivers surrounding the city are also pleasurable pastimes that attract people from all over the country. Bluegill, speckled perch, shellcracker, and largemouth bass are a few of the fish in area waters.

Favorite spots among locals include Lake Seminole, which is considered one of the top five lakes in the United States because it doesn't have the pressure that lakes near cities do; and Lake Jackson, renowned for its big bass. Lake Talquin in western Leon and Gadsden Counties originated in 1927 with the completion of the Jackson Bluff Dam on the Ochlockonee River. The lake is unique because a river channel runs through it, making it the only lake of its kind in Florida.

**Red and Sam's Fish Camp** (5563 N. Monroe Street on Lake Jackson; 850-562-4660; www.rednsams.nu).

This local guide service specializes in freshwater fishing on the surrounding lakes, with emphasis on Lake Jackson. There are canoe and boat rentals, a tackle shop, and a boat launch on site, as well as modest, fully-equipped mobile homes right next to the lake for overnight rental.

**Shell Island Fish Camp/Marina** (located 30 minutes S off Hwy. 363; 850-925-6226).

This is a full-service fish camp and marina, with boat rentals and accommodations on the Wakulla River.

**Shell Point Resort** (located 30 minutes S off Hwy. 367; 850-926-7162).

Shell Point offers boating/sailing, boat ramp/fishing, swimming, nearby golf, a motel, and a restaurant on the Gulf beach.

**TNT Hideaway** (US 98 at the Wakulla River near Crawfordville; 850-925-6412).

Canoe a three-and-a-half mile crystal clear, tree-lined stretch of the Wakulla River, just beyond the Wakulla Springs Wildlife Refuge. An average trip takes about three hours, and you're likely to see turtles, birds, alligators, wild boar, otters, osprey, and herons during your journey. The route is easy for both novices and children to navigate.

**Wacissa River Canoe Trail** (SR 59 W., Wacissa; 850-488-3701).

This easy, beginner canoe trail follows the meandering path of the Wacissa River, a clear, spring-fed stream. The lower section of the river from Goose Pasture to the entrance of the canal can be hard to follow, but stay to the right and look for the canal hidden by willow trees. The trail ends several hundred yards upstream on the Aucilla River at Nutall Rise Landing. Call for a map and access information.

## Golf

**Cross Creek** (6701 Mahan Drive; 850-656-GOLF).

This new facility features a par-three, nine-hole lighted golf course, three-tier driving range, and putting area.

**Hilaman Park Golf Course** (2737 Blairstone Road; 850-891-3935).

An outstanding municipal course, Hilaman features an 18-hole par-72 course with a driving range, putting green, pro shop, clubhouse, and restaurant.

**Players Club at Summerbrooke** (7505 Preservation Road; 850-894-GOLF).

This semi-private, 18-hole, par-72 course features a driving range, a putting green, a restaurant, and a pro shop.

**Seminole Golf Course** (2550 Pottsdamer Street; 850-644-2582).

This is a public 18-hole course, with a lighted driving range, cart/club rentals, individual/group instruction/clinics, and a clubhouse with a restaurant and a pro shop.

## Tennis

**Forest Meadows Park** (4750 N. Meridian Road; 850-891-3920).

Forest Meadows features nine lighted clay courts and six hard courts, three indoor racquetball courts, locker rooms, a spa, and a pool.

**Tom Brown Park** (501 Easterwood Drive; 850-891-3966).

This is a multi-use park with 12 lighted tennis and 12 outdoor racquetball courts.

**Winthrop Park** (1601 Mitchell Avenue; 850-891-3980).

At Winthrop Park there are six lighted courts and two outdoor racquet courts.

## Restaurants and Nightlife

Quincy mushrooms, Vidalia onions, Whigham pecans, Cairo pickles, Jefferson County watermelons—Tallahassee is surrounded by fresh, homegrown vegetables and fruits that routinely show up on the tables at many of the restaurants in town. Hearty, homestyle cooking is one of the area's specialties, along with fresh seafood—grilled or fried—and barbecue.

*Chez Pierre is a popular French restaurant and bar located near downtown.* (Courtesy of the Tallahassee Area Convention and Visitors Bureau.)

**Andrew's Capital Bar & Grill** (228 S. Adams Street; 850-222-3444; open Monday–Saturday from 11:30 A.M. until . . ., Sunday for brunch).

This casual, upscale eatery is a favorite hangout for legislators during session. Steak, chicken, burgers, salads, and pasta are standard fare.

**Andrew's Second Act** (228 S. Adams Street; 850-222-3444; open Monday–Thursday from 6:00 P.M. to 10:00 P.M., Friday–Saturday until 11:00 P.M.).

Upstairs from the Capital Bar & Grill, this downtown dining establishment is a consecutive Golden Spoon winner since 1979. Classic elegance prevails here with beef, veal, and fresh seafood dishes. Andrew's also touts its wine cellar as the largest in North Florida.

**Angelo's** (32 miles SW of Tallahassee off Hwy. 98, Panacea; 850-984-5168; open Monday, Wednesday, Thursday from 4:00 P.M. to 10:00 P.M., Friday–Saturday from 4:30 P.M. to 11:00 P.M., Sunday from 12:00 P.M. to 10:00 P.M.).

Voted one of Florida's top 200 restaurants eight years in a row, this local favorite serves fresh seafood, pastas, and steaks.

**Barnacle Bill's** (1830 N. Monroe Street; 850-385-8734; open daily from 11:00 A.M. to 11:00 P.M.).

"You know where…" Barnacle Bill's on North Monroe is the place for fresh Florida seafood cooked "any way you like it."

**Chez Pierre** (1215 Thomasville Road; 850-222-0936; open Monday–Saturday from 11:30 A.M. to 2:30 P.M., 5:30 P.M. to 10:00 P.M.).

This restaurant features delicious, authentic French cuisine and gracious service in a grand-house setting. Specialties include lamb chops, roasted duck, tournedos, quiche, vegetarian entrées and homemade soups, sorbets and pastries, and an espresso/wine/full bar.

**Dave's CC Club** (Sam's Lane off Bradfordville Road; 850-894-0181; weekends, doors open at 6:30 P.M.).

This legendary blues club features the finest blues worldwide—"it ain't nothin' but the truth!" It also serves Cajun barbecue, touted as the best this side of the Mississippi.

**Marie Livingston's Texas Steak Restaurant & Saloon** (3212 Apalachee Pkwy.; 850-877-2986; open Monday–Thursday from 5:00 P.M. to 9:30 P.M., Friday–Saturday from 5:00 P.M. to 10:30 P.M., Sunday from 11:00 A.M. to 2:00 P.M.).

Billed as the best little steakhouse in Tallahassee, it serves U.S.D.A. choice Midwestern corn-fed beef, plus shrimp, fish, and chicken.

**Mom and Dad's** (4175 Apalachee Parkway; 850-877-4518; open Tuesday–Thursday from 5:00 P.M. to 10:00 P.M., Friday–Saturday until 11:00 P.M.).

In this family-owned and operated eatery, Mom serves up heaping dishes of lasagna, chicken parmesan, grouper piccata, pizzas, and fettucine alfredo—all made with her fresh, homemade pasta and delicious sauces.

**The Moon** (1105 E. Lafayette Street; 850-878-6900; open Wednesday–Saturday from 10:00 P.M. to 2:00 A.M.).

The Moon is an upscale high-energy, multi-level nightclub featuring a disc jockey, laser lights, and state-of-the-art acoustic/video equipment. Live entertainment frequently includes top-name performers.

**Nicholson Farmhouse Restaurant** (15 miles N of Tallahassee on Hwy. 12, Havana; 850-539-5931; open Tuesday–Saturday from 4:00 P.M. to 10:00 P.M.).

A complex of restored farmhouses and country buildings sits on 30 acres of pasture and woods, with the 1828 historic Nicholson farmhouse as the centerpiece. The home is reportedly the oldest home between Pensacola and St. Augustine. Five of the buildings comprise the six-hundred-seat restaurant, famous for its aged hand-cut steaks, grilled seafood, chops, and chicken. You'll also find a gift shop, a barn, a shed with antique farm tools, and a gazebo on the property.

**Posey's Restaurant** (30 minutes SW of Tallahassee on Hwy. 98, Panacea; 850-984-5799; open Tuesday–Sunday from 6:00 A.M. to 9:30 P.M.).

The home of the topless oyster, Posey's serves up Southern-style seafood, mullet, frog legs, oysters, lobster, and fresh Gulf fish.

**Shell Oyster Bar** (114 Oakland Avenue; 850-224-9919; open Monday–Saturday from 11:00 A.M. to 6:30 P.M., Saturday until 6:00 P.M.).

The Shell Oyster Bar is a hole in the wall where the locals hang out, but it has the best oysters in town—raw or fried.

**Silver Slipper** (531 Scotty Lane; 850-386-9366; open Monday–Saturday from 5:00 P.M. to 10:00 P.M.).

Since 1938 the high rollers in Florida's political arena have been wining and dining various parties at this Tallahassee landmark. It's reputed to be the oldest family-run restaurant in the state and a long-time favorite of many legends. John F. Kennedy, Lyndon Johnson, Jimmy Carter, Ronald Reagan, and George Bush have all dined at the Silver Slipper. The booths have curtains you can pull shut for private meetings. Steak and seafood are the house specialties.

## Accommodations

Tallahassee has several of the national chain hotels and motels to choose from, and in the surrounding small towns, there are many bed and breakfasts that cater to tourists.

**Governor's Inn** (209 S. Adams Street; 800-342-7717, 850-681-6855).

Convenient to both FSU and the capitol complex, there are 40 rooms in this upscale downtown inn.

**Inn at Killearn Country Club** (100 Tyron Circle, Tallahassee, FL 32308; 800-476-4101, 850-893-2186).

Located in the center of a residential area north of town, this inn features an Olympic-size pool, eight tennis courts, and access to the private, 27-hole golf course.

**Sweet Magnolia Inn** (803 Port Leon Drive, St. Marks; 850-925-7670).

A rooming house in 1923, the Sweet Magnolia Inn reopened in 1996 as a fully restored B&B. There are seven bedrooms, all with private baths, and five of the baths feature spa tubs for two. You'll also find a light, airy interior with pine floors, antique furniture, and fresh, plump linens on the bed.

Sweet Magnolia Inn is close to Fort San Marcos and St. Marks Wildlife Refuge, so there is plenty to do in the vicinity.

**Wakulla Springs Lodge** (550 Wakulla Park Drive, Wakulla Springs; 850-224-5950).

Part of the Florida State Park system, this magnificent 27-room lodge is situated in the middle of the park, overlooking the swimming area of the springs.

## Shopping

**Bradley's 1927 Country Store** (12 miles N of Tallahassee on Centerville Road; 850-893-1647; open Monday–Friday from 9:00 A.M. to 6:00 P.M., Saturday from 9:00 A.M. to 5:00 P.M.).

Step back in time with a visit to Bradley's Country Store, a Tallahassee landmark since 1927. Although dry goods and commodities are available for purchase, the store's claim to fame is the tasty, seasoned sausage made from Grandma Mary's 1910 recipe. Legend has it that at one time, Mary's husband sold her sausage on the capitol steps.

Recognized as a historic site by the National Register of Historic Places in 1984, the store is housed in its original 1927 tin-roofed building. Other country fare made at the store includes hogshead cheese, liver pudding, cracklings, and coarse ground milled grits.

Another tradition is Bradley's Fun Day, a day-long extravaganza in the fall of arts and crafts, country cooking, and old-fashioned entertainment, all on the acreage around the store and the Bradley's 1893 homestead. Model-A car rides, sugar

*A Tallahassee landmark since 1927, Bradley's Country Store is famous for its homemade sausage.* (Courtesy of the Tallahassee Area Convention and Visitors Bureau.)

cane syrup-making, and old-time demonstrations are some of the most popular events.

**Governor's Square Mall** (1500 Apalachee Parkway, one mile E of the capitol; 850-671-INFO; open Monday–Saturday from 10:00 A.M. to 9:00 P.M., Sunday from 12:30 P.M. to 5:30 P.M.; www.governorssquare.com).

This contemporary enclosed shopping center features the area's largest selection of specialty shops and push cart vendors, from Eddie Bauer, American Eagle Outfitters, Cacique, to the Bombay Company, the Disney Store, and others. Anchor department stores are Burdines, Dillards, JC Penney and Sears. You can also enjoy full-service restaurants such as Ruby Tuesday, Mozzarella's Cafe, Morrison's Cafeteria, and a five-hundred-seat food court.

**Native Nurseries** (1661 Centerville Road; 850-386-8882).

A walk through this quiet, shady nursery is a wonderful way to learn about local flora. The nursery specializes in plants native to Florida, while the gift shop is filled with statuary, accessories, reflecting balls, clothing, and bodycare products for garden lovers.

**Nomads** (508 W. Gaines Street; 850-681-3222; open Tuesday–Saturday from 11:00 A.M. to 6:00 P.M.).

Photography, wearable art, pottery, jewelry, and sculptures by local, regional, and national artists are showcased and for sale at this funky, eclectic gallery near the FSU campus. Themed exhibits are planned throughout the year.

**Tallahassee Mall** (2415 N. Monroe Street; 850-385-7145; open Monday–Saturday from 10:00 A.M. to 9:00 P.M., Sunday from 12:30 P.M. to 5:30 P.M.).

Shop, dine, and play at this regional mall conveniently located off I-10 on North Monroe Street. There are over 90 specialty shops such as Barnes & Noble, Gap, Structure, and Victoria's Secret as well as four major departments stores: Montgomery Ward, Gayfers, Goody's, and Parisian. Twelve fast-food locations and three full-service restaurants are on site. Entertainment choices include AMC Tallahassee Mall 20 with stadium seating and Q-Zar Laser Tag.

### Festivals and Special Events

A major draw for the area is the number of annual festivals. Considered seasonal activities in other parts of the nation, the pleasant

year-round temperatures have turned these celebrations into perennial favorites. Two of the most popular are Springtime Tallahassee
and The Winter Festival. Springtime Tallahassee has now blossomed
into a four-week jubilee in celebration of spring and Florida history. The Winter Festival is a two-week event highlighted by an outdoor evening of lighting the city's holiday decorations.

*January*

### Hernando de Soto Winter Encampment

This living history portrayal of De Soto's 1539 winter encampment features exhibits and interpreters of Spanish and
Apalachee cultures. Free. Call 850-922-6007.

### Rattlesnake Round-Up

Snake handling, cooking, contests, arts and crafts, and entertainment can be expected at this annual event in Whigham,
Georgia. Free. Call 912-762-4215.

*March*

### Natural Bridge Civil War Battlefield Re-enactment

Another re-enactment, only this time it's the Civil War. Interpreters wear authentic uniforms and carry antique or replica
muskets. Call 850-922-6007.

*April*

### Springtime Tallahassee

Moving a state capital seems almost ludicrous in today's
technologically advanced world, but as recently as 1968, there
was talk about relocating the seat of Florida's government to a
more centralized location. To counter such chatter, Tallahas-
sean Betty McCord set out to promote the city's rich heritage
and high quality of life to the rest of the state. Her answer?
Springtime Tallahassee.

Perhaps no other city in the South can boast such a spectacular display of spring as Florida's capital city. And certainly
no other city can match Tallahassee's contributions to shaping
the state of Florida. The festival has now blossomed into a four-
week jubilee in celebration of spring and Florida history, and is
considered by some to be the city's premier event of the year.

*Springtime Tallahassee was started in the 1960s to keep the seat of Florida's government from relocating.* (Courtesy of the Tallahassee Area Convention and Visitors Bureau.)

Several events held throughout the city lead up to the main day of celebration, which literally overflows into the streets of downtown Tallahassee. There are at least 250 arts and crafts booths scattered along sidewalks and in the streets, six stages of entertainment to provide citizens with a diverse selection of musical performances, and a parade with floats depicting the periods of Florida history. Call 850-224-5012. The website address is www.3wstudios.com/springtime.

**Thomasville Rose Festival**

The City of Roses blossoms with themed celebrations including the Downtown Rose Parade and Rose Show. Most events are free. Call 800-704-2350 or 912-225-5222.

*May*

**Humanatee Festival**

Welcome the Wakulla River manatee herd into the area. Held at the San Marcos de Apalache State Historic Site in St. Marks, the festival features live music, arts and crafts, guided tours, and children's programs as part of the entertainment. Call 850-925-6216.

**Southern Shakespeare Festival**
A summer renaissance festival culminates with Shakespeare-in-the-Park. Events are held downtown in the Capitol Commons area behind city hall and are free. Call 850-413-9200. The website address is www.freenet.fsu.edu/festival.

*June*

**Monticello Watermelon Festival**
A local tradition since 1949, the Monticello Watermelon Festival features arts and crafts, a parade, golf tournament, 5K run, rodeo, softball tournament, seed-spitting contest, barbecue, street dance, and the "Watermelon Queen" pageant. Most events are free. Call 850-997-5552.

*July*

**Celebrate America**
Patriotism is popping, literally, at this annual fireworks display at Tom Brown Park. Held on July 4, the festival also includes sporting events and patriotic performances for the 50,000 attendees. Call 850-891-3866.

*August*

**Caribbean Carnival**
Rhythms of reggae, calypso, and salsa fill the air during a West Indian-inspired weekend that includes a parade and carnival village with ethnic crafts, food, and entertainment. Most of the events are held in downtown Tallahassee and are free. Call 850-878-2198.

*September*

**Native American Heritage Festival**
Seminoles, Choctaws, Creeks, and other Native Americans participate in traditional dancing, stickball and blowgun demonstrations, cooking, basket making, dugout canoe building, bead work, flint-knapping, stickball club making, and other skills during this three-week celebration. The event is held at the Tallahassee Museum of History and Natural Science. Call 850-575-8684.

*October*

### North Florida Fair

Here's your chance to see a traditional, small-town fair in full swing. North Florida's and South Georgia's largest event features agriculture, arts and crafts, exhibits, 4-H demonstrations, Nashville stars, and a midway chock full of fun. The fair takes place during October and into November at the North Florida Fairgrounds. Call 850-878-3247.

*November*

### Bradley's Historic Country Store Fun Day

What started as a small fair for sampling Bradley's famous homemade sausage has turned into a day-long celebration of traditional crafts. Demonstrations on cane grinding and syrup making, live music, arts and crafts, and horse-drawn wagon and Model-A rides are a few of the activities. Call 850-893-1647.

### Market Days

The North Florida Fairgrounds overflow with artists and craftspeople selling a wide variety of unique handmade items. This is one of the Southeast's largest and finest arts and crafts shows and sales. Call 850-575-8684.

*December*

### December on the Farm

Sponsored by the Tallahassee Museum of History and Natural Science, this festival highlights farm life as it existed in Tallahassee in the 1880s. Featured demonstrations included cane grinding, syrup making, wood working, and blacksmithing. Call 850-575-8684.

### Harambe Festival

A celebration of African-American culture, the Harambe Festival is a holistic experience of the sights, sounds, and expressions that compose the African-American lifestyle. Local, regional, and national performing, visual, and folk artists provide exhibits, presentations, and performances during the weekend event that culminates Black History Month. In addition to the versatility of performances and the variety of booths, there is a black film festival, a museum displaying African artifacts, a forum for the exchange of ideas and issues concerning black artists, and a Harambe Exchange, which is a brain bowl competition for middle and secondary students on black history.

Created in 1980 as a way to gain exposure for black artists, the festival is now attended by around 15,000 people, and coordinated exclusively by community volunteers. "Besides the opportunity to see such wonderful talent collectively, it is also a way to experience and understand and appreciate what African-Americans have given to this country," says Beverly Barber, one of the founders of the festival. "It's become so popular that we even have people who arrange their vacation around the celebration."

No other name could do this festival as much justice as *Harambe,* which is an East African term meaning "working together for the betterment of all." Call 850-599-3136.

**San Luis Heritage Festival**

Historic reenactments, traditional foods, and music are part of the San Luis festivities in honor of Florida's cultural heritage. The site of this festival, which features a 17th-century Spanish mission and Indian settlement created some two hundred years before Florida became a state, is only one of many archaeological "gems" discovered in the Tallahassee area. Call 850-487-3711.

**The Winter Festival: A Celebration of Lights, Music, and the Arts**

In 1987, city planners purchased about $70,000 in new holiday decorations. Little did they know that a wildly popular winter festival would be one of the results of their purchases. That first year, a small, one-night event in honor of lighting the new decorations was planned to kick off the holiday season. Over six thousand people showed up, and the numbers—and activities— have grown ever since.

Today, the Winter Festival is a two-week celebration featuring family programs, a holiday music and fine arts competition, outdoor ice skating, and cultural arts entertainment. Santa's Enchanted Forest, which is really a city park transformed into a winter wonderland by city staff, is one of the event's most popular attractions. However, the lighting of the decorations remains the centerpiece of the festival.

According to Bill Behenna, senior public information specialist with the city, the entire festival is coordinated by the Tallahassee Parks and Recreation Department and volunteers within the community. "Lots of people eagerly anticipate this festival, and it has grown beyond our expectations," says Behenna. "It's really wonderful to see so many people downtown during the evening, and it's a really neat way to kick off the holiday season." Call 850-413-9200 or 850-891-3866.

## Day Trips

### Havana

This charming old town, once a winter resort for wealthy Northerners and a prosperous agricultural center specializing in tobacco leaf for cigars, is now synonymous with antiquing. Located only 10 minutes north of Tallahassee, many of its restored buildings line the narrow main street, and some of its older homes display interesting and impressive collections of antiques. Unusual shops specializing in dolls, ethnic items, and rocks and crystals, can also be found throughout town.

This movement to a quaint setting where shops could be within walking distance from each other was started in 1985 by Keith Henderson and Lee Hotchkiss, owners of H and H Antiques. Over 30 different shops, art galleries, and cafés have since followed their lead. There are several places of note:

*The Cannery* is a collection of antique dealers, craftspeople, and working artists, all housed in the restored Havana Canning Company plant built in 1934. The Cannery has live entertainment on Friday and Saturday nights, and features *Shade*, a restaurant specializing in New Southern Cuisine. The newest addition is the bottling plant where you can have your own special recipe of sauce bottled and labeled with custom labels. Call 850-539-8401.

*H and H Antiques* is an antique emporium filled with architectural pieces, fine china, original artwork, collectibles, stained glass, and lighting. Call 850-539-6886.

Most shops are open from Wednesday through Sunday. For more information, call the Gadsden County Chamber of Commerce at 850-627-9231.

*Joie de Vivre* is full of all things French. There is a wonderful selection of French CDs, fruit and vegetable tiles, and other gifts with a Parisian or Provincial touch. Call 850-539-1696.

*Wanderings* is an ethnic gallery featuring authentic art, crafts, specialty furniture, jewelry, and gifts from around the world. Call 850-539-7711.

### Monticello

Visiting Monticello is like taking a trip back in time. Here you'll find elegant, turn-of-the-century homes and stately public buildings tucked away on tree-lined, two-lane streets. Many are listed on the National Register of Historic Places. The town's crown jewel is the *Monticello Opera House,* a glorious performance hall where plays and variety shows were shown during the early 1900s. The Opera House closed when movies became en vogue, and it remained closed until the 80s, when the Monticello Opera House, Inc., was formed to save the structure. Now the rambling Victorian building hosts a full season of drama, musicals, ballet, and cabaret.

Other attractions include the *Confederate Memorial Park,* the site of a blockhouse built to defend the town during the Seminole Indian Wars; three nearby rivers for outdoor enthusiasts; quaint bed and breakfasts; and the annual Watermelon Festival, where visitors can indulge in a "slice of the good life." Call the Monticello/Jefferson County Chamber of Commerce at 850-997-5552.

### Quincy

Incorporated in 1828, Quincy is the county seat of Gadsden County. From the 1830s to the early 1970s the city's main industry was tobacco. The locals discovered that growing tobacco under a cloth shade improved its color and texture, thus earning Quincy the nickname "Shade Tobacco Capital of the World." Today, many warehouses and packing houses remain.

Quincy is also known as the "City that Coca-Cola Built" because Mark W. "Pat" Munroe, president of the Quincy State Bank in 1893, was inclined to loan money to customers who followed his advice and purchased stock in a new company called Coca-Cola. Eventually, dozens of the residents became millionaires and, at one time, 68 percent of all Coke stock was held by residents of Quincy. Munroe's home at 204 East Jefferson Street is now leased by the Quincy Garden Club.

Historic grandeur is evident in homes throughout the city, including the magnificently restored *McFarlin House B&B* (1895), *Quincefield Inn* (1892), and *Allison House Inn* (1843). Downtown Quincy was officially listed as a Nationally Registered Historic District in 1980. In 1987 Quincy was designated as a Florida Main Street City and was the recipient of 1996 All American City Award. For more information call the Quincy Chamber of Commerce at 800-627-9231 or 850-627-9231.

**Thomasville**

Known as the "City of Roses" because of the plethora of rose bushes scattered around town, Thomasville continues to be a winter getaway for wealthy Northern families; Ted Turner and Jane Fonda are among the plantation owners in the area. With brick-paved streets, period lamp posts, Southern architecture, and unique boutiques, Downtown Historic Thomasville has kept its old-fashioned charm. There are also several historic sites worth visiting: the *Lapham–Patterson House,* an 1885 restored Victorian home; the *Thomas County Historical Museum* featuring plantation period memorabilia and Civil war relics; *Susina Plantation Inn,* a splendid antebellum mansion built in 1841 on a 115-acre estate; and the *Farmers' Market* on Smith Avenue, where you'll find the best home-cooked Southern food in the region. For more information call the Thomasville-Destination Thomasville Tourism Authority at 912-225-3919 or 800-704-2350; the website address is www.thomasvillage.com.

# Bibliography

Bettinger, Julie and Heidi Tyline King. *Tallahassee: Teamwork, Tradition, and Technology*. Montgomery, AL: Community Communications, 1995.

Brinton, Daniel Garrison. *A Guidebook of Florida and the South for Tourists, Invalids, and Emigrants*. Philadelphia: G. Maclean, 1869. A facsimile reproduction of the 1869 edition. Gainesville: University Presses of Florida, 1978.

Dunn, Hampton. *Yesterday's Tallahassee*. Miami: E. A. Seemann Publishing, Inc., 1974.

Ellis, Mary Louise and William Warren Rogers. *Tallahassee and Leon County: A History and Bibliography*. Tallahassee: Florida Department of State, 1986.

Ellis, Mary Louise and William Warren Rogers. *Tallahassee: Favored Land: A History of Tallahassee and Leon County*. Virginia Beach, VA: The Donning Company, 1988.

*Florida: A Guide to the Southernmost State*. Compiled and written by the Federal Writers' Project of the Work Projects Administration of the State of Florida. New York: Oxford University Press, 1939.

*Florida's Sandy Beaches*. Gainesville: University Presses of Florida, 1985.

Groene, Bertram H. *Ante-Bellum Tallahassee*. Tallahassee: The Florida Heritage Foundation, 1971.

Haase, Ronald W. *Classic Cracker, Florida's Wood-Frame Vernacular Architecture.* Sarasota, FL: Pineapple Press, Inc., 1992.

Hayden, Clara R. *A Century of Tallahassee Girls: As Viewed From the Leaves of Their Diaries.* Atlanta: Foote & Davies Co., ND.

Hostetler, Mark. *That Gunk On Your Car: A Unique Guide to Insects of North America.* Berkeley, CA: Ten Speed Press, 1997.

Hupp, Susanne and Laura Stewart. *Historic Homes of Florida.* Sarasota, FL: Pineapple Press, 1995.

Ketchum, Eleanor. *Tales of Tallahassee.* Tallahassee: Jerry Dye and Associates, 1976.

Klinkenberg, Marty and Elizabeth Leach. *Natural Wonders of Florida: A Guide to Parks, Preserves, and Wild Places.* Castine, ME: Country Roads Press, 1993.

Lanier, Sidney. *Florida: Its Scenery, Climate, and History.* A facsimile reproduction of the 1875 edition with Introduction and Index by Jerrell H. Shofner. Gainesville, FL: University of Florida Press, 1973. Bicentennial Floridian Facsimile Series.

Logan, William Bryant and Vance Muse. *The Smithsonian Guide to Historic America: The Deep South.* New York: Stewart, Tabori & Chang, 1989.

Marsh, Del and Martha J. *Florida Almanac: 1998–1999.* Gretna, LA: Pelican Publishing Co., 1998.

McKinnon, John L. *History of Walton County.* Gainesville, FL: Palmetto Books, 1968.

Mickler, Delia Appleyard and Carolyde Phillips O'Bryan. *Colonel's Inn Caterers: Tallahassee Historical Cookbook.* Tallahassee: Rose Printing Company, 1984.

Morgan, William Herman. *The Seacoast of Northwest Florida: A Geographical Appraisal.* Gainesville, FL: University of Florida, 1962 (dissertation).

Morris, Joan Perry and Martee Wills. *Seminole History.* Jacksonville, FL: South Star Publishing Company, 1987.

Moylan, Marjorie Morrison. *Magnolias and Mavericks.* Moylan, 1992. (self-published)

Paisley, Clifton. *From Cotton to Quail—An Agricultural Chronicle of Leon County, Florida, 1860–1967.* Gainesville, FL: University of Florida Press, 1968.

Riegert, Ray, ed. *Hidden Florida: The Adventurer's Guide.* Berkeley, CA: Ulysses Press, 1990.

Smith, Hale G., Ph.D. *Tallahassee: Historic Scenic Capital of Florida.* Tallahassee: Talla., Inc., 1955.

*The WPA Guide to Florida.* New York: Oxford University Press, 1939. Reprint with introduction by John I. McCollum, 1984.

Turner, Lisa, ed. *Awesome Almanac: Florida.* Walworth, WI: B&B Publishing, Inc., 1994.

Williams, John Lee. *A View of West Florida.* Philadelphia: Printed for HS Tanner and the author, 1827. A facsimile reproduction of the 1827 edition published under sponsorship of the Bicentennial Commission of Florida, Gainesville, 1976.

Willis III, Lee. *At the Water's Edge: A Pictorial and Narrative History of Apalachicola and Franklin County.* Virginia Beach, VA: Donning Company Publishers, 1997.

Womack, Marlene. *Along the Bay: A Pictorial History of Bay County.* Norfolk, VA: Pictorial Heritage Publishing Company, 1994.

# Index

## A

Accommodations:
  Apalachicola, 226-27
  Beaches of South Walton,
    142-45
  Okaloosa County, 110-12
  Panama City, 186-90
  Pensacola, 80-81
  Tallahassee, 278-79
Airlines, 35
Apalachicola, 194-233
Apalachicola oysters, 198-200
Attractions:
  Apalachicola, 207-21
  Beaches of South Walton,
    121, 127-34
  Okaloosa County, 91-100
  Panama City, 164, 165-76
  Pensacola, 52, 54-74
  Tallahassee, 242, 243, 244-70
Average temperatures, 21
  Apalachicola, 201

  Beaches of South Walton,
    120
  Okaloosa County, 89
  Panama City, 160
  Pensacola, 53
  Tallahassee, 240

## B

Beaches, 18-21
  Big Lagoon State Recreation
    Area, 55-56
  Camp Helen State Park,
    164
  Cape San Blas, 202
  Dog Island, 202
  Grayton Beach State Recre-
    ation Area, 130
  Gulf Islands National
    Seashore, 61-62
  Henderson Beach State
    Recreation Area, 95
  Indian Pass, 202-3

Little St. George Island, 203-4
Panama City Beach, 161-62
Perdido Key State Recreation Area, 71
St. Andrews Bay Recreation Area, 174-75
St. George Island, 204
St. George Island State Park, 215-16
St. Joseph Peninsula State Park, 216
St. Vincent Island, 204
St. Vincent National Wildlife Refuge, 217-18
South Walton, 122-27
Topsail Hill State Park, 132-33
Beaches of South Walton, 115-55
Bike rentals:
Apalachicola, 228
Okaloosa County, 107
Seaside, 152
Tallahassee, 264

## C

Camping, 35, 37
Canoeing and kayaking, 37
Apalachicola, 212, 221, 222, 223
Beaches of Fort Walton, 132
Okaloosa County, 93, 100
Panama City, 166, 167-68, 170, 175, 193
Pensacola, 56-57, 70-71, 75-76
Tallahassee, 247, 274
Caring for wildlife, 37-38

Carrabelle, 231-33
Contact information, 35
Apalachicola, 201
Beaches of South Walton, 119
Okaloosa County, 89
Panama City, 160
Pensacola, 53
Tallahassee, 239-40
Crestview, 114
Cycling, 38-39

## D

DeFuniak Springs, 154-55
Diving and snorkeling, 39-40
Apalachicola, 222-23
Beaches of South Walton, 132, 136, 151-52
Okaloosa County, 102, 103, 104-5
Panama City, 158, 171, 175, 177, 179-81, 193
Pensacola, 51, 75
Tallahassee, 258
Dog cafés, 205-6

## F

Festivals and special events:
Apalachicola, 229-31
Beaches of South Walton, 147-49
Okaloosa County, 112-13
Panama City, 191-92
Pensacola, 82-84
Tallahassee, 281-87
Fishing/water recreation, 40-41
Apalachicola, 221-23
Beaches of South Walton, 134-36

Okaloosa County, 100-104
Panama City, 176-79
Pensacola, 74-75
Tallahassee, 273-74
Flora and fauna, 21
Armadillos, 22-23
Herons, 23
Jellyfish, 23
Lovebugs, 23-24
Mosquitoes, 24
Opossums, 24
Sand gnats, 24-25
Sea turtles, 25-26
Shells, 26-28
Atlantic Abra, 26
Coquina Shell, 27
Cross-Barred Venus Clam, 27
Dwarf Surf Clam, 27
Lightning Whelk, 27
Moon Snail, 27
Ponderous Ark, 27
Slipper Shell, 27
Van Hyning's Cockle, 28
Snakes, 28-29
Copperheads, 28
Coral snakes, 28
Rattlesnakes, 28-29
Water moccasins, 29
Spanish moss, 29
Florida Caverns State Park, 192-93
Florida's official, 30

**G**
Geology, 16-18
Golf:
Apalachicola, 224

Beaches of South Walton, 136-38
Okaloosa County, 105-6
Panama City, 181-83
Pensacola, 76
Tallahassee, 275
Gulf County, 233

**H**
Havana, 287-88
Highway information, 41
Hiking, 41-42
History, state, 14-16
Apalachicola, 197-98
Beaches of South Walton, 116-19
Okaloosa County, 85-89
Panama City, 158-60
Pensacola, 49-51
Tallahassee, 235-39
Hurricanes, 42-43

**L**
Lanier, Sidney, 33
Lottery, 43

**M**
Maps:
Apalachicola, 196
Apalachicola area, 194
Beaches of South Walton, 123
Downtown Tallahassee, 236-37
The Emerald Coast, 88
Historic Fort Walton Beach, 98
Okaloosa County, 86
Panama City area, 156

Pensacola, 56-57
Pensacola area, 48
State parks in the Florida
    Panhandle, 34
South Walton area, 116
Tallahassee area, 234
Tallahassee Historic District,
    249
Monticello, 288

## N

Natural habitats, 29-30
Flatwoods, 29
Hardwood forests and ham-
    mocks, 29-30
High pine, 30
Salt marshes, 30
Scrub, 30

## O

Okaloosa County, 85-114

## P

Packing list, 43-44
Panama City, 156-93
Peak season, 44
Pelican picks:
Apalachicola, 204-7
Beaches of South Walton,
    120-22
Okaloosa County, 90-91
Panama City, 163-65
Pensacola, 52-53
Tallahassee, 242-44
Pensacola, 49-84

## Q

Quincy, 288-89

## R

Rental car information, 44
Restaurants and nightlife:
Apalachicola, 205, 206-7,
    224-25
Beaches of South Walton,
    139-42
Okaloosa County, 108-10
Panama City, 163-64, 183-86
Pensacola, 78-80
Tallahassee, 275-78
RV rental companies, 44

## S

Safety tips, 44-45
Seasickness, 45
Seaside, 126, 149-54
Shopping:
Apalachicola, 227-29
Beaches of South Walton,
    122, 145-47
Okaloosa County, 90-91,
    106-7
Panama City, 190
Pensacola, 81-82
Tallahassee, 279-81
Smoking, 45-46
Sports, Tallahassee, 270-73
Spring break, 163
South Walton Turtle Watch,
    120-21
Sunburn, 46
Sunscreen, 46

## T

Tallahassee, 235-89
Tennis:
Beaches of South Walton,
    138

Okaloosa County, 106
Panama City, 183
Pensacola, 77
Tallahassee, 275
Thomasville, Georgia, 289
Time zones, 46-47
Tipping, 47
Tips for travelers, 33-47
Transportation:
    Apalachicola, 201-2
    Beaches of South Walton, 120

Okaloosa County, 90
Panama City, 160-61
Pensacola, 54
Tallahassee, 240-41
Tupelo honey, 204-5

**W**

Walt Disney, 13
Water safety, 47
Walton County Snowbird Club,
    122